Duncan Shaw

The History and Philosophy of Judaism

Or, A critical and philosophical Analysis of the Jewish Religion

Duncan Shaw

The History and Philosophy of Judaism
Or, A critical and philosophical Analysis of the Jewish Religion

ISBN/EAN: 9783337070267

Printed in Europe, USA, Canada, Australia, Japan

Cover: Foto ©Lupo / pixelio.de

More available books at **www.hansebooks.com**

THE HISTORY AND PHILOSOPHY
OF
JUDAISM:
OR, A
CRITICAL AND PHILOSOPHICAL ANALYSIS
OF THE
JEWISH RELIGION.
FROM WHICH IS OFFERED
A VINDICATION OF ITS GENIUS,
ORIGIN, AND AUTHORITY,
AND
OF ITS CONNECTION WITH THE CHRISTIAN,
AGAINST THE
OBJECTIONS AND MISREPRESENTATIONS
OF MODERN INFIDELS

BY DUNCAN SHAW, D.D.
ONE OF THE MINISTERS OF ABERDEEN.

The Law is our schoolmaster, to bring us to Christ.   Gal. iii. 24.
Blame not before thou hast examined the truth: understand first, and then rebuke.
                                                                      Ecclus xi. 7.

EDINBURGH:
PRINTED FOR C. ELLIOT, EDINBURGH,
And C. ELLIOT, T. KAY, and Co. at Dr Cullen's
Head, N° 332. Strand, LONDON.

M,DCC,LXXXVII.

PREFACE.

WHETHER Chriſtianity has gained or ſuffered moſt, by the aſſaults that have been made upon it by Infidels, is a point ſtill problematical. However, if I might venture to offer an opinion upon it, I muſt own, I am inclined to think that it has, upon the whole, gained. A local and temporary loſs it may have ſuſtained, by the rude or ſly arts that have been uſed to deſtroy its credit and influence: But, that it has already reaped many, and will ſtill reap more, advantages from them, is highly probable.

One thing, abundantly evident from the hiſtory of infidelity, is, that, ſince it began to obtain any footing, thoſe records which the votaries of Chriſtianity eſteem

PREFACE.

esteem sacred, have been examined by its friends with more critical acuteness than ever they were before. The consequence is,—that the nature, evidence, and obligations of revealed religion, have been incomparably better understood.

It must, in justice to the enemies of revealed religion, be owned, that, in attempting to run it down, they have tried every art, from which policy could suggest the least hope of success. Those of subtilty and cunning are generally the most dangerous: And these have, of late, been frequently adopted. Our countryman, David Hume, Esq; seems, in a particular manner, to have been fond of this mode of attack. Thus, in his Essay on National Characters, he endeavours to hurt the influence of religion, by the suspicion he attempts to raise against the character of its ministers. In his Essay on Miracles, he expresses himself in a manner that leads to the most dangerous consequences, and has a tendency

PREFACE.

dency to subvert the foundations, not only of Christianity, but of all religion whatever. And, in his Essay on Superstition, how does he slyly endeavour to prejudice his readers against the Christian religion, by the character which he gives of the Jewish? In the two first of these attempts, his design has been exposed by writers, every way equal to the task they have undertaken*.

I have often wondered that none have taken public notice of the thrust given to Christianity in the third. It is true, he says nothing directly against it. But the wound is the more dangerous that it is given obliquely; and he was sagacious enough to know this. He saw very well, that an open and avowed attack upon the national religion, would, to say the least, have been considered as a public affront to those who professed it: And therefore

* Dr Gerard's Synod Sermon, on the Influence of the Pastoral Office on the Character;—and Dr Campbell's Essay on Miracles.

therefore, a deference to the voice of the nation in its favour, as well as other reasons, might have restrained him from any thing that might look like a direct insult upon it.

But, when it is considered to what consequences the attack upon Judaism leads, it has often astonished me, that none of the many friends of Christianity have attempted to prevent them, by exposing the unfair methods by which he has endeavoured to hurt it.

I waited long, in hopes that his conduct in this matter would have been placed in a proper point of light. But as none, so far as I know, have yet attempted any thing with this view, I have ventured to undertake the task, disagreeable as it may be.

I am abundantly sensible, that the investigation of the sentiments of Mr Hume, concerning the Jewish, and, by consequence,

PREFACE.

quence, the Christian religion, may, by some, be thought ungenerous, now that he is gone, and cannot answer for himself. But, to this, I have two or three things to offer in reply.

In the first place, that I had formed, in my own mind, the resolution of making this inquiry, long before Mr Hume died, though, from a variety of incidents, it was not in my power to execute it. And of this, a not obscure hint may be seen in my *Comparative View of the several Methods of promoting religious Instruction*, N° I. of the Appendix.

In the next place, it has often been said, that, as soon as he became author, he resolved never to make an answer to any thing that might be written against him. And it is well known that he never did. Any animadversions, therefore, upon his writings since his death, are not more sure of escaping without a reply, than they would have been before it.

To this let me add, as the principal part of my apology, if any is thought necessary,—That the sly insinuations thrown out against religion still remain in his writings; and therefore that, while this is the case, its friends are called upon to put mankind upon their guard against them. *Though dead, he still speaketh*, and in them continueth to plead the cause of infidelity. And I can see no reason, why, from a false deference to his memory, the friends of Christianity should lie by, and allow his misrepresentations of it to go current, without any animadversions upon them, as if no reply could be made. *De mortuis, nel nisi bonum*, is, in the general, a good maxim. But, like all general rules, it admits of some exceptions. And, in the present case, I humbly imagine there is no room for them. The cause of truth and religion, or, which is the same thing, the truest interests of mankind, are here nearly concerned. And, to suffer an attack, either oblique or direct, to be made upon these, and not endeavour

endeavour to ward off the blow that might be dreaded from it, would, in those who behold it, betray a false delicacy.

A great deal has been said, since his death, by his admirers, to conciliate the good opinion of the public, with respect to his character, both as a writer and a friend to mankind. My situation in life did not allow me the opportunity of a personal acquaintance with him. But, so far as I am acquainted with his writings, I own I am one of the many who admire them, for that elegance, ease, spirit, and beauty, for which they are justly distinguished. I am not, however, blind to their blemishes. And among these, I must take the liberty to say, that the many inuendos, or oblique hints, with which they abound against Christianity, constitute the most exceptionable part of his character as a writer. And this part of his character, from whatever cause it has proceeded,—whether

ther from a sceptical principle,—a pride of understanding, or—a vain affectation of originality of sentiment in all he said, can scarce admit of a defence, though some of his zealous friends have attempted it.

In the course of the following work, I was insensibly led to animadvert upon the calumnies and reproaches thrown out against revealed religion, by other modern infidels, particularly by Tindal, Lord Bolingbroke, and Voltaire. And I must own I could not read what they have advanced on the subject, without a mixture (however harsh it may sound), of pity, contempt, and indignation: *Pity*,—that men who were possessed of character, not only from their rank in life, but also from their abilities as writers, should allow themselves to prostitute this character, in the ignoble service of infidelity, from the silly ambition of being thought, by some, men of superior talents, and of a more liberal

way

PREFACE.

way of thinking than others. With *contempt* of the dishonourable shifts to which they have often been reduced, in defence of their favourite system. And with *indignation*, at that conspiracy which they seem to have formed against the truest interests of mankind in attempting to unhinge their principles; and, by begetting doubts concerning these, to rob them of the most noble grounds of comfort and improvement, without substituting any thing that can compensate for the loss of them.

The character of infidels in private life, we have nothing to do with, any farther than they themselves bring it into view, in their writings addressed to the public. And accordingly in those strictures which I have offered, upon the infidel writers who have come in my way, I have kept clear of every thing that might look like personal reflection.

But, though I would wish to avoid what may seem to strike at individuals,

I hope I may be allowed to obferve in general,—That, however fair the character of fome of them may be, in refpect of an abftinence from fome fafhionable vices, and perhaps for the exercife of fome rare virtues, it may be charged with a very high degree of blame in other refpects. For it ought to be remembered, that there may be many vices, from which one is conftitutionally averfe; and many virtues, to which, from the motives of intereft or character, one may be inclined. But there can be little dependence upon their averfion to the one, or their attachment to the other, when the principles they profefs can give no fecurity for either.

Befides, it ought to be confidered, that there are different ways in which a man's conduct may be criminal in itfelf, and hurtful to others. He may hurt them by his writings, as well as by his conduct and example in life. And therefore, did we know a man, who could fit down

down and deliberately write, in a manner calculated to weaken the hatred of vice and the regard for virtue, among his fellow-citizens, would we call such a one, a good man, or a good member of the commonwealth?—No. On the contrary, we would not hesitate to pronounce him a worse, and more dangerous, member of the state, with all the most shining talents he could be possessed of, than many others who openly transgressed its laws. From such conviction it was, that I have endeavoured, in the following treatise, to expose the mean arts, the gross falsehoods, and groundless calumnies, with which the writings of some of our modern infidels abound, against revealed religion.

The reputation they have acquired as writers, may make this attempt be censured by some as bold. By others, perhaps, it may be thought arrogant. But it is the reputation which they have acquired, that has made me think of it.

But

But for this, they would have been nowise dangerous. The more conspicuous they have become by their literary fame, the more hurt they have it in their power to do. And therefore it becomes an office both of humanity and of religion, to put mankind upon their guard against a misplaced confidence in their oracular decisions.

A vindication of the Jewish religion, of which such an unfair character is given by Mr Hume, was all I, at first, proposed in this Treatise. But I had not proceeded far, in the execution of this part of my design, when I found it necessary to enlarge my plan, and to consider the several Dispensations (as they are commonly called) of religion, in their connection with, and relation to, one another. In this point of light, I humbly think, they ought ever to be considered. For want of a due attention to this,—a subject, the most noble in itself, and the most interesting to mankind, has been

very

very improperly reprefented by fome, and very imperfectly comprehended by others. I fhall reckon the pains I have beftowed on this fubject abundantly rewarded, if what is offered in the following fheets, fhall be found to give the candid reader, a more juft, enlarged, and comprehenfive view of it, than he had before.

After I had formed, and almoft filled up, the plan, upon which the following Treatife is written, *Dr Lowman's Rational of the Ritual of the Hebrew Worſhip* fell into my hands. I read it with all the avidity and attention, that could be excited by a fimilarity of defign and a coincidence of fubjects: And, when I entered upon it, began to think it might make the publication of this unneceffary.

It would be ungenerous, nay unfair, to deny the merit of the performance. It has a large fhare of it, and well deferves an attentive perufal from thofe, who are
defirous

defirous of information upon the fubject of which it treats. But, when it is obferved, that the plan upon which this treatife is written, is more comprehenfive than that of Dr Lowman, and that fome of the moſt important fubjects handled in it, are placed in a very different light, from that in which they have been commonly viewed, the author hopes he will be vindicated, by the candid public, from fo much as the imputation of vanity, in the offer which he makes of it to them.

In treating the fame fubject, it was impoffible to avoid all coincidence of fentiment. But where any fentiment is more largely infifted on by Dr Lowman, I have directed the reader to it by a note.

The author is abundantly aware, that, for the fentiments advanced in this performance, he is in danger of cenfure, from different claffes of his readers:

From Sceptics and Infidels, for the freedom with which he has offered a critique

upon

upon the writings of some of their most admired authors: And from a few of the friends of revealed religion, for receding from the generally received opinions, in some speculative points. But he hopes both will examine with candour what he has advanced, before they condemn any part of it. If he is in an error, he will be glad to be set right by either; and can assure them, that, whatever shall be offered with this view, shall receive the same candid regard from him, which he asks from them.

INTRODUCTION, Page 17

PART I.

Of the Divine origin of the law, - 23

CHAP. I. *Of the constitution of the Jewish church,* 33
Sect. I. *Of the character of the Deity,* 34
Sect. II. *Of the worship required from Israel,* 65
Sect. III. *Of the times devoted to the services of religion,* 126
Sect. IV. *Of the places of public worship,* 138
Sect. V. *Of the offices of religion,* 160
Sect. VI. *Of the preparation required for the services of religion,* 176
Sect. VII. *Of the style and manner, in which every thing relating to religion under this economy was expressed,* 185
CHAP. II. *Of the political state of Israel, as interwoven, or connected with their religion,* 207
Sect. I. *Of the propriety of the residence of the visible symbol of the Divine Presence among the Israelites, for the purposes both of religion and of government,* 208
Sect. II. *Of the happy correspondence betwixt their civil and religious government,* 213
Sect. III. *Of some of the most exceptionable parts (as they are commonly reckoned) of the administration of the theocracy under which Israel lived,* 219

PART II.

Of the Duration of the Mosaic economy, 240

Sect. I. *That the Duration of it was never intended to be more than temporary,* 241
Sect. II. *That the Mosaic dispensation of religion was intended to prepare the world for the reception of the Christian,* 252

PART III.

That the Gospel is the last dispensation of God's grace to mankind, in the way of religious discovery, - 299

PART IV.

Contains some general corollaries from the subject of the preceding treatise, 304

Sect. I. *That the preceding view of the dispensations of the Divine grace to mankind, exhibits to the devout and contemplative mind, the richest fund of moral entertainment and improvement,* - - 305

Sect. II. *That the Jewish religion is worthy of God for its Author, and was perfectly suited to the purposes of its institution,—the genius of the people, and—the circumstances of the times, for which it was principally intended,* - 311

Sect. III. *That, if we would rightly understand the New Testament, we must accurately study the Old,* 339

Sect. IV. *That a serious review of the subject of this inquiry, will enable us to adduce a proof of the Divine origin, both of the Jewish, and of the Christian, religion,* - - 345

INTRO-

ERRATA.

Page 67. line 29. After *all men*, add *circumcised*.
69. line 1. note, For *he*, read *Abraham*, had an, &c.
179. line 26. For *exedunt*, read *excedunt*.
201. line 26. note, For *Tykes's*, read *Sykes's*.
270. line 1.——After *off*, add *all*.
277. line 4.——After *as*, add *of*.

INTRODUCTION.

IT is the great excellence of the Christian religion, that the more it is studied, the more its nature, design, and tendency must be admired, and the more our faith in its divine origin must be confirmed. This, I know, is a position that will not be admitted by some. Nay, the opposition given to this religion, in an age of so much knowledge, and so distinguished for accurate investigation, as the present is, may perhaps be thought a proof of the contrary.

The opposition given to it, has indeed been great. The pert Wit,—the profligate Debauchee,—the conceited Sciolist,—the loquacious Prattler,—the affected Pyrrhonist, have, all of them, made it the subject of their censures. Nay, it must be owned, that the opposition even of the literary kind, which it has received in the present age, has been great; as great, if not greater, than any it has met with since its first appearance.

In the imagined force of this acknowledged fact, the enemies of Christianity are apt to boast and exult. But there is no such cause for triumph as they may imagine. What opposition has been given to it, may be easily accounted for, without inferring any thing prejudicial to its origin, evidence, or honour. It has proceeded from a variety of causes. In some, from a sceptical humour, which is become fashionable in a certain class of mankind, as if characteristic of a superiority of genius and understanding: In others, from mere ignorance, or, at least, a superficial knowledge, of religion: In not a few, from the check it would give to the indulgence of their criminal pursuits: And, in all, from the prejudices they have somehow contracted against it. An attention to those facts which fall within our own notice, will justify this account of the matter.

Influenced by one or other of the above considerations, it is not to be expected that they would be over-scrupulous as to the mode in which they chose to carry on their attacks against Christianity. Neither, indeed, have they been so. Many are the posts which they have seized, from which they have hoped to annoy it. But (how agreeable to observe?) all of them such, as have showed either their imprudence in the choice, or their weakness in the defence, of them. What has been wanting in strength, they have endeavoured sometimes to supply in art and policy: Few of them have had the honesty to throw off the mask. Though enemies to religion at heart, they commonly appear in the guise of friends; and,

under

under pretence of vindicating, have often wounded, its honour.

It is not my design to trace them through all their mazes and windings in the manner of their attack upon Christianity, and to expose all the unfair and ungenerous arts with which it has been conducted. Such a design, were I equal to it, would open a large field of controversy, and require no small time and labour to execute it properly. My design shall be comprised within narrower bounds.

I have often thought (and am happy to find a writer of distinguished character in the republic of letters of the same opinion), that, in the many defences which have been offered of Christianity, too little attention has been paid to the doctrines and religion of the Old Testament. For " Christianity (as this
" author very properly expresses it) is but the
" last link in a chain of truth, that consists
" of several others; and he that would pre-
" tend to show a chain of truth, must show
" not one link only, but several; and show
" that they are linked with the first, and
" with one another *."

A sentiment such as this, was what first suggested the design of the following sheets. I soon became confirmed in my purpose of carrying it into execution, upon recollecting the disrespectful manner in which a certain writer is pleased to express himself with respect

---

* Barrington's Miscellan. Sacr. Vol. III. Pref. p. 8.

respect to the Jewish religion †, and the dangerous influence which the character he gives of it, might have upon weak and unsettled minds. Nor are there wanting reasons for the proposed inquiry into the nature of the Jewish religion, from the uncautious manner in which (as shall be shown afterwards) even some of the friends of Revelation have spoken concerning it.

I had not proceeded far in my original design, when I found myself led into a train of sentiments, which made an enlargement of my original plan necessary. And, if the whole is but candidly examined, it is hoped the several branches of it will be found to have a close connection with each other.

The design of Part I. is to vindicate the Jewish religion against those, who, by attempting to expose it, would, in an indirect manner, make an attack upon the Christian.

The Jews, taking the advantage of what is advanced in this part in favour of their religion, might perhaps improve it as an argument to justify their constant attachment to it, and to represent Christians as criminal in not submitting to it. The design, therefore, of Part II. is to show, that, though the Jewish religion was originally from God, yet what was properly positive in it, carried evident marks of only a temporary and local obligation.

The

---

† David Hume, Esq; in his Essay on Superstition and Enthusiasm.

The Jewish dispensation having, in consequence of the primary design of God in it, given place to the Christian; it is proposed in Part III. to show, that this is the last dispensation of the Divine grace to mankind, in the way of religious discovery; and that no other can be reasonably looked for.

The Fourth, or last Part, is intended to bring into view, some of the many useful corollaries fairly deducible from the preceding inquiry.

From this short analysis of his design, the Author flatters himself that the Reader will have a pretty distinct view of it. What may be necessary for the illustration of it, shall, for the sake of order, be arranged under the following plan; and the propriety of the manner in which the several parts are filled up, is submitted to the review and judgment of the candid Public.

THE HISTORY AND PHILOSOPHY OF JUDAISM.

PART I.

Of the Divine Origin of the Law.

WHOEVER is in the least acquainted with the sacred writings, cannot fail to have observed, that the word *Law*, which frequently occurs in them, is of very different acceptation. My design does not make it necessary to inquire into the several meanings of it. Let it suffice for our present purpose to observe, that, by it, we are here to understand that scheme of religion, which was published to Israel by the ministry of Moses, and professed by them, through all the ages both of their republican and regal state.

When the Apoſtle Paul ſpeaks of it*, he evidently takes the Divine authority of it for granted; and therefore does not ſo much as offer, or attempt, a proof of it. He conſiders it as making a part of that original plan, which the Divine wiſdom had deviſed for promoting the religious inſtruction and improvement of mankind. And this, allow me to obſerve by the by, was no ſmall preſumption in its favour. For, when it is conſidered by whom this conceſſion was made, a more than ordinary degree of weight muſt be allowed to it.

Our Apoſtle had been educated in one of the ſtricteſt ſects among the Jews, and in the ſchool of one of their moſt celebrated Rabbis. Trained up in the profeſſion of the Jewiſh religion from his earlieſt infancy, it is well known, he, for a conſiderable while, diſcovered the ſtrongeſt attachment to it.

When afterwards he ſaw cauſe to renounce this, and adopt the Chriſtian ſcheme of religion, might it not have been reaſonably expected, that, as his learning furniſhed him with ſufficient ability to diſcover the flaws of it, had there been any, his zeal for that which he had now embraced would have prompted him to publiſh them to the world? But when, in place of this, we find him admitting the evidence and authority of that religion, even after he had renounced the profeſſion of it; what leſs can we infer from ſuch conduct, than that both appeared to him to be

---

* Galat. iii. 24.

be of divine original? But, whatever they may have appeared to him, neither the one nor the other will be admitted by some to be deserving of this character, without a proof: Nay, the claim of both to it has been warmly controverted.

Not satisfied with nibbling at the external evidence that is adduced in support of it, they are more bold. They have daringly attacked the very nature and constitution of it, and roundly asserted it to be incompatible with the character of the Deity, from whom it is said to proceed, or those sentiments which sober reason would teach mankind to form of Him. Nay, some of them have gone farther. They have attempted a proof of the charge they bring against this religion, by singling out, and endeavouring to expose, a few of the *seemingly* exceptionable branches of it, or events connected with it.

Among the moderns, *Tindal*, *Voltaire*, and *Bolingbroke*, have distinguished themselves, by their rude attacks upon revealed religion. And in the respectful band of assailants, *David Hume*, Esq; has always been ambitious of the honour of appearing among the foremost, ever since he has been capable of wielding an offensive weapon. His sentiments on this subject are too remarkable to escape the notice of any who are acquainted with his writings.

In his Essay on Superstition and Enthusiasm, he calls *Judaism*, one of the most *absurd and unphilosophical superstitions, which have yet been known in the world*, that is, (according to the definition he gives of superstition in the beginning of the same essay), the most absurd and unphilosophical species of *false religion.*

It must, however, in justice to Mr Hume, be owned, that, though his opinion of this religion runs in the above terms in some editions of his essays, he has been *graciously* pleased to soften the manner in which he expresses it, in others.

In the London edition, anno 1764, he is pleased to affirm this of *Modern Judaism* only. But why this restriction here, which was not in a former edition? Does it not betray the very design which it was intended to conceal? Had he not, in a former edition, used the expression of *Judaism* in general, none would have taken offence at what he says of modern Judaism. For, if we may form our sentiments of it from their Talmud, which consists of the Mishnah and Gemara, and may be said to contain the whole of their religion; it will appear such a composition as will justify the severest epithets that could be bestowed upon it. But there can be no doubt that, by the phrase, *Modern Judaism,* he meant only to evade the offensive appearance, which the reproach thrown out against Judaism in general had, as it stood in a former edition. Thus he might flatter himself, that the stricture he makes upon Judaism in this form, would be less liable to censure than in the other. But the veil he uses, while it is thin enough to be seen through by the penetrating eye of the

sceptic

sceptic and infidel, is too thin to conceal his design from those to whom he does not wish it to be made known *.

Were

---

* The suspicion which Mr Hume has excited against himself, from the different manner in which he speaks of Judaism, in different editions of his Essays, is greatly confirmed by some other parts of his writings, in which he seems to be more off his guard, and which may serve as a key to his meaning in this.

In support of this remark, and for the satisfaction of those who have not immediate access to the places alluded to, I beg leave to quote them, and to be indulged a few observations upon them.

In his Natural History of Religion, (London edit. anno 1764,   ) he introduces a dialogue between a *Sorbonist* and a priest of *Sais*. In this he makes the priest to own, that it would be mad to cut one anothers throats about the preference of a cabbage or a cucumber, provided the Catholic would confess, that all those are still madder, who fight about the preference among volumes of *sophistry*, ten thousand of which are not equal in value to one cabbage or cucumber. And here he directs the reader to the following note, at the foot of the page.

" It is strange that the Egyptian religion, though so absurd,
" should yet have borne so great a resemblance to the Jewish;
" that ancient writers, even of the greatest genius, were not
" able to observe any difference betwixt them. For, it is
" very remarkable, that both Tacitus and Suetonius, when
" they mention that decree of the senate under Tiberius, by
" which the Egyptian and Jewish proselytes were banished
" from Rome, expressly treat these religions as the same; and
" it appears that even the decree itself was founded on that
" supposition. ' Actum et de sacris Egyptiis, Judaicisque pel-
" lendis: factumque patrum consultum, ut quatuor millia li-
" bertini generis *ea superstitione* infecta, quis idonea ætas, in
" insulam Sardiniam veherentur, coercendis illic latrociniis:
" Et si, ob gravitatem cœli interissent, vile damnum. Cæteri
" cederent Italia, nisi, certam ante diem, profanos ritus exuis-
" sent. *Tacit. Ann. Lib.* 2. cap. 85."

" Externas ceremonias, Egyptios, Judaiosque ritus compes-
" cuit, coactis qui superstitione eâ tenebantur, religiosas vestes,
" cum

Were the infinuations thrown out againſt this religion juſt, we ſhould have the beſt reaſon to pity the vaſt numbers who have been, and ſtill are, impoſed on by it: Nay, to ſuſpect the

" cum inſtrumento omni, comburere, &c. *Sueton. Tiber.*
" cap. 36. Thoſe wiſe Heathens, obſerving ſomething in the
" general air and genius and ſpirit of the two religions to be
" the ſame, eſteemed the difference of the dogmas too fri-
" volous to deſerve attention."

From the above quotation, does it not appear highly preſumable (not to ſay more), that the Judaiſm, which he calls an abſurd and unphiloſophical ſuperſtition, was the *Ancient*, though, to cover his deſign the better, he, in ſome later editions, endeavours to ſoften the matter a little, by applying this deſcription to what he is pleaſed to call *Modern Judaiſm?* But, whatever may be in this conjecture, one thing is abundantly evident, that the Jewiſh religion, which he here compares with the Egyptian, was that which was *anciently* profeſſed: And of this he ſpeaks, in the way of ſly infinuation, with equal difreſpect as of the other. Here he brings them into an invidious compariſon with one another, and from the opinion of Tacitus, Suetonius, and the Roman ſenate concerning them, would infinuate that there was no difcernible difference betwixt them. But what can be more unphiloſophical and uncandid than ſuch a conduct in Mr Hume? For, what though all theſe ſpeak of the two religions as pretty much the ſame, this can be no proof that they were ſo. It amounts to no more, at beſt, than a proof of *their* opinion. But, what regard can be had to this, when there is the greateſt reaſon to think it was founded upon their ignorance of theſe religions, concerning which they ſo poſitively determine? Neither is this a mere aſſertion, without evidence to ſupport it. For, let any one look into the account which Tacitus gives of the Jewiſh religion (Tacit. Hiſt. lib. 5.), and he muſt be ſatisfied, that he was almoſt an entire ſtranger to the nature and genius of it. And it is not improbable, but Suetonius and the Roman ſenate might have been equally ſo. In them, ſuch an opinion might have been, in ſome meaſure, pardonable. From the coincidence in ſome points betwixt theſe religions, they might imagine the reſemblance which the one bore to the other greater

the authority of that religion which we ourselves profess, or rather to give it up all at once, as an imposture likewise. They must stand or fall together, so close is their connection with each other.

To greater than it really was, as it does not appear that they gave themselves the trouble of a minute inquiry into the nature or genius of either. But as Mr Hume must have been better acquainted with both, does it not appear uncandid to mention the opinion of these authors, in a manner that shows his approbation of it, and as if he thought, that it should form a just prejudice against the Jewish religion, that the Egyptian (which he owns to have been absurd) was thought to be so like to it?

Mr Hume is equally inaccurate in the character he gives of this religion, as in the epithet by which he would distinguish it. The very phrase of an *unphilosophical religion* is, so uncommon,—so little authorised by use, that it required an explanation to give it currency, and yet he has not been pleased to offer any.

I acknowledge the term *unphilosophical* is often used in a loose manner for *irrational*. But when such a writer as Mr Hume uses a word of equivocal meaning, he ought, by a proper definition, to fix it, otherwise he creates a suspicion of unfavourable design.

Perhaps Mr Hume may have thought, as certain legislators did of old, that every nation ought to be left at liberty to express their homage to the Deity, in that manner that appears to them the most proper; and that religion should be deemed more or less philosophical, in proportion as it appeared more or less agreeable to the genius or circumstances of the people for whom it was designed, or that mode of government under which they lived. What makes it probable that he considered the determination of the mode of religion, or rather, the modelling the outward form of it, as the province of the philosopher or magistrate, and meant to suggest some such idea, is —what he throws out in a note under this very essay. There, speaking of clergymen, as an order of men set apart for the care of sacred matters, and to conduct the public devotion with the greater decorum and order, he considers their designation to this office as a thing purely political. For, when he

To prove any species of religion *absurd and unphilosophical*, it would be necessary to make it appear to be inconsistent with the nature and character of the Deity,—unsuited to the genius

he speaks of such designation being made by virtue of the *laws* (he surely means those of the state), would he not insinuate that as this, so every thing else that related to religion, was to be settled by these?
 To trace Mr Hume thus far, seemed necessary to develope the character he gives of Judaism. I shall be sorry if I have done injustice to his meaning in the interpretation I have given of it. I have observed the rule universally approved in the interpretation of all authors; that is, I have endeavoured, where his meaning was obscure, to explain it by other places where it was less so. And I humbly imagine, that, if he be allowed to be consistent with himself, I have done him no injustice in the comment made upon him. If we consider the obscurity as undesigned, it reflects upon him, both as a writer and a philosopher. For, in either of these characters, he ought to have studied more accuracy and perspicuity: Or if, to avoid this imputation, his admirers will have it to be designed, they do not mend the matter. They pay a compliment to his head at the expence of his heart, and make candor to truckle to mean artifice. But happy it is for the honour of this religion, that the merit of it is not to be determined by the opinions of a Tacitus, Suetonius, or a Hume, but by the decision of reason and the common sense of mankind; to the examination of which, it is, without fear, submitted.
 Since writing the above note, another edition of Mr Hume's essays, published at London anno 1770, has fallen into my hands. Finding a variation in a former edition, I had the curiosity to look into this, and was not a little surprised to find it differ greatly from all the former. For, in this, the observation concerning Judaism and Popery (which, in former editions, had been called the most absurd and unphilosophical superstitions that had yet been known to the world), is entirely left out.
 How to account for this, is somewhat difficult. Had this edition been posterior to his death, the omission might have been

genius, situation, and circumstances of those whom it principally respects—or, inadequate to the great ends proposed by it. Could this be made appear in the case under consideration

been suspected to have been designed by the Editor, to avoid what might appear disrespectful to religion, especially as the insinuation contained in it seems to have been wantonly introduced. But, as this edition was published in the author's lifetime, it is not to be imagined that any such freedom would be used, without his knowledge and consent. And should this be admitted, still it remains difficult to account for the matter.

The insertion of the epithet, *Modern*, when speaking of Judaism, in his edition anno 1764, seems to indicate a design, by thus softening the observation, to remove the offence given by the first manner of its appearance. And very possibly, finding that this alteration did not answer that purpose, he has, in the last edition, omitted it altogether. But here I must beg leave to observe, that there lies no small objection against his conduct, if considered even in this point of view. It must have proceeded, either from a conviction of the impropriety of the remark, or a fear of offending by it. And neither of these principles are sufficient to justify the part he has acted.

If the last was the principle upon which he struck out this paragraph,—as a philosopher and a candid inquirer, after truth, he ought to have paid no regard to it.—Satisfied of the justness of the remark, he should have allowed it to remain, assured that truth would, at last, prevail; and in hopes that the uncommonness of the sentiment, might prove the means of exciting a proper inquiry into it, and thereby establishing it.—Or if, in consequence of his own review, or the sentiments of others, he saw reason to alter his opinion,—to drop the remark was not enough. Upon the supposition of an alteration of his sentiments, he ought to have acknowledged his error. He could not but see the unfavourable aspect, which the manner of expression used by him had upon the character of the Deity, the generally allowed author of this religion, and upon the religion of Jesus so closely connected with it; and therefore he ought, in justice to both, to have guarded all, with whom his opinion might have

any

tion, the moſt ſtrenuous ſupporters of this religion would be obliged to give it up. To inquire how far it is ſo, ſhall be the deſign of the firſt part of this Treatiſe. And here I ſhall endeavour, by an analyſis of this religion, to evince, that, rightly underſtood, there is nothing in it derogatory to the character of the Deity,—unſuited to the genius of the people to whom it was firſt publiſhed,—or that age of the world in which it was inſtituted: Nay, that it had an admirable propriety in it, with reſpect to all theſe; while, at the ſame time, it ſerved to prepare the world for the reception of the Chriſtian religion, to which it was intended to be an introduction.

For evincing theſe things, it will be neceſſary to take a narrow inſpection of the particular ſtructure of this religion, or, at leaſt, of thoſe things in it which may be conſidered as diſtinctive and characteriſtic. And that we may proceed in this examination with the greater regularity, we ſhall digeſt what may be neceſſary for this purpoſe, under the following diviſions.

C H A P.

---

any weight, againſt the dangerous tendency of it. It is not enough, that, in ſome editions, he kept out the exceptionable and hurtful paſſage. As long as it remains in former editions, its baneful influence will continue.

Nor would ſuch an acknowledgement have reflected any diſhonour upon him, either as a philoſopher or an honeſt man. Nay, in both theſe characters he would have gained greatly by it. As the error he maintained had been made public, and he had reaſon to think, that, from its palatableneſs and the ſanction of his name, it might continue to produce the moſt unhappy effects, he ſhould have done all in his power to prevent them.

CHAP. I.

Of the Constitution of the Jewish Church.

THE religious and civil polity of the Jews were so interwoven and blended together, that he who would form a just notion of either, must not view the one independently of the other, but as they stand closely connected.

Never was there a church more exactly formed than this was, upon a model that might be called truly divine. Every thing that related to, or had the most distant connection with, religion, was settled by the particular appointment of its glorious Author. Not only the great articles, but even the minutiæ (if I may use the word) of the religious service of this people,—what related to the time, place, and other circumstances of it, were all prescribed by God.: And all, in an evident subserviency to the honour and interests of religion,—the genius of the Jews in particular, and—the situation of the world in general.

A candid view of it, is all that is necessary to satisfy the inquisitive upon this subject.

SECT. I.

Of the Character of the Deity.

THE first thing that naturally falls to be considered in any religion, is the character it gives to that Being, whom its votaries are taught to consider as the object of their homage, worship, and service. And the reason is plain; because the religion must ever be of a piece with the sentiments, which such a character is calculated to inspire.

To judge of the propriety of the views in which this institution of religion represents the Deity, it will be necessary to lead back your thoughts, not only to the æra of its commencement, but a little farther.

The birth of the Jewish church may be considered as having taken place at the call of Abraham, whose posterity the Israelites, or Jews, were. And accordingly we find, from the sacred history, a most signal providence exercised over them, in the manner of their descent into Egypt,—of their residence there, and—of their triumphant deliverance from it. But it was in the plains around Sinai, that God first appeared in the character of their supreme magistrate, and formed them into a civil and religious society, of which he was himself to take the principal direction.

In some of the more early, rude, and uncultivated ages of the world, God was pleased to maintain an intercourse with mankind,

under

under some visible appearance. And, in those ages, when the feelings of mankind were far from being tender, and their minds were but little cultivated by science, such method of communication seemed very proper, if not necessary, as shall be shown afterwards. But when idolatry had gained a footing in the world, and the notions and worship of the true God had become greatly corrupted, perhaps from an abuse of these sensible appearances, as well as from other causes, then did the erection of the church of Israel become necessary, for correcting the gross errors that obtained in the different systems of religion, and, by restoring the religion of the true God, for diffusing the knowledge of it in due time through the world.

Accordingly, who that can read, but must admire the propriety, as well as grandeur, with which the foundations of the Jewish church were laid, by the descent, the visible descent, of God upon Mount Sinai? The scenery and apparatus for this equally illustrious and tremenduous event, were every way worthy of, and proportioned to, the grand occasion. So full of awful majesty, that nothing could be better calculated to inspire the minds of the attending Israelites with the most profound reverence and veneration, or, by these means, to engage a most respectful homage and obedience to the dread Sovereign of heaven and of earth. Every thing in the scene itself, and the circumstances that attended it, were such as could not fail to beget

get the moſt ſublime and exalted ſentiments of the Deity, in the minds of all who were looking on, and to tranſmit the like ſentiments to thoſe who ſhould afterwards hear of, the ſolemn tranſaction.

But, does it not deſerve to be taken notice of, that, while every thing was conducted through the whole of this awful ſcene, ſo as to excite the moſt exalted idea of the greatneſs, majeſty, and holineſs of the Deity, every thing was carefully avoided that could give the leaſt encouragement to idolatry,— that ſin to which Iſrael was ſo prone, and which was ſo diſhonouring to God? And particularly, may it not be remarked, that, leſt a bodily preſence upon this occaſion might be conſtrued favourably for it, there was nothing like this to be ſeen? A circumſtance this, which ought to have been conſidered by Iſrael as a ſtrong hint againſt idolatry, or the expectation of any viſible appearance among them. And accordingly, from this time downward, if I miſtake not, we hear no more, or at leaſt but ſeldom, of ſuch appearances.

Now let this tranſaction be properly conſidered, and does not every circumſtance in it appear worthy of that truly glorious Being who makes the principal figure in it? And is it not accompanied with a ſolemnity, every way proper to be obſerved at laying the foundations of a church, that was to be honoured as the depoſitory of the ſacred oracles, and to become the happy inſtrument of ſpreading

spreading the knowledge and triumphs of religion, through the world?

The Israelites having, by their long residence in Egypt, in a great measure, forgot the notions of Deity they had received from their religious ancestors, it was no wonder, that, by being accustomed to hear among the Egyptians, of the descent of their gods in visible shape, their religious sentiments should have been much corrupted. With the greatest beauty, therefore, does God, who honoured them by taking to himself the character of *their God*, while he descended in a visible manner, to show the concern he took in them, descend in such manner, as, in place of leading to any mean sentiments of him, was the best adapted to raise their veneration and esteem of him, to the highest degree they were capable of.

Before we come to consider the different characters, under which the Deity was pleased to manifest himself to this people, allow me to take notice of a circumstance, which is not generally attended to. What I mean is,— that he did not all at once, nor in the didactic way, manifest himself to them, but by gradual discoveries, as they were able to bear them. This observation the better deserves our notice; because it will be found to be a beautiful illustration of the propriety of that mode in which he chose to instruct them, in the knowledge of his nature, perfections, and character.

To this let me add, that the discoveries

made of himself, were always suited to the occasions upon which they were vouchsafed; while at the same time, the occasions themselves, considered together with his manner of acting, served to make every new character he assumed to be better understood, and, by consequence, to make their knowledge of him be greatly enlarged and improved.

In support of this opinion, it might be made appear, were it necessary, that the various names by which God was made known to Israel, were all of them expressive of some particular excellence in his character, and such as discovered the utmost propriety in the application of them.

Names were not originally mere simple and arbitrary sounds, imposed at random. As soon as language was formed, and the meaning of the words which composed it was fixed, names were generally expressive of the nature or quality of the things to which they were applied. Instances of this almost innumerable occur in the sacred history *.

Nay, at first, the imposition of names was considered, as the most compendious and instructive way of conveying the knowledge of what was remarkable in the nature, qualities, relations, or circumstances of the person or thing to which they referred. Of this opinion seem to have been some of the ancients of the most respectable character for knowledge and learning †.

It

---

* Gen. ii. 23. Ch. iii. 20. Ch. iv. 1, 25. Ch. v. 29. Ch. xvii. 15.
† Thus Plato (in his Cratyl.) tells us— τα πρωτα ονοματα ὁ Θιοι εθηκεν.

It is very true, we find, as early as Plato's time, a very injudicious application made of names, in so much that we should run a risk of mistaking the characters of the persons to whom they were given, were we to judge merely by them. But this is no proof, that they were not in earlier times considered as characteristic of something remarkable in the person to whom they were applied. It is, I think, a strong presumption of the contrary. Because it is not at all to be wondered, that parents should, from their partiality for their children and the hopes they might entertain from them, give them names of which they might afterwards prove unworthy. The judgment which, they might have observed, was formed of the characters of persons, from the names by which they were called, might account for the conduct of many of them in this respect.

The Rabbis reckon up no less than ten names, by which, they say, God is spoken of in scripture. And were we to make an etymological analysis of each of them, we should find them, as was hinted before, significant of some particular perfection, for which he is distinguished.

The first name by which we find the Deity spoken of is *Elohim*, which we render *God*. About the meaning of this English word, or

the

θησει. In another part of his Cratyl. he says —το ονομα μιμημα τι εστι τυ πραγματος—εστι δε που και το ονομα μιμημα, ωσπερ το ζωγραφημα.

See a good deal on this subject in Gale's Court of the Gentiles. Part I. Book i. chap. 10.

the idea to be conveyed by it, the learned are not agreed. Some confider it as expreffive only of the fupreme excellence, or perfection of the Divine nature- Others, as including alfo the idea of dominion and authority, and, by confequence, the relation of *Lord* and *Sovereign*. My prefent purpofe does not make it neceffary to fettle this point. It is not what he is called by us, but what he was called in early time, and by the firft men, that we are to inquire into.

If we admit the Hebrew to have been the primæval language, we find that the word *Elohim* was that by which the fupreme Being was firft fpoken of.

It is true, it may remain a doubt (and a doubt very difficult to refolve) whether this name, or that of *Elohim-Jehovah*, that is, *Lord God*, which was given him afterwards, were the names originally given: Or, whether they were only made choice of by the hiftorian, as what he judged the moft proper to be ufed in the defcription he was to give of his operations and government. The laft (as I fhall endeavour to fhow afterwards) is, I humbly think, the moft probable. But, in whichever of thefe views they are confidered, —whether as the original names given to the Deity, or as a proof of the hiftorian's accuracy in the application of them, it is much the fame to our purpofe, which is to fhow that names, according to their primary and moft early ufe, were intended to convey fome tolerably

rably diſtinct idea of the perſon or thing, to which they were applied.

In the hiſtory which Moſes gives of the Creation, he is led to conſider God only under the character of the Creator. Accordingly it deſerves to be noticed, that, through this part of his hiſtory, he ſpeaks of him by the name *Elohim* or *Elhim*, which, it is probable, comes from a root that ſignifies *ſtrength* or *power*. And who may not obſerve an admirable propriety in the choice of ſuch a name, as expreſſive of that very perfection, the exertion of which was particularly required for the production of the Univerſe?

Every reader, who is in the leaſt acquainted with the idiom of the Hebrew language, muſt obſerve from the termination of this word, that it is uſed here in the plural number. It is almoſt needleſs to take notice (there are few that do not know) that, from thence, ſome have not heſitated to infer the doctrine of a plurality of perſons in the Godhead, or divine Nature. This is but one inſtance, among many thouſands, of the unhappy effects produced, in the interpretation of Scripture, by a violent attachment to ſyſtems. For why put a meaning, ſo evidently forced, upon the word, when it can, in perfect conſiſtence with the ſubject upon which it is uſed, admit of one much more natural?

The ſacred hiſtorian having, in his account of the creation, ſeen meet to ſpeak of its great Author, under a name expreſſive of his power, could there be any impropriety, nay,

nay, would there not be a great beauty, in suppofing that he ufed this word in the plural number, to intimate that to him belonged all *Strengths;* that is, that he was not only powerful, but omnipotent? I will not take upon me to fay, that this was the original reafon for the ufe of the word in this form; but I cannot help thinking, that the idiom of the Hebrew language feems to favour this account of the matter. And, if it does, there can be no occafion for having recourfe to an explication that feems quite foreign to the fubject to which it refers. But to return from this digreffion.—To this let me add,

That in early time, long before his appearance to Mofes, he was known to the Fathers by the name of *Shaddai*, which fignifies *Almighty*, or *All-fufficient:*—A name admirably expreffive of his greatnefs, and calculated at once to command the reverence, and encourage the truft and confidence, of mankind.

When the world is formed, and creatures are placed in it, and, on this account, the exertion of his care and government became neceffary, the facred hiftorian varies the name by which he fpeaks of the fupreme Being. He calls him not only *God*, but Jehovah, or the *Lord;* and often unites two titles into one, thus, *Elohim-Jehovah, Lord-God*—and *El-Shaddai, God-Almighty.* This he feems to have done, as if he meant to give a character of him,—to point him out to his intelligent creatures, as not only their Almighty Creator, but alfo their Sovereign Lord; and,—at the

fame

same time, to convey to them this comfortable instruction, that he who made them was not indifferent about them, but that, as they were bound to reverence and serve him, from the relation which subsisted betwixt them, so they might rest assured that he would protect and defend them.

Had not the sacred historian meant to convey such ideas as these, why should he not have continued the use of the name under which he first spoke of the Deity? Or, why should he change it at the only time, when first there could be any propriety in it? Or why not use them separately, but thus compounded?

It must indeed be acknowledged, that the names *God* and *Lord God* seem afterwards, in the course of this history, to be used indiscriminately. And a very good reason may be assigned for this, namely, that the historian having, by the judicious application of them at first, shown the propriety of them, there was no necessity for a scrupulous and critical attention to the distinction afterwards.

In forming our notions of the divine character, we may be very ready to mistake, by the deductions we draw from verbal criticism, or etymological disquisitions. A more certain way to acquire a just idea of it, will be to consider the accounts, which, upon different occasions, God is pleased to give of himself. And these are often minute and particular, as if he would thereby teach us, that the knowledge of him deducible from thence

was

was more to be depended on, than that which is to be learned from the names by which mankind chofe to fpeak of him.

In the firft ages of the world, fome vifible appearances of the Deity might be neceffary, to affift mankind in their conceptions of him. But as their fentiments muft have been derived chiefly from the volume of creation unfolded before them, (for yet they were incapable of comprehending the more fublime notions which Revelation was to communicate) he was often characterifed by the title of, *The Poffeffor of Heaven and of Earth**; in both which, as in legible characters, they might read many of his divine perfections.

After the covenant entered into with Abraham, God is often fpoken of under the character of, *The God of Abraham and the God of Ifrael*†. And this alteration in the manner of addrefs, is not without reafon. Duly attended to, it will be found to have great beauty and propriety in it.

When, in the progrefs of time, the world had become fo corrupted in their notions of religion and the Author of it, that they, in a great meafure, neglected the one and forgot the other, God made choice of Abraham, as a perfon proper on many accounts, for beginning the fo neceffary reformation. What he began, was to be carried on by his defcendants. And therefore, that God might preferve upon their minds the defign of this choice, and excite in them an ambition of

promoting

* Gen. xiv. 19. † Exod. iii. 6.

promoting it, he gracioufly condefcended to be called, *The God of their Fathers—The God of Abraham, The God of Ifaac, The God of Jacob,* and—*The God of Ifrael**.

I know thofe who are no friends to Revelation, reprefent fuch a choice as partial, and inconfiftent with that regard which might be expected from God, confidered as the indulgent Parent of the univerfe. But I muft be excufed if I fhould fay, that they have taken but a very imperfect view of the fubject, who can confider it in this light. It is fo far from being an evidence of a defect of regard, that it is a proof of a very high degree of it. For it was *then* the moft proper, if not the only, method of preferving a fenfe of the true religion in the world, amidft the almoft univerfal corruption that prevailed.

It was, befides, admirably calculated, as fhall be fhown afterwards, Part II. § 2. to draw mankind, without any force offered to their reafon or liberty, to the knowledge of the truth.

It is true, the Jews, elated with the diftinction made betwixt them and the nations around them, came, at laft, to confider themfelves as the fole favourites of Heaven; and, under the influence of this conceit, to treat the reft of mankind with contempt. But fuch conduct can prove no more, than their inattention to the original defign of their felection from the reft of mankind. Had they but

---

* Exod. iii. 15.

but properly attended to this, it muſt have had a very different effect upon them. In place of producing a ſupercilious haughtineſs of conduct towards them, it would have engaged them to all the offices of kindneſs in their power.

No doubt the diſtinction made, betwixt them and the nations around them, was a plain indication of the divine pleaſure, that they ſhould avoid all unneceſſary intercourſe with them, ſo long as the nations remained addicted to idolatry, and the wicked courſes which were the conſequences of it.

But the reaſon of this ſeparation was not becauſe the nations around them, conſidered in a national capacity, were unworthy of being admitted into ſocial intercourſe with Iſrael; but becauſe, from ſuch intercourſe, Iſrael would have been in danger of being corrupted by them, and ſo the very end for which they were ſeparated from them would have been defeated. And now, when, from the event, we are enabled to judge of the propriety of the meaſure, muſt he not be very blind, or very prejudiced, who does not admire it?

The great deſign (as has been hinted already) of the ſelection of Iſrael was, that they might be like a city ſet upon a hill,— that they might become the objects of univerſal obſervation, and that the reſt of mankind might thereby be gradually allured to the knowledge, worſhip, and obedience of the true God. And if, from an acquaintance
with

with human nature, and the hiftory of mankind in the fucceffive ages and different countries of the world, we may judge what probably would have been the confequence of a more free intercourfe at that early period, we fhall be forced to conclude, that the corruption, which was become pretty general, would foon have become univerfal. At leaft, there is reafon to think, that a reformation could not have been effected by any means fo fuitable to the nature of man, as thofe by which it was brought about. Confidered, therefore, in all thofe points of view, this character of the Deity, which has afforded a handle to our modern wits to difplay their talents for obloquy and cenfure, ftands not only fully juftified, but appears with a propriety fufficient to recommend that religion in which it is thus portrayed.

It is obfervable, through the whole facred record, that, as the Deity is reprefented in a variety of characters, fo always in that which is beft fuited to the particular occafion and circumftances in which he is brought into view.

Thus when Mofes, upon the firft intimation of God's defign to fend him into Egypt to refcue his people from the oppreffion which they groaned under, afked by what name he would choofe to make himfelf known to them, he anfwered, " Thou fhalt fay unto " the children of Ifrael, *I am* hath fent me " unto you*."

It

* Exod. iii. 14.

It is well known, that, among the ancients, Jews, as well as Heathens, confidered the knowledge of names as a moſt important fcience. They entertained a foolifh and fuperftitious conceit, that not only the nature of the perfons and things to which they were applied was to be learned from them; but alſo, that many of them were of ſuch a wonderful compofition, that they might, by them, obtain oracles, cure difeafes, and perform a variety of miracles. Hence fome have thought, that the reafon why Moſes was ſo defirous of knowing the name of God, was that he hoped, from fuch difcovery, to be able to do the greateſt wonders by the ufe of it. But this feems to be a conceit of much later times, and it is highly probable never once entered into the mind of Moſes. The reafon of his inquiry (of which we are informed verfe 13.) is much more rational.

The ancients (as I obferved before), and particularly in the Eaſt, feldom gave names without fome evident defign. They were originally expreffive of the temper, character, or circumftances of the perfon to whom they were given.

Moſes very reafonably conjectured, that, upon his arrival in Egypt, Ifrael would inquire into the character of the God who fent him; and therefore might conclude that he would make choice of one the beſt fitted to convey to them the knowledge of him, and thereby to make the deepeſt impreffion upon them.—Nor were his hopes difappointed. For he, he, with a condefcenfion, and, at the fame time, dignity worthy of himfelf, and fuch as befpake a juft fuperiority to every other, calls himfelf, *I am that* (or who) *I am.*

Ifrael, from the obfcurity and fervitude in which they had been kept in Egypt, had very probably but narrow and contracted views of the true God, having had but a very imperfect idea of him, from the revelations made of himfelf to their anceftors, before their defcent into this country. And therefore, had Mofes only told them that the Lord God of their Fathers had fent him to them, they might have imagined that he was no more than fome local and fubordinate deity, and fo would have derived but little comfort from thence. But when he tells them, that the *I am* had fent him, he led them ferioufly to reflect upon the meaning of this character, and, by thefe means, gradually to develope it.

This character, *I am that I am*, which God affumed to himfelf, founds, it muft be owned, a little uncouth, and does not, all at once, convey a determinate idea along with it. But the very fingularity of it, and the obfcurity that attended it, could not fail to have the happy effect of fixing their thoughts upon it, and making them inquire into the defign and propriety of it.

It is well known, that, according to the genius of the Hebrew language, the meaning of any important word may be fixed and determined

termined by a due attention to the root from which it is derived.

Whatever speculations have been formed concerning the word *Jehovah* (and they have been many), all are agreed as to the derivation of it, and deduce it from a root which signifies *To Be*. And if, as critics allege, and the Hebrew doctors allow, the original word may be rendered so as to apply to the *Past*, *Present*, and *Future* time, and to signify *I was, I am, I shall be*, then it is evident that it was admirably fitted to convey the idea not only of self-existence and independence, but also of eternity and immutability.

A strong presumption that, in this sense, the word which we render *I am*, was to be taken, is,—The construction put upon the inscription in the temple at Delphi. Plutarch tells us, that, over the place where the statue or image of Apollo was erected, the word EI was engraven in golden letters. After reciting the various conjectures concerning the meaning of it in this place, he mentions the opinion of *Ammonius*, which is,—that, among the many titles given to Apollo, *this* was one:—that it was the ordinary form in which his votaries saluted him when they entered into his temple; and—that it was intended to express their veneration for him, and the opinion they had of his self-existence, independence, and immutability*.

Similar to the inscription on the temple of
Apollo

---

* Plut. in Lib. EI. apud Delph.

Apollo at *Delphi*, is that on the temple of Minerva at *Sais*, *I am whatever was, or is, or shall be, and my veil hath no mortal ever taken off* *. Now, is it not probable from both, that this title of God, *I am*, was early and well known, and that from it have been borrowed the inscriptions just now taken notice of?

The interpretation given of this title of God is rendered probable, not only by what has been offered above, but also by the translation of the Septuagint, Εγω ειμι ο ων. And here perhaps it may not be unworthy of notice, that these translators render the word in a manner that conveys the idea of personality and intelligence, as well as of self-existence, by using the masculine, in place of the neuter, gender.

Considered in this view, it is not improbable, that they meant to guard against the Pantheistic scheme, which had been adopted by some long before their time †, and which, by representing the Deity under the character of the Το Εν or the Το Παν, led to consequences, not only the most absurd in themselves, but the most hurtful to the interests of true religion.

But, while we offer these strictures upon the character or name by which God would have

---

* Plut. de Isid. & Osirid:—Εγω ειμι παν το γιγονος, και ον, και εσομενον, και τον εμον πεπλον ουδεις πω Θνητος απεκαλυψεν.

† The Septuagint translation was not made till about 240 years before the Christian æra; but we know that the Pantheistic scheme obtained long before that time.

have Moses to announce him to Israel, it deserves to be taken notice of,—that the rest of the answer which he gave to the inquiry made by Moses, seems to have been intended to account for the, at first, apparent obscurity of it, and to strengthen their confidence in, and expectations from, him.

For, when he thus speaks, does he not seem to give a hint, that there was no being with whom he could compare himself, and therefore that it was difficult to give such an explanation of his nature as mankind could understand? And while this hint served as a proper check to their too prying inquiries into the nature of the God of Israel, who was the true God, did it not also serve to expose the pretensions to Deity made by the Egyptian gods, whose origin was so well known, that all could say *who*, and *what*, they were?

And now, as the sacred historian informs us *, that it was at this time God first made himself known by the name *Jehovah* †, may

we

---

* Exod. vi. 3.

† Who does not know what whimsical conceits many of the Jewish Rabbis have entertained concerning the word *Jehovah*, and what a mighty pother has been made by the cabbalistical writers, about the manner, lawfulness, and wonderful effects, of the right pronunciation of it? Some of them alleged, that the right pronunciation of it, after having been communicated by God himself to mankind, had been lost on account of their wickedness. But it is no wonder (without having recourse to such a cause for it) that the proper pronunciation of it should not be agreed on. Because, as this entirely depends on the manner in which the vowels are

disposed

we not discern a great propriety in the choice of this season for the discovery? One reason is very obvious.—The ideas of eternity, self-existence, disposed of, it is evident this must be various. And accordingly we find it is so, among the different nations that use the word. Neither, so long as the same idea is conveyed by it, does this diversity matter much. And when it is remembered that they held it *unutterable*, not so much on account of their ignorance of the right pronunciation, as from the imagined unlawfulness of expressing it, nothing can be more absurd than any dispute about the manner of doing it.

Foolish as their conceits were concerning the lawfulness and manner of pronouncing it,—that, with respect to the wonderful virtue ascribed to it, is no less so. For, were you to believe some, the right pronunciation of this wonderful name (or the *Tetragrammaton*, as it was called, because consisting of four letters), was a powerful spell, by which the most extraordinary miracles might have been performed. Nay, so ignorant and superstitious were some of the Jews, that they ascribed all the stupenduous miracles which were performed by our Lord, to his having got possession of this profound secret, by stealing it out of the temple.

The Jews hold that this name is incommunicable, or, at least, never given by the sacred writers to any but the true God. In this they are right, though the reason is not what they allege,—any special sanctity that belongs to it; but that, according to its original meaning, it can apply to none other. It was, at the time taken notice of above, that God assumed to himself the name *Jehovah*. It is very true, we find frequent mention made of it, in the sacred history, long before this time.—And the reason is obvious. The use of the name *Jehovah* had become familiar among the Israelites long before Moses wrote the book of Genesis; and therefore, as no title could be more expressive of the nature and several of the perfections of God, he often uses it in the account he gives of times, persons, and events, long prior to the first discovery of it, and in this followed the phraseology of his own time, and not of the times whose history he recorded.—If the reader would choose to know more on this subject, he may consult Calmet's Dictionary, under the article *Jehovah*, and the Ancient Univ. Hist. vol. iii. p. 356. edit. 8vo.

existence, independence, and immutability (all which the title conveyed), were too abstract and profound to be early entered into.

Previous to a proper conception of these, a considerable improvement of the human mind was necessary. And though I will not say, that, when this character of the Deity was made known to Israel, they could fully comprehend it; yet it so evidently conveyed the idea of a vast superiority to the gods of the Egyptians, as admirably served to remove all the fears they could entertain from them, in the opposition they might be supposed to give to their removal.

Nay, to assert a superiority over the gods of Egypt, and thereby encourage their confidence in him, who called himself *The God of their Fathers,* does not seem to be all that was intended by the appropriation of this name to himself.—It served to convey a still more important instruction. His superiority might have been allowed in perfect consistency with the system of Pagan theology, which admitted of different classes or orders of divine beings. Such an acknowledgment as this, had it been made by the Egyptians, in consequence of what they saw Moses do in the name of his God, would have been no great honour to him. Nay, it would have been in fact a degradation of him into a mere local and tutelary deity; and, in place of overturning, had a tendency to confirm them in the erroneous faith of Polytheism. In the enunciation of his commission to Israel, it deserves to be taken

ken notice of, that Moses never descends so low as to institute a comparison betwixt his God, and those of the Egyptians. In the character under which he speaks of him, *I am that I am*, or, as some have rendered it, *I am he who am*, he asserts his sole and absolute right to the dominion and sovereignty of the universe; and thus, by what amounted to a denial of the divinity of the reputed gods of the Heathens, he undermined the very foundation of idolatry, which was one great design of God in the selection of Israel, and the many extraordinary dispensations of his providence towards them.

When God speaks of himself by a new title, as the reason for assuming it is generally apparent from the history, so the import of it will be found to be, for the most part, explanatory of it. A proof of this observation we have in the next character of the Deity, which we shall take under our consideration, and which is as remarkable as the occasion upon which it was assumed.—The Lord proclaims this to be his name (Exod. xxxiv. 6, 7.), *The Lord, The Lord God, Merciful*, &c.

A few days before this, Israel had, in a most provoking manner, disclaimed a regard for the God who had done so much for them, by making a *golden calf**, and falling down before

---

* It may, to the unlearned, appear strange, that Israel should have fallen into such a gross species of idolatry. But when it is considered that the Egytians, among whom they lived so long, were wont to worship their gods, *Isis* and *Osiris*, sometimes

before it, to worship. No wonder that so rude an affront, from a people distinguished by such a series of favours, should kindle the displeasure of God against them. Moses intercedes for them, and, as an evidence that he had found grace in his sight, God makes himself known to him by this name, *The Lord, The Lord God*, &c.

No doubt, in circumstances of such aggravated guilt, they not only trembled when they thought on God, but feared that they had for ever forfeited his favour, and that he would be gracious no more.

In such a situation, how opportunely does this declaration come from God himself, and with what affecting solemnity is it given! In this character, every line may be considered as forming a distinct feature, and all unite to give beauty, dignity, grace, and perfection to it.

The reader will be pleased to indulge me in

a

---

sometimes under the emblem of a living bull and sometimes under the image of it, this will account for their conduct in this instance, and for the choice they made of this figure in preference to any other. We are not to imagine, that by this action Israel renounced all faith in the true God. It only showed their proneness to worship him under some visible emblem, as the Egyptians had been accustomed to worship their gods. But admitting this, which is the only apology that can be offered for them, yet if we will consider the proofs they had of the divine presence among them,—the solemn manner in which the Law had, but a few days before, been delivered to them, and—the express terms in which the use of images was forbidden in the worship of God, their conduct must appear not only highly absurd, but equally criminal, and deficient in regard to him.

a few passing observations upon it. The Deity calls himself *The Lord, The Lord God*, or *The Strong-God*, that, by reminding them of this part of his character, he might secure their reverence and respect, and show them that it was not for want of power that he did not punish them.

The perfection of *Power*, which commanded respect, was also fit to encourage confidence, especially when they were, at the same time, told that he was *merciful and gracious*. He calls himself *merciful*, to show that he was disposed, not only to pity their weaknesses, but also to pardon their sins, and to relieve them from the miseries which were the consequences of them. But, at the same time, lest they should, from that pride for which they were so remarkable, imagine that any merit in themselves was the spring of the mercy shown them,—he tells them, that, in all this, he acted from pure grace and favour, or—benignity of nature.

They had often offended him; but he appeals to themselves, if they had not found him, in their experience, *long-suffering and slow to wrath*; nay, *abundant in goodness and truth:* possessed of a 'goodness that triumphed over all their unworthiness, and equally exceeded their hopes, as it did their merit:—A goodness, the exercise of which was secured to them, not only from the pleasure of communicating it, but also from a sacred and inviolable regard to his promises, made for the

the encouragement of their faith and confidence.

But as there was some danger, that the display of so much goodness might, (though intended to remove their fears) by an unhappy perversion of it, beget presumption, he adds with the greatest propriety, that he would by no means *clear the guilty;* that is, those who continued such. How grand, and, at the same time, amiable, this account of the Divine character! Is it not such an aggregate of perfection as must render him to whom it belongs, the deserved object of the highest reverence, esteem, confidence, and hope, with those to whom he has thus manifested himself?

Another title, under which we often find God introduced in the sacred history, is, *The Lord of Hosts**, or Armies.

Abstractedly considered, this may appear a character of the Deity very ungracious, and such as could only inspire terror, and so unfit the mind for that filial and ingenuous confidence, that was necessary to render the service of his subjects any way liberal. But the least acquaintance with the history of this people, to whom he makes himself known under this character, will evince the propriety of assuming it.

The people of Israel, in order to effect their settlement in the land of Canaan, and afterwards to maintain it, were obliged to engage

---

* 2 Sam. vi. 2.   2 Sam. vii. 26.

engage in many bloody wars with its inhabitants and the neighbouring nations. Compared with these, they were but a handful. No wonder, therefore, that, conscious of their own inequality, they should have been dismayed, when, at any time, they found it necessary to encounter them. In what terms, then, could God address them, better calculated to rouse their courage and engage their confidence, than by calling himself *The Lord of Hosts;* and thus teaching them to consider him as their Leader and General, interested for their protection, honour, and success? Viewed in this light, how naturally would they be led to take the field under his auspicious conduct, against the most formidable enemy that could start up to oppose or disturb them?

From the reason just now assigned, it is very probable, the title of *The Lord of Hosts* might have taken its rise.

I know there is another account given of the matter, and,—even according to that, the propriety of it must be readily admitted.

We are informed that, very early, there prevailed a gross species of idolatry in the East.—" Indulging themselves in some of the
" most fanciful speculations concerning the
" nature of the universe in general, and of
" this world in particular, and the influence
" which the sun and moon had upon it, mankind came at last to be persuaded (or pretended to be so) that the sun and moon were
" so many deities. From an admiration of
" the

" the grandeur of their appearance, and of
" their various phenomena, motions, and in-
" fluence, the tranfition to an adoration of
" them was very eafy. Nay, led away by a
" fpeculating humour, they, in procefs of
" time, affumed into their apotheofis, fome
" of the moft illuftrious of their anceftors,
" who had, by their heroic and good fervices,
" deferved well of their country, and now be-
" gan to be thought upon with a kind of en-
" thufiaftic gratitude. And to this deifica-
" tion they might be ftrongly prompted, from
" a conceit they entertained,—that, imme-
" diately after their death, their fouls remo-
" ved to fome of the luminous bodies they
" faw moving, in fuch awful majefty, over
" their heads, and that,—as minifters of the
" fupreme Deity, they might be highly fer-
" viceable to them *."—" They had alfo their
" demons and genii, beings of an order far
" fuperior to men, but inferior to the celeftial
" deities †."

Now as thefe notions prevailed long before the time of Mofes, it is not improbable, that, to them, there might be a reference in this truly grand title of the God of Ifrael. And if we will but fuppofe, that thefe demons, deified heroes, and the heavenly luminaries in which they were thought to have taken up their refidence, were confidered as the hofts

of

---

* See Vol. I. Part i. Sect. 2. of the Comparative View of the feveral Methods of promoting religious Inftruction, from the earlieft down to the prefent time.
† Vol. I. Part i. Sect 3.

of Heaven (and there are many places of sacred writ that seem to favour this conjecture*) there must appear a great deal of beauty and dignity in this character of the Deity. It not only distinguishes him from the gods of the nations, who were some of this host, but ascribes a superiority to him over them all. This opinion concerning the origin and import of the title, *Lord of Hosts*, has had some learned advocates for it †, as well as the former. And whichever of them the reader shall see meet to adopt, he will, I hope, admit, that, considering the circumstances of Israel at that time, there was a great propriety in it.

There prevailed among the Heathen nations an opinion of local deities. Hence the distinction of, *The Gods of the Hills*, and *The Gods of the Plains* ‡, as if each had his province or department assigned to him, and—of gods presiding over certain countries, as if they were committed to their special tutelage and guardianship §.

To counteract the influence of these opinions, which had a tendency to dishearten the Israelites, should they, at any time, be obliged to engage their enemies out of their own country, or within the particular province or jurisdiction of any of the other gods,—their God does, in effect, tell them, that he

---

* Deut. iv. 19. Chap. xvii. 3. Nehem. ix. 6. 1 Kings, xxii. 19. Pf. ciii. 20, 21.
† Mede's Works, Disc. on Luke ii. 13, 14.
‡ 1 Kings xx. 23, 28.
§ 2 Kings xviii. 34, 35.

he was the God of the hills as well as of the plains, and that his government and superintendance extended equally to both.

Nay, to remove all ground of fear, from the suppofed interpofition of any of thofe nominal deities in favour of their votaries, he is reprefented to his people as *The God of gods and Lord of lords* *;* that is, as one to whom, all, who were called gods, were to be confidered as fubordinate and fubjected.

The reader will, I hope, permit me to take notice of one title or character more, which God affumes to himfelf. The folemnity with which it is introduced, and the comfort and inftruction with which it abounds, feem to point it out, as particularly deferving of the attention of thofe to whom he addreffes himfelf. Thus faith *The Lord, The King of Ifrael, and his Redeemer the Lord of Hofts, I am the Firft, and I am the Laft, and befides me there is no God* †. To difcern the beauty and propriety of this addrefs, it will be neceffary to recollect the character of the people to whom it is made. They had, upon many occafions before this, difcovered a very ftrong propenfity to idolatry, and often fhamefully relapfed into it, notwithftanding all the pains that had been taken to guard them againft it. Here, therefore, God once more addreffes them in a manner that led them to infer, not only the priority of his exiftence to that of every other Being, but alfo that, as he derived it from

none

---

† Deut. x. 17.   † Ifa. xliv. 6.

none other, so it should remain for ever unimpaired by the greatest length of time. All this the Heathens, and those infected with their principles, might admit, without any prejudice to their system of religion. For, according to their Theogony, the acknowledgement of one supreme Deity, did not forbid the belief of others whom they supposed to be generated and subordinate to him,—whom, like him, they believed to be immortal and without end of time. With the greatest propriety, therefore, does God draw the conclusion to which the preceding observations concerning his nature did fairly lead, but which he knew the deceitful influence of their prejudices would prevent them from making, namely, that *besides him, there was no God*, that is, none who deserved the title, however the folly of some might dignify them with it. And here, before I have finished the remarks proper to be made upon this important passage, is it not deserving of notice, that the Prophet is at the greatest pains to guard against the application of this character to any but him, to whom it, of right, belonged? And for this purpose, he tells those to whom his commission led him, that it was, *The Lord Jehovah, King of Israel, Their Redeemer, The Lord of Hosts*, and not any other, who had thus pronounced concerning himself, *I am the First, and I am the Last, and besides me there is no God*.

There are several other characters under which the Deity is presented to the view of Israel, all of which, were we to consider them separately,

separately, would be found to have the same propriety, which has, in so striking a manner, marked those already taken notice of. But it is unnecessary to mention any more of the characters, by which he was known under this dispensation. Those already taken notice of, may serve for the purpose on account of which they are adduced.

Plato informs us, that the great *Socrates* wished for a discovery of the true names of the Deity, as the most probable way of arriving at a just knowledge of him *. What he so evidently desired, we find, from the above induction of titles which form the character of the Deity, the people of Israel have been favoured with. And now, instead of calling such discovery, or the manner in which it was made, *absurd and unphilosophical*, it is submitted to the impartial reader, whether both do not appear to be the reverse. For surely, their natural and direct tendency was,—to beget in the minds of the Israelites, the most respectful sentiments of the Deity,—to form their tempers and lives for religion, as individuals,—to nourish their national confidence in him, as a community,—and to do both in a manner the most promising of success, because the best adapted to their genius,—the circumstances of time and place in which they were situated, and the prejudices of various kinds, and of the most powerful influence, under which they laboured.

But,

---

* Περι Θεων ἡμιν ἰσμεν, ὁτι περι αυτων, ὁτι περι των ονοματων, ἀτια ποτε αυτους καλοσι, &c. Plato in Cratyl.

But, not to infist on observations of this nature at present, as they may perhaps be made with greater advantage afterwards, upon a reflex view of our subject, we proceed to the consideration——

SECT. II.

Of the Worship required from Israel.

IT is impossible to contemplate the character of the Deity, without being led, by a natural train of sentiment, to think of the worship that is to be paid to him. This is an homage justly due from creatures, who have an immediate, constant, and absolute dependence upon him. The reasonableness of offering a worship to the Deity being once admitted, the next inquiry comes to be into the nature of it, and the acceptable manner of performing it.

Against the nature of the worship required of Israel and the manner of performing it, there are not a few objections raised by those who are disposed to cavil. They are at great pains to represent it, in both these respects, as unworthy of the Deity to recommend,—below him to accept, and such as must mislead those who are called to be engaged in it.

The charge is bold; and would need to be well supported, to deserve regard. For this purpose, they allege that no worship but what is spiritual can be acceptable to the Deity, who is himself a pure Spirit; and therefore

E that

that a manner of worship so loaded as this is, with a multitude of external rites, can never be so: Nay, that it has a tendency to beget in the minds of the worshippers, the grossest sentiments of him; and, by these means, instead of improving, to corrupt both their principles and manners.

It is very readily admitted, that a worship which is spiritual, that is, which proceeds from, and is animated by, a true devotion in the heart, can alone be acceptable to a Being such as God is. Nor does the Mosaic institution of religion, require, or approve of, any other. This is an assertion that will not, I know, be admitted without a proof, especially as, it must be owned, appearances are against it.

The best way to investigate this proof, is to take a particular view of the worship enjoined. And when we have done so, we shall, I hope, in the issue, find that it is no other, than what sober and unbiassed reason must approve. The mode of performing it, may, at first, appear incompatible with this character of it; but if it can be made appear (as I hope it can) that it was perfectly suited to the genius of the people of Israel and the circumstances of the times in which it obtained, and also admirably calculated to promote that spirit of devotion, which it was intended to express, it will be readily allowed to be justly deserving of the character I have given of it.

Before we enter on the consideration of the nature and manner of the Jewish worship, the rite

rite of *circumcifion* claims our attention. This was the rite of initiation into the Jewish church, and falls very properly to be inquired into, before the examination of its particular services.

Concerning the origin of this rite of the Jewish religion, various opinions have been entertained. Among the ancients, *Herodotus, Diodorus Siculus, Celfus,* and *Julian,* and among the moderns, *Marfham, Shaftefbury, Middleton, Voltaire,* and others, have maintained (for what reason is hard to say, if not to difparage it) that it did obtain in Egypt, long before it was practifed by Abraham.

That it did obtain pretty early among the Egyptians is not denied; though I humbly think, not near so early as the advocates for this opinion would allege.

What moft of the ancients, and all the moderns, have advanced on this subject, has taken its rife from what *Herodotus* and *Diodorus* have written concerning it.

That the reader may judge for himfelf, it may not be improper to lay before him, in a short extract, the sentiments of both upon it. Herodotus fays (to give his opinion in Englifh, for the fake of thofe who may not have accefs to the original), " That the Colchians, Egyp-
" tians, Ethiopians, are alone, of all men,
" απ'αϱχης from the *beginning*. And that the
" Phenicians and Syrians who were in Pale-
" ftine, acknowledge they were taught this
" rite by the Egyptians. But, with refpect
" to the Egyptians and Ethiopians, I cannot
" take

" take upon me to say which of them received
" it from the other, for that it seemed to be
" of ancient standing *."

Diodorus, writing of the Jews and Colchians, both which he seems to have considered as colonies from Egypt, observes in support of this opinion,—" That their children were cir-
" cumcised according to an ancient custom
" which obtained in Egypt, and was borrow-
" ed by them, from thence †."

That the sentiments of these writers, are, by no means, decisive upon this subject, will evidently appear from the following remarks.

In the first place, may it not be observed as to Herodotus, that he speaks not a word of the Jews? And it can with no degree of certainty, be inferred that he meant them, by the Phenicians and Syrians in Palestine. But, should this be granted, pray, where is the proof of the fact he alleges? It rests solely upon his *ipse dixit*, or, at least, upon the information of the Egyptian priests, to whom he was obliged for all his intelligence in this matter. But who can admit this authority to be sufficient to support such an opinion, when it is considered that it is, if not expressly contradicted by the Jews themselves, rendered improbable from a variety of considerations, which all seem to indicate a quite different origin of this practice ‡?

Who

---

* Herodot. lib. 2. cap. 104. † Diodor. Sicul. lib. 1.
‡ Josephus observes (Antiq. lib. 1. cap. 8) that, by the indulgence

Who that is, in the least, acquainted with the national character of the Egyptians, can be ignorant of that pride for which they were distinguished? And is it not probable that they might be, from thence, prompted to affect the honour of originality in this, as in all the other religious rites which they practised? To have acknowledged that they derived them from any other, would have been a condescension not to be expected from them.

But why insist, from this passage of Herodotus, that the practice of circumcision was derived from Egypt? There is no necessity for such an interpretation. It needs imply no more, than that the practice was a very early one. So indeed he, in effect, himself explains it. It is true, he says, this practice was among the Egyptians, ἀπ'ἀρχῆς. But this does by no means imply that they were the first who used it; but only that the use of it was so early among them, that they could not fix the precise time of its origin. And that Herodotus

dulgence of Pharoah, he had an opportunity of conversing with the most learned in his kingdom—that he was high in reputation among them for his knowledge; and that he took the opportunities thus given him, to set them right, as to many of their rites and ceremonies in religion; and therefore is it not more probable that they would have borrowed from him, for whom they had such a veneration, than that he should borrow from them?

It is true, it may be alleged that the authority of Josephus upon this point is but of little weight. On a point of such antiquity, it may be considered as no more than the authority of Rabbinical traditions. But surely it deserves as much regard upon the one side, as Herodotus and Diodorus do on the other.

tus meant no more by this phrase, is presumeable from the reason he assigns for the difficulty of determining, whether the Egyptians learned it from the Ethiopians, or the Ethiopians from the Egyptians, namely, that it *seems to have been of ancient standing.* And might not the Egyptian priests have said, with the greatest propriety, that it was of ancient standing, when they gave this information to *Herodotus,* even though we should suppose it introduced into Egypt, long after it was practised by Abraham and his descendants.*?

Diodorus, it must be owned, is more express. But it is evident, that the account he gives of the origin of this practice in deducing it from Egypt, proceeds upon a mistake. He supposes the Jews, as well as the Colchians, to be a colony from Egypt; and from thence concludes, that, because the Colchians very probably borrowed this rite from the Egyptians, so did the Jews also.

Thus, from these few remarks, the boasted testimonies of Herodotus and Diodorus, must evidently appear to be far from decisive upon this point. But, were they even as explicit as could be desired, would there not be a degree of unfairness in giving credit to them, because they favour a particular hypothesis, while yet a very different account of the matter is given by another author, who lived much

---

* Circumcision was instituted in the 99th year of Abraham's age, that is, A. M. 2107, or ante Christ. 1893.—And Herodotus was not born till an. ante Christ. 484, that is, 1409 years, after the institution of circumcision.

much nearer the times and events of which he writes, and who had the fulleſt information with reſpect to every thing he records concerning them?

But, to paſs over what theſe ancient authors have ſaid upon the ſubject, with theſe few curſory remarks, let us examine the matter in another light, and we ſhall find that there are the ſtrongeſt preſumptions againſt their alleged origin of this practice.

It muſt be admitted, becauſe evident from the Moſaic hiſtory, (unleſs its authority could be diſcredited) that Abraham went into Egypt upwards of twenty years before we hear any thing of circumciſion*. And as it is not to be doubted but he would become acquainted, during his ſtay there, with the great lines of their religious ſyſtem †, might it not be imagined, that this very circumſtance would have determined him againſt the uſe of the rite, he is ſuppoſed to have borrowed from them?

It is evident that his journey into Egypt, was not till after his call from Haran, in Chaldea. And if we ſuppoſe him, as ſome have

---

* Abraham was 75 years of age when he left Haran and travelled into Egypt, but it was not till he was 99 that he circumciſed Iſhmael, &c. See Gen. xii. 4. compared with Gen. xvii. 23, 24.

† His acquaintance with the Egyptian ſyſtem of religion, is preſumable from what has been obſerved in note, p. 68. But, leſt this account, as coming from a Jew, might be ſuſpected, let me obſerve that it is, in the great lines of it, confirmed by Melo and Nicolaus Damaſcenus. See Shuckford's connection, &c. Vol. II.. p. 34, 35.

have done, to have been expelled his own country for his averſion to idolatry*, or, according to the ſcripture account of the matter, choſen to be the ſupporter of the religion of the true God, againſt the ſpreading influence of idolatry, is it to be imagined that he would make choice of a rite from the religion of ſuch groſs idolaters, eſpecially as there was nothing inviting in it, but, on the contrary, every thing that could diſſuade from it? Or, if we could ſuppoſe that Abraham might, from ſome motives unknown to us, have been determined in favour of this rite, I would aſk,—Is it to be imagined that God, to pleaſe Abraham, would have adopted it into that religion, which, by the means of his family, he was to teach the world? Is there not rather reaſon to think, that the uſe of it among the Egyptians would have determined him againſt it? eſpecially as it is well known, that one reaſon, and a principal one too, of the choice of Abraham and of the laying the foundations of his church in his family, was to counteract the influence of that idolatry, which was then like to overſpread the world.

The only objection of weight that ſeems to preſs hard upon this account of the origin of circumciſion, is—the ſuppoſed improbability that

---

* Joſephus tells us (Antiq. lib. 1. cap. 7.) that he was the firſt who taught openly that there was but one God, the creator of all things;—that becauſe he defended this opinion, and enforced it upon others, the inhabitants of Chaldea and Meſopotamia roſe ſeditiouſly againſt him, and that to avoid their outrage he fled to the land of Canaan.
See alſo Judith v. 8.

that the Egyptians would have borrowed it from the Israelites. Thus some would represent the matter. " Considering the high con-
" tempt which the Egyptians entertained of
" the Israelites, and their religion :—Of the
" one, on account of the servile state to which
" they were reduced; and—of the other, on
" account of the impious and impure abomi-
" nations, with which, in their opinion, it
" was stuffed; is it not extremely improbable,
" say they, that they would adopt such a
" bloody rite, from so detested a religion, and
" transmit it, as sacred, to their descendants?"

In the objection, thus stated, it must be allowed, there is something very plausible. But, at the same time, it is humbly contended, there is nothing conclusive.

It is readily granted that the aversion which the Egyptians had to the Israelites at first, joined with the nature of the rite itself, might have greatly prejudiced them against it. But when, under the auspicious and popular administration of Joseph, the Egyptians came to think better of the Israelites, might they not have become better disposed towards their religion also? And if, as *Philo* hints, they could be either weak or superstitious enough to imagine, that the great increase or population of Israel was owing to the use of this rite, we can easily conceive how their pride might stoop so far as to adopt it into their religion.

Nay, another reason may be assigned for the Egyptians adopting this rite from the religion of the Israelites. It is well known that
the

the Heathens admitted an intercommunity of worſhip, in honour of each others gods. And; upon this principle, might not the Egyptians, according to their ſyſtem, have joined with the Iſraelites, in the uſe of this rite preſcribed by their God? Or, if the averſion they had to the Iſraelites would have prevented their ſhowing this mark of reſpect to their God, might it not, according to another principle of their religion, be accounted for, even from the terror of his greatneſs?

They had received many irrefragable proofs, not only of the great power, but alſo of the ſuperiority, of the God of Iſrael to their own Deities, eſpecially, in the manner, the triumphant manner, in which he wrought their deliverance from the bondage under which they groaned. Might they not, therefore, have adopted this rite of his inſtitution, (if we ſuppoſe the adoption of it ſo late) in hopes that, by ſuch a mark of honour and reſpect, they might be able to court him over from their enemies to themſelves, as was often attempted in other caſes, by evocatory ſacrifices?

I do not ſay upon which of theſe principles, or if upon any of them, the Egyptians adopted the rite of circumciſion. But I humbly imagine any of them is ſufficient to remove the force of the objection, which would deny its derivation from the Iſraelites, on account of the alleged improbability of it.

But ſhould it ſtill be inſiſted on, that, for the reaſons mentioned in the objection, it is improbable

bable that the Egyptians fhould have borrowed this rite from the Ifraelites, yet, why fhould it from thence be inferred that the Ifraelites borrowed it from them? Such an opinion muft reft upon the authority of Herodotus and Diodorus; and yet, it concerns the advocates for it, to affign a good reafon, why a greater regard fhould be paid to the teftimony of thefe in fupport of it, than to that of Mofes againft it. And till they do fo, I cannot underftand why a preference fhould be claimed.

But not to infift on a larger proof of the Divine origin of this practice *, let us attend to the defign of it; and the propriety of inftituting fuch a rite, will be found to ftand juftified, againft all the torrent of ridicule that has been directed againft it.

To underftand the defign of it the better, it will be neceffary to attend to the time and occafion of its appointment.

A certain writer †, juftly celebrated for his learning and his regard for religion, entertains a very fingular opinion, as to both.

He fuppofes it to have been one of the original inftitutions, appointed immediately after the fall; and that though retained here and there, it had been left off in Abraham's country,

---

* See what relates to the origin of circumcifion largely handled by Dr Findlay, in his vindication of the Sacred Books, againft the cavils of M. Voltaire.

† See Forbes's Thoughts, concerning religion, natural and revealed, and the manner of underftanding revelation, tending to fhow that Chriftianity is, indeed very near, as old as the creation.

country, where idolatry began to prevail; and therefore, that it was renewed when he was selected to be the father of a people, who were to become the keepers of the sacred oracles? He also supposes that the original intention of it was,—to be a memorial to mankind of the evils brought upon them by an improper gratification of appetite, and thus to guard them against an undue indulgence of it for the future.

But, great as the regard is which is due to such an author, I must be allowed to say, that there seems to be no foundation for this opinion, in the sacred history. Every circumstance in the appointment of this rite to Abraham, seems to indicate that particular time to be the æra of its institution.

We have an account of the institution of circumcision Gen. xvii. 10. &c. From this, it evidently appears to be connected with the covenant which God had before entered into with Abraham, and had confirmed at this time.

The promise of a son made to Abraham, at so advanced a period of life, was not more acceptable to him, than the accomplishment of it must have appeared improbable. According to the ordinary course of nature, appearances seemed to be against it. No wonder, therefore, if his faith should need something to confirm it.

Abraham, from the very first mention of the promise made to him, seems to have entertained no doubt of the accomplishment of it, it, in due time. Accordingly we are told (Gen. xv. 6.) that "he believed in the Lord, "and he counted it to him for righteouſ- "neſs." But though, at receiving the promiſe, he ſeems to have given full credit to the performance of it, yet as, betwixt the making of this covenant and the renewal of it, a conſiderable time had intervened, without any appearance that looked more favourable, than when it was entered into, he aſks God, verſe 8. whereby he might know that he ſhould inherit the promiſed land.—This he did, not ſo much from any diffidence he yet had in the Divine promiſe, as from an apprehenſion or fear, that a delay in the accompliſhment of it, might, at ſome unguarded moment, and in ſome diſadvantageous ſituation, ſtagger his faith in it.

From a gracious regard, at once to the ſincerity and weakneſs of his faith, God is pleaſed to grant him what he aſked. And, for this purpoſe, he appoints the uſe of a rite, which might, at once, ſerve as a memorial of his promiſe and a confirmation of that faith in it which was required, and was neceſſary to animate all the ſervices of religion.

It is evident from the ſacred hiſtory, that the covenant God entered into with Abraham, included his poſterity. And as, from thence, a long ſucceſſion of ages became neceſſary to carry the ſeveral parts of it into accompliſhment, did not this circumſtance require the inſtitution of a rite, that ſhould continue till it did take place, that ſo a remembrancer of God's

God's promise might, at no subsequent period, be wanting?

"Be it so, but (may it be asked) might not a rite less liable to exception have been pitched upon for this purpose?" To this it might suffice to reply—that the choice must be allowed to belong to God, without his being under any obligations to assign the particular reasons of it. But, though we do not pretend to guess all the reasons which there might have been for it, we may discern enough to vindicate the institution.

I already observed, that one great design of the institution of this rite, was to confirm not only the faith of Abraham, but of his posterity, in the promises made to him. From this consideration, there arises an evident ground of propriety in it. Had God pitched upon any sign that should but rarely occur, or was not always to be seen, we may conceive, that, in many cases, where the assistance of it might be needed, it might be wanting. Whereas, by carrying about this sign in their very flesh, they never could be in circumstances, where they had not still present to them, what was sufficient to confirm their faith in the Divine promises, made to their ancestors.

Closely connected with their faith in the Divine promise, was the influence it was calculated to have upon religious practice. To this, such a rite was admirably subservient. Like every other rite in this religion, it had an important moral couched under it. It reminded them of the promise of God, and so

encouraged

encouraged them in his fervice. It, at the fame time, not obfcurely hinted to them the nature of it, and the obligations they were under to mortify every irregular appetite, by reprefenting the indulgence of thefe as incompatible with the character of a people devoted to God, or who would hope that their fervices would be acceptable to him.

It had an excellent moral tendency in another point of view.

In the circumftances in which it was appointed to Abraham, it not only ferved as a proper confirmation of his faith, by being a memorial of the Divine promife. It was alfo an excellent proof and illuftration of his faith and piety, in fubmitting to an operation of fo much pain and danger, and at a period that feemed to fruftrate all the great hopes which the Divine promife was calculated to raife in his mind. Now, let it be confidered, that the defign of God in the felection of Ifrael, was not fo much to diftinguifh them by their defcent from Abraham according to the flefh, as by the imitation of his faith and other virtues. And what could be better calculated for this purpofe, than fuch an exhibition of them? As often as they thought on this rite, fo extraordinary in itfelf, it is almoft impoffible but they muft have thought on their illuftrious anceftor, who firft fubmitted to it. And as in this inftance of his obedience, they were naturally led to difcern the faith, piety, and devotion that animated his conduct, were they not from thence led to the imitation of him

in

in thofe virtues, which fo eminently dignified his character, and rendered him fo great a favourite of Heaven? This could not fail to recall him often to their remembrance, and to beget in their minds fentiments of the higheft efteem and refpect for him. And nothing can be more natural, (if they did not fuffer themfelves to be feduced by the influence of paffion) than to copy the manners of one they had fuch juft reafon to admire. And now let us but reflect upon the circumftances of thofe early ages,—that the revelations yet vouchfafed to them were but few,—that the ufe of letters was probably altogether unknown among them, and,—confequently that any knowledge they had of religion, could have been communicated only by tradition, and it is humbly fubmitted, if, in fuch a fituation, this inftitution was not admirably expreffive of the above purpofes intended by it.

Befides the reafons for the inftitution of this rite, which have been already taken notice of, there is another which muft not be overlooked, and that is,—that it feems to have been intended as a badge of diftinction, betwixt the defcendants of Abraham and the nations around them*; which, by the by, is a fhrewd prefumption, that, when the practice was begun

by

---

* This is not only evident from the facred record, and from the teftimony of Jofephus; Tacitus alfo fhows the general opinion in his time, concerning the defign of it, when he fays —" Circumcidere genitalia inftituere, ut diverfitate nofcantur." Hift. lib. 5.

by Abraham, it did not obtain in Egypt or any where else.

Before that time mankind were pretty much agreed in the worship of the one true God; and therefore such a rite, considered as a badge of distinction, was unnecessary. But when, now, they became divided into the worshippers of many gods, there must appear an evident propriety in it, as the use of it served for a virtual acknowledgment of the true God, and their determined resolution to adhere to his service.—That in this sense it was to be understood by those who submitted to it, seems evidently to have been the sentiments of the Apostle Paul (Gal. v. 3.), who says—*That every one who is circumcised becomes a debtor to the whole law.*

We may also be able to trace some not obscure hints of such a design by this rite, in the practice of subsequent ages, which seems to have a reference to it. We know that the votaries of particular deities, were distinguished by their special signature; such as,—a thunderbolt for Jupiter,—an ivy-leaf for Bacchus, &c.—And these marks or brands, which were esteemed sacred, were considered as public marks of their consecration to the service of that deity *. Could we imagine that this custom had obtained before the institution of circumcision (and of this kind some think

F were

---

* See Spencer de Legib. Ritual. Hebræor. lib. ii. cap. 14.—Mede's Works, p. 511.—See also something on this subject, though applied to a different purpose, Lowman's Rational, &c. p. 236.

were the rites, alluded to Levit. xix. 28. practised by the Heathens at the funerals of their
friends, and with a view to render the infernal
deities propitious to them), we should be apt to
think, that it had been intended as a counter-
distinction of the worshippers of the true God.
But, as there is reason to think, that the use
of such signatures, punctures, or marks, is of
a much later date, or, at least, that such an
application of them is so, the probability, I
think, is—that it had taken its rise from the
practice of circumcision. And so it becomes
a presumptive evidence, that one of the original
designs of it was,—to serve as a distinction of
the worshippers of the true God, from those
of the fictitious deities around them.

It is true, this rite, by being afterwards
adopted by other nations, ceased to be any
longer characteristical of the Jews. But it
was not, on that account, to be superseded.
This was but one end of its institution. The
use of it was continued for its subserviency to
the other ends proposed by it. And it deserves to be taken notice of, that, as it was
necessary to preserve such a distinction betwixt
Jews and Gentiles as should keep the former
from being corrupted by the latter,—so, when
circumcision (for the reason just now mentioned) ceased to be sufficient for this purpose,
a pompous ritual was instituted, which, at the
same time that it served for other valuable
purposes, answered equally well for keeping
up this distinction.

This much seemed necessary in vindication
of

of the original, and in illustration of the design, of this rite, by which mankind were to be initiated into the church of God, under a part of the Abrahamic and the whole of the Mosaic dispensations *. And as, from what has been offered on the subject, the reasonableness of it, will, I hope, be admitted, let us now address ourselves to the particular business of this section,—the consideration of the religious worship required of Israel.

This may be considered as consisting of two parts,—the more ordinary and stated, and—the more solemn and occasional.

At first sight, neither of these seems to have a very favourable aspect upon a pure and rational devotion: But a more narrow inspection will remove these prejudices, and give us quite different sentiments concerning them.

The subject of sacrifice is one of those upon which the learned have bestowed great attention,

---

* When, in the course of this work, I speak of what are commonly called, The *Patriarchal*, *Abrahamic*, *Mosaic*, and *Christian* dispensations of religion, it may be proper, once for all, to inform the reader, that I do not consider them as so many different dispensations, independent of, and unconnected with, one another, but as so many parts of a great whole: though, to avoid the trouble that would necessarily arise from the frequent mention of this distinction, I use the ordinary and vulgar mode of expression, with respect to them. Properly speaking, there has been but *one* dispensation of God's grace to mankind, from the beginning,—but *one* religion that has derived its origin from God: What is called the different dispensations, or, if you will, modifications of it, being no more than the gradual openings of his plan, as the circumstances of the world, and the improvements of mankind, would admit, and seemed to require.

tion, and yet have run into very different sentiments.

In an inquiry of this nature, the principal design of which is to judge of the propriety and importance of the rite, our first concern should be to be satisfied of its origin; for, if it is of human, and not of divine, institution, we have nothing to do with it.

The antiquity of the practice is universally acknowledged, but the origin of it differently accounted for.

A certain author *, not only to discredit the practice, but to reach a stroke against religion, represents it as the pious fraud of some designing priests, who, taking the advantage of the ignorance, superstition, and credulity of the people, promoted the trade of so gainful a butchery, from the hopes of reserving some of the choice pieces for themselves. To this purpose he expresses himself upon the subject.
" It is probable that the Heathen priests, who
" shared with their gods, and reserved the
" best bits for themselves, had the chief hand
" in this, as well as in all other gainful super-
" stitions, while the deluded people, who many
" times suffered by the scarcity of provisions,
" were at vast expence in maintaining these
" holy butchers, whose very trade inspired
" them with cruelty. And it is probable,
" that this absurd notion prevailed, like all
" other absurdities, by degrees; and that, at
" first, sacrifices were only religious feasts,
                                      " either

---

* Christianity as old as the Creation, Vol. I. p. 79.

"either in commemoration of some national
"benefit, where, after God, their great Be-
"nefactor, was celebrated, they commemora-
"ted their particular benefactors:—or else,
"feasts were made on a private account by
"the master of a family, upon shearing his
"sheep, gathering in the fruits of the earth,
"&c. where those who assisted him were en-
"tertained, and joyfully joined in giving
"thanks to the Author of those blessings, with-
"out destroying or burning any part of the
"creature given for their use: And the ma-
"ster of the family, was, no doubt, master
"of the ceremonies, at his own feast. But
"this simple method not pleasing certain
"persons, who were resolved to have the best
"share in all those religious feasts, they per-
"suaded the people, that it was necessary
"some part of the flesh of animals should be
"burnt to feed the hungry nostrils of the
"Deity, delighted with the sweet savour of
"burnt flesh; and the better part to be reser-
"ved unburnt for themselves, to whom the
"slaying of the animals, and the offering them
"up, was appropriated."

This indeed is such a shameless, and, at the same time, such a weak, attack upon religion and its ministers, that it is perhaps doing it too much honour to take notice of it. Few words are necessary to expose, either the ignorance or malevolence from which it proceeds. It affords scope for many severe strictures. I beg leave, however, to dismiss it with one remark,—that had the author but allowed himself to consider, that the practice, even of animal sacrifice, was in use long before the institution of a regular priesthood (though he would, to serve his purpose, insinuate the contrary), he might have been ashamed to assign it, either to the avarice or luxury of the priests.

Others, viewing this as a practice glaringly absurd, have supposed that it took its rise from an opinion that the objects of worship, were of like passions with those who offered it. From thence they imagined that mankind, in their early, rude, and uncultivated state, imparted to their great and common Benefactor, a share of those things in which they most delighted themselves, not doubting, because they were pleased with them, but he would be so too.

This is the opinion of the author of Philemon to Hydaspes, or *The History of false Religion*.—In support of this hypothesis, he has offered very little, though, I humbly think, it would require a great deal, to gain credit to it,—much more indeed than is necessary to vindicate that which it opposes.

Other schemes have been adopted to account for the origin of this practice, which, though more plausible than any of the former, do not appear to be well founded.—I shall mention one of them.

Some have supposed the practice to be coeval with, or, at least, to have commenced soon after, the fall of man, and to have continued, without any appointment of God, to

be

be the mode in which mankind chose to express their devotion, till, soon after giving the law, it received the divine sanction. Then, say they, God was pleased, by a special appointment of it and the whole ritual that concerned it, to indulge Israel in a practice of which they seemed passionately fond, and, by introducing a reformation, to guard them against the abuses into which they were apt to run. Dr Spencer argues warmly in favour of this opinion *.—So does also Grotius †. And both seem to think, that a very clear hint in support of it is given by the prophet Jeremiah, chap. vii. 22.

I must own I am greatly surprised to find so great a stress laid upon this passage, by such learned men. For surely, if it is but candidly attended to, it must be allowed to contain nothing against the Divine institution of sacrifice, long before the time they would fix for it.

It is acknowledged, that, prior to the giving of the law, or rather the worship of the golden calf, we find no account of the institution of sacrifice: But the reception it had from Israel, long before this time, is no small presumption in favour of a much more early origin. This of itself seems to contain a tacit acknowledgment, that both Moses and Israel were fully satisfied of its divine origin, though the time of it was so far back, that they could
not

* Vide Spencer Differt. Secund. de Origine Sacrificiorum.
† Grot. de Veritate, &c. lib. v. cap. 8.

not eafily fix it, elfe it would not have had fo much regard paid to it, by either.

A pofitive decifion in favour of the Divine inftitution of facrifice, fo early as we find the firft mention made of the practice, we do not pretend to. But if, in a cafe (fuch as this) where we have an account of the practice, but none of the origin of it, the greater degree of probability ought to determine our judgment, we muft, I humbly think, give it in favour of its Divine origin. Every circumftance in the early hiftory of this practice, feems to plead for this opinion.

The firft inftances of facrifice which we find any mention of in fcripture, (the oldeft hiftory we have) are thofe of Cain and Abel,—And with refpect to them, the attentive reader cannot but obferve, that, when they addrefs themfelves to this act of religion (for fuch it evidently was) there is no hint, either from the hiftory or their practice, that would give us the leaft caufe to fufpect that it was of their invention. But, if we could imagine them forward enough to venture, in the firft tranfports of their zeal, to worfhip God, without any direction from him, is there the fmalleft reafon to think, that animal facrifice would have been the mode they would have pitched upon? Perhaps there might appear fomething plaufible in the oblation of the fruit of trees, cakes of bread, honey, &c. as a tribute of gratitude, to God, confidered under the character of their generous Benefactor. But how it fhould ever enter into the human mind to imagine, that
the

the effufion of the blood of an innocent animal could be acceptable to the Deity, muft, independent of an appointment of God himfelf for this purpofe, be ever difficult to reconcile with any principle of reafon. Let *this* fact be but duly attended to, and it will be found to plead ftrongly for the divine origin of facrifice. For, confidering how different the tafte, fentiments, temper, and interefts of mankind are, it is humbly fubmitted, whether it be, in the leaft degree, probable, that, had this been no more than a human invention, there fhould have been an univerfal, or, at leaft, next to univerfal, confent in it? This is what has never happpened in any other inftance or mode of worfhip. And what reafon can be affigned, that is even plaufible, why it fhould have happened in this? Nay, were there not many reafons, which (abftracting from a higher than human authority) would have made them ftrike out againft it?—Or, could we fuppofe mankind (from what principle no matter) to have adopted this practice, yet what reafon could we have to imagine that it would have met with the Divine approbation? And yet do we not find the moft exprefs declaration of fuch fervice being accepted in many inftances, and, in fome, in a manner that feems not obfcurely to indicate the Divine appointment of it?

Thus, with refpect to the very firft facrifices we have an account of, are we not told, that God had refpect to Abel and his facrifice, becaufe (according to the information of an apoftle) apoſtle*) he offered it through faith, that is (for it can mean no leſs), in dutiful obedience to the Divine command that required it, and in humble dependence upon the Divine bleſſing which was promiſed to reward it?—Nor is this all. We have an inſtance, even of a direct command from God himſelf, with reſpect to ſacrifice, prior to the alleged inſtitution of it in the plains of Sinai. It is in the caſe of Abraham Gen. xxii. 13. I know it may be ſaid that this was a particular caſe, and that from it we can infer nothing with reſpect to the practice in early times. But if we will conſider how Moſes, by the ſpecial command of God, appointed the whole ceremonial relating to ſacrifice, we cannot doubt but Iſrael was before well acquainted with the practice of ſacrificing. The manner in which he proceeds is evidently ſuch as preſuppoſes this †.

Having thus, from the moſt probable reaſons, evinced the Divine origin of the practice of ſacrificing, it may not be improper, before we offer a vindication of it, to take a view of the original deſign of it.

When, in theological writings, mention is made of ſacrifice, it is often in a very indefinite ſenſe. In the common acceptation of the word, it ſignifies thoſe animals that were devoted

---

* Heb. xi.
† See on the Divine Origin of Sacrifices, Shuckford's Connection of ſacred and proph. Hiſt. v. i. p. 79. Shuckford on the Creation and Fall of Man, Pref. p. 95. and Dr Richie on the Particular Doctrines of Revel. vol. i. p. 144.

devoted to God, and actually offered up upon his altar. Strictly speaking, however, it means any thing devoted to a holy and pious use; and so includes all the offerings of a religious kind, that were made unto God.

The sacrifices in use, under the Mosaic œconomy, were of different kinds, and received different denominations, according to the several lights in which they were viewed, or the purposes to which they were applied. The sacred history has not made an exact distribution of them, into their several classes. They may, however, all, or the most remarkable of them, be comprehended under the following— *The Expiatory*, *Fœderal*, *Eucharistic*, or *Votive*.

It is not necessary to be very nice in the several distinctions under which they are to be considered. It will be of more importance to ascertain the original design and intention of them.

As to this, very different sentiments have been entertained by those who have written upon the subject; and into these they seem to have been led, by too narrow and contracted views of it, and an attachment to some favourite system derived from thence, in conformity to which they labour to explain every thing that relates to it.

Thus, some have considered sacrifice as no more than a tribute paid by man, in humble acknowledgment of his dependence upon, and obligations to, God. Others have considered it as an oblation of prayer and praise, expressed in the silent language of action, or, according

cording to the simplicity of those early times, in signs and symbols. Many have considered them as a vicarious substitution of the animal to be sacrificed, in place of the offender,—the instituted mode of a confession of sin, and the means of obtaining the pardon of it. Not satisfied with any of these views of sacrifice, others have represented the design of it to be penal, and considered sacrifice as a mulct to be levied upon the sinner, with an intention to lead him to repentance, and thereby procure him the remission of his past offences, and to deter him from the commission of the like in future, by rendering it thus expensive to him. Some imagining that men would choose a method of engaging the friendship of the Deity, similar to that which is practised in contracting and maintaining friendship with one another, look upon sacrifice, as a sacred or religious entertainment, in which the Deity vouchsafes to hold intercourse and correspondence with them, as his guests. And there are not a few, who maintain that the *principal* design of sacrifice was to be a mystic hint, or typical representation, of that great sacrifice that was to be offered to God, in the death of his Son, for the reparation of his injured honour.

My design does not require that I should enter into a minute and critical examination of these, and the other schemes that have been adopted by learned men, on this subject. All of them seem to have confined their views too much, in the consideration of it. None of of thefe fchemes, can give either a juft, or a full, idea of the original defign of this practice. Nay, if we will view it unwarped by prejudice, we fhall find that it comprehends more than them all.

The reafons for which men might be defirous to addrefs the Deity, may be eafily figured out to be many, according to the variety of circumftances in which we may fuppofe them placed. And facrifice was, in thofe early ages in which it firft obtained, intended to be expreffive of their devotion in all thefe.

The *Burnt-offering* or Holocauft was, of all others, the moft ancient, and, according to fome, the only kind that obtained before the giving of the law at Sinai. What makes this the more probable is,—that, in the firft ages of the world, the fituation of mankind did not admit a complicated fervice in religion: And therefore it is reafonable to fuppofe, that God would, in condefcenfion to the imperfection of their ftate, make it as fimple as poffible.

What the rites were, that, in this early period, attended the oblation of burnt-offerings, we cannot pofitively fay, becaufe we have but little relating to this, handed down to us. But one thing may be juftly prefumed, and that is,—that, as it was of Divine inftitution, the whole ceremonial relating to it would be fixed by God. And if we will but attend to what was afterwards enjoined in the law of Mofes concerning it, we may from thence

thence conjecture some of the early uses that were made of it.

According to some, it was intended to be a general act of devotion,—an acknowledgement of the honour and worship due to God, under the characters of their Creator, Governor, and Lord. And, according to others, it might be used in acts of particular devotion, and answer all the purposes which sacrifices of the expiatory, eucharistic, and precatory kind, did afterwards: that is, might, according to the temper and mood of the worshipper, answer as a solemn confession of sin, and an oblation of prayer and thanksgiving. Different instances might be adduced of such an application of it. But it is unnecessary. Every one's own reading will suggest many of them.

When mankind became greatly increased, and formed into societies, and God saw proper to enlarge the ritual of religion, the ancient mode of sacrificing was still retained, but became more restricted in the purposes for which it was used.

Under the Mosaic œconomy, the oblation of *burnt-offerings* was presented for sins in general, considered as an obstruction of the Divine favour. When they found it necessary to confess their sins, with any particular specification of them, *sin-offerings* were appointed for this purpose. And as prayers generally accompanied the one as well as the other, both might, not improperly, be called *precatory*.

In the courſe of the Divine providence, mankind were furniſhed with many occaſions for thankſgiving, both as ſocieties and individuals; and,—to excite, inflame, and expreſs a Spirit of gratitude, ſacrifices of the euchariſtic kind were appointed. Of this ſort were moſt of the *peace-offerings*.

In thoſe early ages, when the world was, as it were, in its infancy, and mankind ſtood in need of every degree of tenderneſs in the manner in which they were to be dealt with, God was graciouſly pleaſed, the more ſucceſsfully to engage their dutiful ſervice, to deal with them in the way of covenant. And that the tranſaction might affect them the more, and the better ſecure their obedience, by encouraging their faith in the promiſed reward of it, certain ſacrifices were appointed to accompany it, and from thence theſe have, by ſome, been denominated *Fœderal ſacrifices*.

The people of Iſrael could not but ſee that they, in a particular manner, owed the fruitfulneſs of the land in which they were ſettled, to the bleſſing of the Divine providence. Gratitude would naturally prompt them to acknowledge this by ſome act of religion. The offering of the *firſt-fruits* was appointed for that purpoſe.

I might run through the conſideration of the other kinds of ſacrifice. But my deſign does not make it neceſſary to enter more particularly into this. All I propoſe is only to inquire into the propriety of the practice in general, which has, by ſome, been ſo much

inveighed

inveighed against. And therefore, to what has been said of sacrifices adapted to particular occasions, I beg leave only to add,—that there was one species which went under the name of the *daily sacrifice*, because it was to be offered every day, evening and morning. And this was of that nature, that, having a respect to the whole society, it might be considered as an act of national devotion,—in an humble confession and acknowledgment of sin, and prayer for the pardon of it.

And now, from the imperfect view (and it is no more) which we have exhibited of the design of this ancient practice, may I not, with some degree of confidence, appeal to the candid reader, as to the usefulness of it?

From this account it is evident, that sacrifice was offered to God by Israel, not, as the Heathens imagined, from an opinion of the pleasure he took in the streams of a victim, the smoke of an altar, or the fumes of a libation. No.—They were offered to God, as a very significant expression of the worshipper's devotion,—of those pious sentiments which possessed his breast and animated his religious service. Thus, did they not contain an acknowledgment of the greatness and majesty, the purity and holiness of the Deity,—their constant dependence upon and obligations to him,—their hatred of sin,—their sorrow for it,—their confidence in his mercy, and their hopes from thence of pardon,—their determined resolution of a more faithful service for the future,—their delight in a religious
intercourse

intercourse with him, and—their desire of doing every thing that appeared proper to maintain and preserve it? And now, considered in all these points of view, must it not be allowed to be a most instructive and significant mode of devotion? This, I humbly think, cannot be denied. But whether another, less liable to exception and more proper for these purposes, might not have been devised, falls now to be considered.

After having offered what may be considered a proof of the Divine origin of sacrifice, such inquiry may appear unnecessary. And indeed, if the proof is admitted, here we might allow the matter to rest. The propriety of the institution, is the natural consequence of its being the appointment of unerring Wisdom. Any difficulties that might attend the account given of it in the sacred history, would be no good argument against the wisdom of it. Many, wise and good, might be the reasons of the Divine conduct in this and many other cases, though at present they may be beyond the reach of our weak and limited understanding. But it is one great excellence of all the Divine institutions, that they carry such reasons along with them for the appointment of them, as can bear to be scanned and canvassed, and must approve themselves to every impartial mind. An abundant proof of the justness of this observation, we will, I hope, have, in an investigation of the probable reasons of the insti-

G tution

tution of sacrifice. These will appear to be such, as are sufficient to justify it.

Those who are disposed to cavil, will perhaps allege, that all the ends, above-mentioned, might have been answered equally well without such an appointment; and that all, which, it is said, was signified by sacrifice, might have been expressed in the more simple language of words, either prescribed for this purpose, or left to the choice and discretion of the worshipper. But, if we will look back to the times when this practice was enjoined, we shall find it could not.

In proof of this let me observe, that, in the early and rude age, in which this practice first obtained in consequence of a positive appointment, the use of letters was entirely unknown, and consequently the communication of knowledge very difficult. And, therefore, nothing could be better fitted, in such circumstances, for the attainment of those ends, than that emblematical and symbolical method, which so early obtained. When we consider sacrifices, with all their attendant rites, as the appointment of God, and the means of promoting the instruction, devotion, and comfort of man, we cannot entertain the least reasonable doubt, but God would, at the first institution, explain and ascertain the meaning of every part of it. And, if this be admitted, the propriety of such method of preserving and communicating knowledge, will be abundantly apparent, because admirably adjusted to those early ages,

ages, which could scarcely admit of any other.

Let us reflect upon the simplicity of those ancient times, and in what manner could the sincere worshipper better express his devotional sentiments,—the sentiments of a heart strongly agitated with different passions,—reverence, grief, fear, hope, joy, &c. than in some such manner as this? Actions, looks, signs, are the first language in which the soul expresses itself.

Besides, let it be considered, that, in those early, rude, and uncultivated ages, the feelings of mankind were far from being tender. This made it difficult to make a deep impression upon their minds. Must we not, therefore, see a particular aptitude for this purpose, in the appointment of sacrifice? An exhibition of this kind, could not but deeply affect the spectators, as well as the worshippers themselves. By a pathetic address to their senses, it would lead them into a train of the most serious and devout reflections:—Such as were the most proper not only to accompany this particular service of religion, but also to have the most powerful influence upon the whole deportment of life:—to beget in their minds the most sacred reverence and veneration for the object of their worship;—the most implacable abhorrence of sin, the cause of his displeasure, and of their own danger, and—the most determined resolutions against it, ever after. That was the natural and direct tendency of sacrifice, had it been performed without any, the leaft, ceremony attending it.

This was alfo the tendency of all the pomp that preceded and accompanied it. Nay, this was not only the tendency, but feems alfo to have been the original defign, of the fplendid and coftly apparatus for this purpofe.

None can be fo weak as imagine, that the many wafhings and purgations enjoined, previous to the oblation of facrifice, were required for their own fake, or any intrinfic value in them. There might, in the appointment of them, be a regard had to their fubferviency to health, in the Eaftern countries, where an attention to cleannefs was fo neceffary for this purpofe. But, confidered as rites of religion, they muft have had a moral couched under them. To the ignorant, this might appear a piece of gaudy fhow. But furely, the more knowing, even under that dark difpenfation, would eafily fee, that it was intended to infpire their minds with the moft refpectful reverence for the Deity, and—an opinion of the neceffity of holinefs, in all their approaches to him.

It is true, the Jews, degenerated from the devotion of their pious anceftors, and miftaking the meaning of thofe ufages in which they expreffed it, came, at laft, to fatisfy themfelves, with the fcrupulous, literal, obfervance of their ritual. And for this, God fharply reproved them:—reproved them in a manner, which fhowed even to demonftration, that the devotion he required was very different

different from what they performed, and— that they miſtook the original intention of the ritual he enjoined, when they reſted in the outward obſervance of it *.

In thoſe early ages, ſuch a ſymbolical and emblematical language might be well underſtood, and could not fail to be very emphatic. But it is eaſy to ſee, how, in the progreſs of time, the original meaning might come to be loſt, and afterwards to be interpreted to quite a contrary purpoſe. This, by the by, is a proof, that this œconomy was intended to be only of a temporary duration, and did gradually verge towards a period.

This method of religious worſhip, notwithſtanding all that has been ſaid in defence and illuſtration of it, may appear to ſome ſtrongly marked with impropriety. But ſuch probably judge according to the ideas of modern times, which are far from being a proper ſtandard of judgment in the caſe. To form a proper deciſion upon this point, it is neceſſary to look back to thoſe early ages in which the inſtitution took place, and to the genius of the people among whom it firſt obtained; and then, both the ſeeming impropriety, and the offence ariſing from it, will vaniſh at once.

I know it is alleged that the inſtitution of ſacrifice, which is generally aſcribed to a Divine origin, and was, at firſt, confined to brute animals, did, at laſt, lead to the barous

* Iſa. i. 10—15.

barous practice of human sacrifices: And particularly, that the command of God to Abraham, concerning the sacrifice of his son Isaac, has been pleaded as the origin and excuse of it*.

But what if it should be granted, that the sacrifice of the human, did take its rise from that of the brute, kind? This can argue no more, at best, than the abuse of an institution, originally wise and proper: and an abuse too, which might have been easily avoided, had mankind but attended to the primary design of the institution, and not pretended, by affecting a superior wisdom, to improve upon it. Nothing can be so reasonable, but mankind, if they will indulge a proud and inventive imagination, may corrupt. And as this has actually been the case, in the following periods of this practice, nothing can be more unfair than the attempt to discredit the institution, from the alleged bad influence, which, in the case of Isaac, it might have had upon the practice of the Heathen nations around.

Whether human sacrifices were, at that early period, practised, is not altogether certain. Abraham's receiving the command, without any apparent surprise, is no proof, as is alleged by some, that the practice had been received and become frequent. His conduct

---

* See Shaftesbury's Charact. Vol. III. p. 110. edit. 12mo; Christianity as old as the Creation, Vol. I. p. 80. Ancient Universal Hist. Vol. III. p. 336. edit. 8vo.

conduct might be eafily accounted for, without any neceffity of fuppofing this. But, whether the practice of human facrifices was prior or pofterior to the intended facrifice of Ifaac, it could, with no degree of reafon, be confidered as receiving the leaft countenance from it.

If we fhall fuppofe human facrifices to have obtained (which indeed is not improbable) before this period, what could be conceived to be a ftronger difcouragement to the practice, than the ftop put to the facrifice of Ifaac, when the father's hand was lifted up to perform it? Did not this fhow that, unlike the gods of the Heathen, his God took no pleafure in altars ftained with human blood?

Little as the intercourfe of one nation was, at that time, with another, it is not improbable but many muft have heard of this remarkable event. Abraham's rank in life,—his travels into Egypt,—his victory over fome confederate princes, who made an irruption into the country, where his brother Lot fettled, and carried him away captive,—the many natural connections he had formed with fome, and—the political alliances he had contracted with others, of the neighbouring ftates, could not but make them acquainted with fo remarkable an occurrence of his life, —point him out as a perfon of diftinguifhed character to all around, and fo render them in fome meafure interefted in what concerned him, and make them inquire after his profef-
fion,

sion, his hopes, and his religion*. And if we can imagine (what indeed is very natural) that they had, on this account, conceived a veneration for him, is it not very probable, that they would construe this interposition of Heaven, in the intended sacrifice of his son, as a public check to a practice but too frequent among them? And so, in place of encouraging, had it not a tendency to put a stop to it?

But let us, for argument's sake, suppose the practice of human sacrifice to have taken place posterior to the order for sacrificing Isaac; yet I humbly think it would be both unreasonable and unfair to ascribe the origin of it to this. For, if we suppose the neighbouring nations to be acquainted with the occasion of the injunction given to Abraham, they must have seen that there was nothing in it, that could authorise them to plead his example as a precedent in this practice. But let us suppose them ignorant of the original design of this injunction, and therefore disposed to reason from the obligations upon him, to the obligations upon themselves; yet surely we cannot suppose them acquainted with the command of God that required, without supposing them acquainted with his command, equally express, to put a stop to it. And what good reason can be assigned, why they should

---

* Dr Shuckford observes (Connection of Sacred and Prophane Hist. Vol. I. p. 308.) that the fame of Abraham had spread far and near over the East, and had reached to India, and that probably all Persia was full of it.

should pay such a deference to the Divine command in the one case, and so little in the other? When the command requires a service that is agreeable, we wonder not that it should meet with a cheerful and ready obedience. But this was so much the reverse, that mankind (it might be thought) would naturally seek for excuses to justify themselves in the neglect of it, and would think themselves fully authorised to renounce such practice, when they heard of a Divine command, expressly forbidding it in the case of Abraham.

What has been offered, in answer to this objection thrown out against sacrifice, from the alleged bad consequence of such an institution, has been more from a regard to the imagined, than the real, force of it. There is nothing, so far as I remember, either in sacred or profane history, that would seem so much as to insinuate, that human, was the consequence of animal, sacrifice. And it is incumbent upon the advocates for this opinion to ascertain the fact, before they can plead any thing upon it. Nay, I may even go farther, and say, that could the fact be established, that the one took its rise from the other, this would be no conclusive argument against the institution, but an evidence indeed of the most corrupt abuse, of it. Many are the reasons that may be figured out (and some, though not all, we know) why God chose to call Abraham to so severe a trial, and they are such as are sufficient to justify this part of the

the Divine conduct; while the stop put to the execution of the command, by an interposed prohibition, served to give a check to a practice he wished to discourage *.

I know that objections have been started, unfavourable to this part of the Mosaic institution, from the supposed countenance it gives to the practice *of human sacrifices*, in the law relating to things devoted to God (Levit. xxvii. 28, 29.), and in the approved conduct of Jephtha, in consequence of a solemn vow he had made (Judges xi. 30. and Heb, xi. 32.) But my design does not lead me to a minute confutation of all that has been thrown out against the practice of sacrificing, as authorised by God. And therefore I shall pass over what is argued from the topics just now referred to, with observing, that the places of sacred writ upon which they are grounded, may admit of a very easy and natural interpretation †, without giving the least countenance to the practice, in behalf of which they are pleaded. Such an application of them shows the straits to which our modern infidels are reduced, when they are obliged to have recourse to such shifts to extricate themselves from them.

Upon the whole, 1 hope it is evident, from what has been observed upon this subject, that the practice of sacrificing, considering its early

---

* See an excellent discourse on the subject of Abraham's offering up his son Isaac, by Mr Grove of Taunton, Vol. II. Serm. 7, 8, 9.

† See on this subject, Grove's Works, Vol. II. Serm. 8.

ly origin, has nothing improper in the institution of it But, on the contrary, that it stands justified, from the consideration of the age in which it at first took place,—the genius of the people among whom it obtained, and the ends intended by it. And therefore the charge of *absurd and unphilosophical* will not apply to sacrifice, considered as a branch or part of Judaism. But, to proceed,

Let us consider the more solemn and extraordinary parts of the Jewish worship. These may be said to consist in the observance of certain festivals appointed by their law, and celebrated with a pomp proportioned to the events to which they referred. Most, if not all, of them, were memorials of events signal in themselves, and important in their consequences to the commonwealth, and the remembrance of which, accompanied with corresponding affections of soul, had a powerful tendency to promote their improvement in virtue and holiness. This was indeed the nature, design, and tendency of every one of them. They all pointed to the same end, though by different means. This will perhaps best appear by an induction of particulars.

To begin with the consideration of the *Sabbath*.

My design in this section, does not lead me to inquire into the time of the institution of this sacred day. This will fall to be considered Sect. IV. It is sufficient for our present purpose, that an appointment for the observance fervance of it is admitted All we are here concerned with, is the wifdom and propriety of fuch an inftitution.

I need not obferve that, though the word *Sabbath* is fometimes put for thofe holy days in general, which, by an abftraction from ordinary bufinefs, were devoted to any of the fervices of religion, we are here to underftand by it, the *feventh* day in the hebdomodal or weekly revolution of time.

The original defign of the inftitution of the Sabbath (whether we confider it to have taken place at Sinai or fooner) feems to have been to commemorate the accomplifhment of the great work of creation. Some think the deliverance of Ifrael from Egyptian bondage, happened on the fame day which was originally devoted to this great purpofe. If fo, the inftitution of this day would anfwer the additional purpofe of being a memorial of this illuftrious event alfo. But how far the appointment of a particular inftitution for this purpofe was proper, is what now claims our attention.

Not to trouble myfelf, or the reader, with Rabbinical conceits concerning the manner of obferving the Sabbath, it is evident, from the appointment of the facred reft to be obferved,—the double facrifices to be offered, and—the holy convocation to be held upon it, that it was the defign of the legiflator to give every degree of folemnity to it, that could render it duly honoured and refpected. And if we will but reflect upon the grandeur

deur and importance of the events, the remembrance of which it was intended to perpetuate, or—the advantages that would naturally result from the frequent and serious review of them, we can remain no longer in any doubt about the propriety and usefulness of such an institution: Nay, both must be very apparent.

Let us consider, that man, from his very nature, evidently appears to be designed for religion, and was sent into this world to be prepared, by its salutary discipline, for a state of greater perfection and happiness in another. Now, what could more conduce to promote this improvement, than those solemnities of devotion, into which the reflex view of the great works of God would naturally lead him, by an easy train? Would not the first of those glorious events, I mean that of creation, have an admirable tendency to inspire the mind, with a just sense of the greatness, wisdom, and goodness of God,—of our dependence upon him, and the obligations we are under to honour and serve him? While the latter, as an event in which the Jews were particularly concerned, served to give a noble elevation to their devotion, by ministering the most proper fuel to their gratitude. And, if we will but reflect, that, long before the giving of the law at Sinai, a very gross superstition had begun to prevail, by which angels and the planets were supposed to have a very considerable influence over the several portions of our time, and the events which

happened

happened during any of thefe, according as they fell under the rule of the one or the other of them, may we not fee the propriety of renewing the appointment with refpect to the Sabbath, at this time? Did it not ferve to teach Ifrael, that the God to whom this day was dedicated and whom they worfhipped, was none of the imaginary Deities of the Heathen, but the fame who created, and continues to govern, all things?

This much the remembrance of thefe events was calculated to produce, even in private. But, when we call to mind, that this day was appointed to be obferved among them as a *holy convocation*, it is eafy to conceive how this circumftance might become fubfervient to the purpofes of a more exalted devotion, refined pleafure, and proportionable improvement.

For what particular purpofes this convocation was required, is a point not agreed upon, either by Jews or Chriftians. In this, as in moft other cafes, where there is room for it, they have run into different opinions.

I muft own, that, to me, it appears probable, that the devout Jews affembled on the Sabbath, to hear the fcriptures read and expounded to them, and to join in acts of focial devotion.

This we know, from the teftimony of an Apoftle*, was early the practice, though, according to fome, it did not begin till after the

---

* Acts xiii. 27. and. xv. 21.

the erection of synagogues, in the time of Ezra. It is very true, the inquiry which the Shunamite's husband made into the reason of her desiring to go to the prophet, when it was neither new-moon nor sabbath †, would seem to indicate that there were stated times of assembling at his house, and very probably for the prpposes of religious instruction and devotion: And this was long before the days of Ezra.

But it is not so much upon either of these places of sacred history that I build my opinion, (though these seem greatly to favour it), as upon the reasonableness of the practice itself. For, when we consider the Sabbath devoted to the religious remembrance of these two most illustrious events,—the creation of the world and the redemption of Israel from Egyptian bondage, nothing could be more reasonable than that the people, when assembled for this purpose, should endeavour, by proper acts of devotion, to stir up each other to a grateful celebration of the Divine praises. And if the reasonableness of this conjecture is admitted, who but must see the propriety and advantage of such an institution? For, must it not be owned, that there is something in a genuine, spirited, and social devotion, that can scarce fail to command regard,—to compose and elevate the mind,—to kindle the fire of devotion, and fan it into a lively flame,—to make the deepest impression upon

---

* 2 Kings iv. 23.

upon the spectators, and—excite such a holy emulation in their breasts, as would be satisfied with no degree of devotion in themselves, short of what they so much admire in others? As live coals, when separated, are ready to die, but, when put together, not only preserve, but increase, each others heat; so public devotion, when it appears easy and natural, communicates its warmth to all who are within the sphere of its influence, and renders them susceptible of the best impressions, by giving them a taste and relish for things spiritual and divine.

All these advantages, and many more, we owe to the institution of the Sabbath. For, without such an institution as this, it is highly probable that mankind would never have agreed upon any proper times for the exercises of social devotion. And so they would have been either altogether neglected, or, at least, but seldom and slightly performed. What more is necessary to be taken notice of upon this subject, will fall under consideration Sect. IV. The above is sufficient to vindicate the usefulness and excellence of the institution, which is all that was proposed in this place.

Another piece of the more solemn worship of the Israelites, was that practised at the festival of the *passover**. Of the institution itself.

---

* Whence this festival derived its name, is generally admitted. Some, however, have mistaken its etymology, and, considering it as typical of the sufferings of our Lord, have imagined

itself,—the design of it,—the preparation required for it, and—the rites which were to attend the celebration of it, we have an historical account, in the 12th chap. of Exodus.

From the sacred history we find that God, in many instances, chose to perpetuate the memory of the most illustrious events of his providence, by some rite or ceremony instituted for this purpose. The ordinance now under consideration, was of this nature, and intended to be a memorial of an event, truly great in itself, and important in its consequences to Israel.

Let any but read the account given of this institution without prejudice, and I will venture to say, he must admit not only the propriety of the original design, but also of the continuance of it, through the successive ages of their commonwealth. The event which gave rise to it, was one of the most grand recorded in history, and carried after it a series of the most beneficial consequences;

and gined that it was called *the Passover* from the Greek word πασχω, which signifies, " to suffer;" because, at the time appropriated to the celebration of this festival, our Lord was crucified. This was the ignorant conceit of some of the primitive fathers. A much more natural derivation of the name is suggested from one of the instructions given to the angel, who was employed in the destruction of the first born of the Egyptians, in the night which preceded the day of the march of the Israelites out of Egypt. He was directed to sprinkle the door-posts of the houses of the Israelites, with the blood of a lamb, which should be a sign to him to *pass over* these. Hence the festival, which was instituted in commemoration of this extraordinary deliverance, is called *the passover* or *pascha*, from the Hebrew word, *pasach*, " he passed by."

and therefore did it not deserve to be handed down, to the most distant ages, by the institution of a proper memorial? And is not such an institution admirably calculated to perpetuate the memory of an event, which, however grand and important, would otherwise, very probably, have been soon forgotten?

Those who are disposed to cavil at the propriety of the institution, may allege that the events referred to were such, that Israel could never have allowed them to fall into oblivion;—that they were so nearly interested in them, that they could never have let the impression made by them be effaced;—nay, that they could not fail to have transmitted them, from one generation to another, with every mark of honour, esteem, and regard.

This, all this, would have been no more than the deserved return for such distinguished kindness. But God, forseeing how ready they would be to forget them, instituted this ordinance to secure them as much as possible against it, and did not choose to rest the transmission of so glorious an event, upon so precarious a foundation. Those of that generation who had shared in this glorious salvation, and been the witnesses of the dreadful destruction in which the first born of the Egyptians were involved, could never forget an event, productive of such a series of blessings to them: Nay,—it is probable they would not fail to communicate it to their children. But it is as probable, that, in proportion as the times were removed from that in which this happened,

happened, the impreſſion made by it would become ſtill more faint, till, at laſt, it would be quite effaced and eraſed from the mind. A more effectual method, therefore, could not be deviſed to prevent this, than the annual celebration of this feſtival, and that on (what may be called, though not ſtrictly, according to the Jewiſh computation of time) the anniverſary of the day, on which it was firſt inſtituted. The ſo frequent return of it, would ſerve to renew the impreſſion, before that which had been made upon a former occaſion could be worn out.

It deſerves to be taken notice of, that the whole ſolemnity (including the feaſt of unleavened bread, which immediately ſucceeded it, and is often conſidered as a part of it) required a ſpace of ſeveral days. Very probably the deſign was, that the duration of it might, by the ſucceſſion of rites uſed on this occaſion, not only excite and inflame thoſe affections, with which it became them to remember ſuch an event, but that, by continuing the impreſſion ſo long, it might alſo make it the more deep and laſting.

Beſides this general advantage which it was calculated to afford, there were many others of a particular nature which it could not fail to produce. An attention to the ſeveral parts of this emblematical ſervice, would convey the moral inſtruction intended by it. Thus, for example, what could more fitly repreſent the neceſſity of a careful preparation for an approach to God, or of purity in the services of religion, than the course they were required to go through, previously to their attendance on this sacred institution?— What could more properly remind them of the grief and sorrow with which they had been obliged to bear their servitude in Egypt, than the bitter herbs with which they were required to eat- the paschal supper? How could they set about eating it, with their staves in their hands, &c. without reflecting on the haste with which they were obliged to fly, from the grievous oppression of their cruel task-masters?—Or, how could they think of the glorious Author of that deliverance, of which this ordinance was intended to be a memorial, without recollecting the obligations they lay under to him, and thus showing every proper religious regard to him, from a principle of gratitude, of all others the most liberal and ingenuous? And if to this we add, that several parts of the ritual enjoined in this ordinance, were intended (which is not at all improbable *) to produce

and

---

* It is certain that, before the institution of the Passover, idolatry had risen to a most enormous height, among the Heathen nations, and particularly among the Egyptians. It is, therefore, perfectly consonant to the wisdom of God to suppose, that, while he meant to preserve alive upon the minds of the Israelites, by such an institution as this, a due sense of their obligations to him for the deliverance he had wrought for them, he should, at the same time, so contrive the ritual to be observed in it, as to guard them against those rites which disgraced the religious solemnities of the Heathens, and for some of which the Israelites might have perhaps discovered too great a fondness.

We

and keep up in the minds of the Israelites, an abhorrence of the impurities and superstitions, which obtained in some of the Heathen, and particularly the Egyptian, festivals; what service of religion could be better calculated, under such a dispensation, to raise admiration, to interest the heart, to excite all the tenderest, which are its finest, feelings, and—convey the most useful moral instruction along with it? And, considered in all these points of view, must not the wisdom and propriety of this institution stand abundantly justified?

The feast of *weeks* was another grand and solemn festival among the Jews. This is spoken of in Scripture under different names, and each carries the reason along with it. Thus it is sometimes called, *the feast of weeks* *, because it was to commence seven weeks after the first day of *the feast of unleavened bread* †.

We are informed that the Egyptians, very probably in adoration of the constellation *Aries*, were wont to worship that creature, about the time of the vernal equinox, when the sun entered that sign. Hence, therefore, some have thought, that God appointed a lamb to be sacrificed at this time, that Israel might, from this, learn, what little regard was due to the god that was thus represented.

Plutarch and others inform us, that the Heathens, in the celebration of some of their religious festivals, were wont to tear and eat the flesh of animals, and to consult the entrails of those which were slain, for the purposes of augury and divination. And therefore, could we suppose God to have had an eye to these practises, it was not, without the greatest propriety and beauty, that he enjoined a practice quite the reverse of them, in that service which he required, at the Passover. See Spencer de Rit. Hebræor. cap. 4. De Paschate.

* Exod xxxiv. 22.   † Levit. xxiii. 15.

And it is called *the feast of harvest**, or of the *first fruits* †, because this being the season of harvest in that climate, the first fruits of it were required to be offered to God, accompanied with certain sacrifices of the animal kind, that were appointed for this purpose ‡.

From the name of the feast of weeks, it has, by Greek writers, been called *Pentecost*. Under this denomination it is spoken of in the New Testament; and the reason is, because it was the fiftieth day from the Passover. And as the promulgation of the law at Sinai, happened about the fiftieth day from the departure of Israel from Egypt, (as may appear from an easy computation), hence it has been considered as a remembrancer to them of that truly interesting epoch in the annals of their nation. And, considered in any of these lights, it must be allowed that neither the design, nor tendency, of such an institution can, with any propriety, be deemed *absurd or unphilosophical.*

The fruits of the earth, especially those which are the produce of a painful and laborious culture, men are apt (if not reminded of the contrary) to consider as the effect of their own diligence or the reward of their industry, and so, while they enjoy the gift, either to forget the giver, or think themselves nowise obliged to him. It is easy to see how the indulgence of either of these sentiments, must have had the most baneful influence upon

---

* Exod. xxiii. 16.   † Numb. xxviii. 26.
‡ Levit. xxiii. 10, 11, 12.

on the human heart and conduct. And therefore what could be more wife than an inftitution, which had the moft direct tendency to guard againft both, and infpire fentiments of a conftant dependence upon, and of the warmeft gratitude to, God?

To this let me add, that it is highly probable, that, before this time, there prevailed a notion among the Heathens, that the clemency of the feafons, and the fertility of the earth, were owing to the favour of certain dæmons, or inferior deities, who prefided over them. And if this is admitted, muft we not difcern an additional beauty and propriety in fuch an appointment, as the direct tendency of it was to correct this error, and turn both their attention and their gratitude to the true God?

Befides what has been already obferved, upon this part of the fubject, there is another thing deferves our attention, and that is,—that, from a coincidence of the delivery of the law with the time of their harveft, this inftitution was probably intended to be a memorial of the firft as well as of the laft. And if we will but confider the importance of the law itfelf, and the awful folemnity with which it was announced, will it not be admitted that it muft have been a matter of the greateft moment to them, to have been ever kept in mind of both? And if fo, what could be more proper for this purpofe, than the obfervance of an inftitution appointed with this very view?

There yet remains another great religious festival of the Jews, to be taken notice of, I mean, that of *Tabernacles*. The appointment concerning the feast itself, and the manner of observing it, may be seen Levit. xxiii. 36. It lasted eight days; and the first and last days of the festival which were called the Great Hosanna *, they celebrated in many solemn processions, and with great joy and mirth.

This sacred feast was called *The Feast of Tabernacles*, because Israel was required during the whole of this solemnity, to dwell in booths, made of the branches of trees, and adorned with the most agreeable foliage. This was intended to lead back their thoughts to that important period, during which their ancestors sojourned in the wilderness, and to remind them of the Divine providence, in defending them against the inclemencies of the season, when they had no other accommodation but what their humble tents afforded them. Many were the emotions of piety and devotion, which the remembrance of these events, excited by this (if I may be allowed the expression) scenical representation of them, was calculated to nourish in their minds: And therefore such as must lead the candid to an approbation of the appointment concerning it.

It

* The word *Hosanna* (which is Hebrew) properly signifies, *Save, I beseech thee;* and was an exclamation of joy, used at the feast of Tabernacles, and intended not only to express their gratitude at the remembrance of their deliverance from Egypt, but also their hopes, according to some, of future greatness under the Messiah.

It does not fall within my design to take notice of the many stories of the Rabbis, with respect to the manner of celebrating this festive service. I am concerned with no more, than what received a sanction from the law of Moses. Permit me, however, to take notice of one thing, and that is,—that, as the best institutions may be corrupted, this seems to have been so, in some of the later periods of the Jewish state. For, according to the best information, in place of remaining sacred to a grateful and devout service of God, it became prostituted to a frothy and giddy levity, and presented scenes of the most indecent merriment. This I take notice of, because it may account for what Plutarch says (in his Sympos.) concerning the Jews,—that they celebrated this festival, in honour of Bacchus*. This shows how little, even men of learning among the Heathens, were acquainted with the religion of the Jews, and how little regard is to be paid to the reflections they often throw out against it. Had Plutarch been as well acquainted with the genius of the different religions that then obtained, as might have been expected from his character, as a priest of Apollo, he might have easily avoided this error. He might have known that the religion of the Jews did admit of Divine honours to none, but their own God. But ignorant, in a great measure, of the nature of their

---

* The Author acknowledges himself obliged to Dr Jennings for this observation. See his Jewish Antiquities, Vol. II. p. 232.

their religion, and not giving himſelf the trouble to examine whether the tumult that attended this, one of the ſervices of it, was enjoined by its ritual, or ſuperinduced by the ſuperſtition of its votaries, he raſhly concludes their feaſt of Tabernacles to have been inſtituted and obſerved in honour of Bacchus, from the reſemblance which he imagined the one bore to the other, in the time and manner of their celebration. But to return from this digreſſion.

Beſides the particular advantages already taken notice of, reſulting from the devout obſervance of each of theſe inſtitutions, allow me to obſerve that there were ſome of a general nature, which all the three were calculated to promote.

Theſe were feaſts which, according to the law, could be no where celebrated but at Jeruſalem, after God had erected the temple there, and which all the males of Iſrael were required to attend. What a wiſe inſtitution was this? Separated, in a manner, from all the reſt of the world, or, at leaſt, having but little intercourſe with them, what could be of greater importance to them, whether in a civil or religious ſenſe, than a happy union among themſelves? And what could have a more direct tendency to promote it, than the frequent intercourſe which was hereby encouraged, and the communion they had in the offices of life and religion?

Beſides theſe occaſions, which were all of the feſtive kind, there was another ſeaſon of devotion,

devotion, which deservedly challenges our attention, in this review. The one I mean, —is *The day of expiation or great atonement.* It was observed as a day devoted to solemn fasting, and on which they were called to afflict their souls.

You have an account of the institution of it, Levit. xvi. 29. and xxiii. 27. From this it appears that it was celebrated from the evening of the ninth, to the evening of the tenth, day of the seventh month, with the most affecting solemnity.

With respect to this, as well as every other part of the Jewish worship and ritual, the Rabbins, indulging a fruitful fancy, have offered many wild and extravagant conjectures. Thus, for instance, some have alleged, that the design of the institution was to be a memorial of the fall:—Others, of the defection of Israel, in the affair of the golden calf. But there is no end to conjecture,— and here it is altogether unnecessary. If we will attend to the words which contain the institution, they clearly enough indicate the intention of it, which was,—to call upon the nation to take a serious review of their conduct during the preceding year,—to make a public confession of their sins, and,—by the oblation of the most solemn sacrifices and prayers, to intercede for the pardon of them.

A service of such a nature could not but appear highly interesting to every one concerned. And that nothing might be wanting that could tend to engage the hearts of the
spectators,

spectators, and compose them into a corresponding devotion, (it is deserving of notice) every part of the ceremonial gone through, was pompous, solemn, and affecting.

In the services of this day, the high-priest was called to act. And some of them were competent for him only to perform, such as, —the confession of his own sins, and those of the people, upon the head of the scape-goat, —the immolation of the sacrifices appointed for this day,—his entrance into the most holy place,—his intercession for the people, and,— in conclusion of the whole, the solemn benediction pronounced upon them. Add to all this,—the careful preparation required of the high-priest for this service,—the attention with which every part of it must have been performed, and—the danger he run from the least miscarriage; and it is submitted to all who will allow themselves to judge impartially, whether every circumstance and appendage of this service, did not carry in them a striking propriety.

To us who are accustomed to less operose services, there may, at first, appear an unnecessary multiplicity of rites and forms, thro' the whole of this sacred transaction. But the propriety of the whole, or of its several parts, is not to be judged of, from an attention to our particular taste or situation, but from an attention to the genius of the people and the age to which it referred. And in such circumstances, it will appear highly conducive to the most valuable purposes. For, was it not

not admirably calculated to inculcate upon that people (and in a manner, too, the moſt fit to touch their hearts) their conſtant dependence upon God, both as a nation and as individuals,—the narrow infpection he takes of their conduct,—the neceſſity of a ſerious review of it themſelves, and of a deep contrition of ſoul, for the tranſgreſſions of the Divine law with which they were chargeable, and,—at the ſame time, to engage their humble addreſſes to the Divine mercy, from the encouragement they had to hope for pardon? And, confidered in theſe ſeveral points of light, muſt it not be admitted to be an ordinance of religion, of the moſt admirable tendency?

Thus I have confidered ſome of the moſt remarkable branches of the religious worſhip required under the Moſaic œconomy. I know there are other inſtances, not a few, in which a certain religious ſervice was required of Iſrael, ſuch as thoſe which reſpected the oblation of the firſt-fruits,—the firſt-born, and—the obſervation of the feaſt of trumpets, new-moons, and jubilee. But as, in all theſe, there was ſomething political blended with religion, I ſhall paſs them over, at leaſt, in this place. And I hope it will ſuffice for our preſent purpoſe to have ſhown, by the few remarks we have made upon the inſtitutions that have come under our confideration, that they were all of them worthy of that wiſdom from which the Chriſtian, as well as the Jew, contends they are derived;—that the defign
which

which runs through them all, was kind and gracious; and—that the ceremonial which accompanied each of them, had a congruity in it, correfponding to the occafion and purpofe of their appointment.

It is impoffible to confider worfhip independently of the circumftances of time and place, and therefore I proceed to treat,

SECT III.

Of the Times devoted to the Services of Religion.

FROM the hiftory of the Jewifh church, it appears that there were certain times fixed for the performance of every part of its fervice, and that thefe returned according to the determined rotation.

We have already confidered fome of the moft remarkable branches of their worfhip. The time for the performance of each, or, at leaft, moft of them, was fixed with a precifion that could not eafily admit of a miftake.

There have been more difputes concerning the *Sabbath*,—the time of the inftitution, defign and duration of this ordinance, than about all the reft.

Some have thought that there was no Divine appointment with refpect to it, till it was made in the wildernefs to Ifrael. And in fupport of this opinion, they allege that the words

words Gen. ii. 2, 3 *, should be interpreted, not as containing the institution of the Sabbath, from the accomplishment of the work of creation, but from the time in which the observance of it was enjoined to Israel, of which, say they, God here spoke by way of anticipation.

What seems principally to have led to this opinion, is the silence of the sacred history upon this point, previous to the æra just now mentioned. But I must own I have often wondered, that men of learning could lay so much stress upon a circumstance of so little importance.

Many others there are of incomparably greater importance, which plead for the early institution of the Sabbath. Among these I might take notice of the mention made of *weeks* †, or a septenary division of time, which obtained long before the promulgation of the law. And, as this must be admitted, it will be no easy matter to account for it upon any other supposition, than that of the so early existence of this institution, because there is no natural division of time, from the revolution of the sun, or any of the planets, that could have suggested it.

The

---

* " On the seventh day God ended his work which he had
" made, and he rested on the seventh day from all his works
" which he had made. And God blessed the seventh day and
" sanctified it, because that he had rested from all his works,
" which he had created and made."

† Gen. xxix. 27.

The allotment of a certain portion of time for the worſhip of God, may be conſidered as a dictate of the light of nature itſelf. And, as we cannot imagine that man, immediately after his creation, when a ſenſe of the Divine kindneſs was freſh upon his mind, would neglect a proper acknowledgment of it, by acts of homage ſuited to the ſimplicity of thoſe early times; ſo nothing could be more natural than to imagine, that he would allot certain periods, which, by their regular revolution, would call upon him to this religious ſervice. And, if we will but ſuppoſe man to be acquainted with the hiſtory of the creation,—the order of the Divine progreſs in it, —and the ſolemn reſt that enſued upon the accompliſhment of it, there would be nothing improper, if I ſhould ſay, that he might conſider this as a hint for his choice of the time to be obſerved in commemoration of ſo glorious and intereſting an event, and—as proper as any other for the purpoſes of religion.

What appears reaſonable in theory, it is highly preſumable, was true in fact. For, let it be obſerved, that, when Moſes makes mention, for the firſt time, Exod. xvi. 23. of the Sabbath, he does not drop the leaſt hint from which it could be inferred that it was a novel inſtitution, that had never before been heard of. On the contrary, he gives reaſon to think that they were well acquainted with it, ſince he offers little more with reſpect to the obſervance of it, than what related to the manner in which they were to behave about the manna.

manna. And this he does for a reason, which would have induced him to be equally minute and particular as to the observance of the Sabbath, had the circumstances relating to it been the same, that is, had it been a thing quite new to them.

Nay, does not the injunction to *remember* the Sabbath day to keep it holy, hint at the institution of it, long prior to the command at Sinai? And is not this conjecture greatly confirmed by Deut. v. 12. where, to the command enjoining the religious observance of the Sabbath, it is added, *As the Lord, thy God, hath commanded thee?* When? It can only refer to the primary institution of it, at the creation.

The opinions have not been more various about the time of the institution of this ordinance, than about that fixed for the observance of it,—whether the seventh day in rotation from the creation of man, or one day in seven, without regard to this particular order.

If we will allow the words Gen. ii. 3. to contain the institution of the Sabbath from the earliest beginning of time, it is, I think, probable that it was the intention of God, that the seventh in succession should be sacred to the memory of the stupenduous event of the creation, and those exercises of devotion, which the remembrance of it would naturally lead to; and that, accordingly, it was so observed by the pious in the patriarchal age.

But

But as the Israelites might, during their captivity in Egypt, be hindered from such a religious observance of it as they could have wished, and so might, at last, be led into a forgetfulness of it altogether, therefore some have thought that this might be the reason for the Divine renewal of the appointment.

I must own, this does not strike me as the reason of it. Grievous indeed was their oppression in Egypt. But as, from the promises made to their ancestors, they had reason to hope for a deliverance from it in due time, it is not, I think, probable, that they would have allowed themselves entirely to forget an appointment so sacred, and, they might believe, so important, because the first which God had given them. Nay, if we will suppose, according to an early tradition concerning this ordinance, that a septenary division of time obtained so early as this among the Egyptians (and it is far from being improbable), this, of itself, would, in a great measure, prevent the forgetting it.

A much more probable reason may be assigned, for the law concerning the Sabbath, at Mount Sinai. It is supposed to have had a particular reference to their deliverance from Egyptian bondage, and to have been appointed on the seventh day after their passage at the Red Sea, by which it was completed, as a memorial of this illustrious event. Many reasons there are which make this probable.

In

In the first place, we find that the seventh day, counting backward from the appointment with respect to the Sabbath (Exod. xvi. 22, 23.) was not a Sabbath. For, on that day, Israel, by the special command of God, who directed all their motions, made a march from Elim to the wilderness of Sin: And this, we are sure, he would not have allowed them to have made, had this been a Sabbath, on which, by his own authority, he required men to rest. Is not this, therefore, a strong presumption, that, by this new appointment, he made an alteration in the order of the seventh day, to be henceforth observed by the Jews as their Sabbath?

I know it is alleged by some who admit the early institution of the Sabbath, that, though the observance of it was enjoined as a memorial of creation, it was only at the giving of the law, that a strict rest was enjoined to be kept on this day *.

If this opinion is admitted, I acknowledge it will greatly weaken, if it does not entirely take away, the force of the above argument for the alteration of the seventh day for the Sabbath. But still there are other reasons that make it highly probable.

One day in seven seems to have been appointed by God, in commemoration of the creation; and therefore the obligation of it is continued. But what makes it probable, that, at this time, he altered the day, and appointed

---

* Grotius de Veritate, &c. lib. v. § 10.

ed the seventh from their passage at the Red Sea, is—that he requires this appointment to continue in force, *through all their generations**, that is, during the continuance of their commonwealth †.

The revolution of the Sabbath once in seven days, served to keep them in mind of the design of the original institution; while the revolution of it in this particular order, served to perpetuate the memory of the glorious event of their deliverance. And if there was no foundation for this opinion, with what propriety could the Sabbath be said—*to be a perpetual covenant and a sign betwixt God and his people* ‡? or why should God require them to remember that he brought them out of Egypt, as often as they observed the Sabbath §?

From this some have imagined that the institution of the Sabbath respected only the people of Israel. Had there been originally no reason but what regarded them solely, such conjecture might be admitted. But the appointment of a day in seven for the purposes of religion, respects all mankind as well as them. Accordingly we find it engrossed in those laws of a moral nature, and consequently

---

* Exod. xxxi. 13, 16.

† That in this sense the phrase may be here understood, is evident from the many other places where it occurs, and in which it cannot so well be understood in any other; such as Gen. xvii. 7, 9, 12.—Exod. xii. 14, 17, 42. Exod. xvi. 32. Exod. xxix. 4. Exod. xxx. 21. Exod. xl. 15. Levit. xxiv. 3.

‡ Exod. xxxi. 13.   § Deut. v. 15.

ly of a perpetual obligation, delivered by God at Mount Sinai.

This hint, with refpect to what may properly be called the Jewifh Sabbath,—the feventh day in fucceffion from their paffage at the Red Sea, fuggefts a reafon better than is commonly given, for the alteration of the day, (henceforth to be obferved) from the Jewifh to the Chriftian Sabbath. By the particular ordinance of God, the obfervance of that enjoined Ifrael was only to remain *during their generations*, that is, during their commonwealth; and therefore, the reafons of it being peculiar to them, it was to ceafe with them. And if there be any ground for the conjecture of fome learned men,—that our Sabbath is the feventh day, in the revolution of time from the creation, there is a particular beauty and propriety in the return to it from the Jewifh, the obligation of which has now ceafed. For, thus it becomes at once a memorial, of two the moft illuftrious events recorded in hiftory, —the creation and redemption of man.

This much may fuffice with refpect to the original inftitution of the Sabbath, and the various changes in point of time, which it has undergone.

Befides the feventh day devoted to the purpofes already taken notice of, there were feveral others to be devoted to the fervices of religion. A part of every day was defigned for the oblation of the morning and evening facrifice. And every folemn feftival was fixed to certain feafons, as may be feen by looking into

into the account which the sacred historian gives of their institution.

I know some exclaim greatly against this religion, for the time necessarily taken up in the services of it. This they would represent as incompatible with the duties of civil and social life, and as the occasion of great and frequent danger to their country, from the insults of their troublesome neighbours to which it exposed them. But it is only a superficial view of things that can lead to this opinion. A due attention to the temper and circumstances of the people, for whom it was principally designed, will lead us to admire the propriety of this ritual.

When Israel left Egypt, difficult was the task which Moses had to manage. He had not only a religion, in a great measure, new to teach them. He had also all those prejudices to remove that could be supposed to arise from an attachment to the old. All this was necessary before they could be settled in the land destined for them, and required a considerable time. The wilderness was, in many respects, a very proper school for acquiring this important branch of knowledge. While in it, they were, from the little intercourse they had with the people around it, not only in no danger of being corrupted by them, but they were also supported, all this time, by the bounty of heaven, in an extraordinary manner, and so had abundance of time to attend to it. It is true, they were, during their stay in the wilderness, exempted from the more operose and

expensive

expensive services of religion, because their situation would not admit of them. But, abstracting from these, it furnished them employment enough. And indeed, considering the humour of this people, and the extraordinary propensity, which, upon many occasions, they discovered to idolatry, there must appear an admirable propriety in its being made so much the object of their study and attention.

It may be alleged, that, should this be admitted to have been proper, during their residence in the wilderness, it cannot be said that it was so, after their settlement in Canaan. But this I am so far from being sure of, that the contrary appears to me very probable. Even after their settlement in Canaan, it is well known, that, upon every the slightest occasion, they were ready to be seduced into the idolatrous practices of their Heathen neighbours. What, therefore, could be more wise than an institution of religion, which, by employing their time at home, would allow them but little intercourse with those around them, since it could almost never be indulged without manifest danger of corruption?

Nor can it be alleged, with any justice, that this almost continued succession of religious services did encroach upon the functions of civil or social life. Considered as a nation, and circumstanced as they were, it is evident that it was never intended, that they should enter into the busy scenes of an extensive commerce. Thus their views and their

their schemes were greatly circumscribed. Their own country, by the special providence of God, afforded them what was necessary to render them, not only easy at home, but respected abroad. And thus, exempted from the hurry and bustle in which others around them were involved, they were left more at liberty, like a nation of priests, to attend to, and perform, the offices of religion. Nor did the genius of their religion, had it been rightly understood, lay any restraint upon the exercise of benevolence, where circumstances called for it, even upon the Sabbath-day, more than any other. A proof of this we have in many instances, in the conduct of our Lord. One very striking is—that, when the Jews sought to slay him, because he healed a man upon the Sabbath-day, he, in vindication of himself, shows that the institution of the Sabbath, did, by no means, forbid such good offices; and—that, in this, he only acted in imitation of his heavenly Father, who, upon Sabbath-days, as well as others, exerted that unremitting energy, upon which the being of creation depended*.

It is acknowledged that, at certain times, thrice in the year, and during the celebration of some of their grand festivals, the attendance of all the males was required, first at the tabernacle, and afterwards at the temple, and that under the highest penalties. This, it must be owned, was a peculiarity in their religion,

* Jo. xv. 17.

religion, that could, with no propriety, be transferred into that of any other people. It would have expofed them to the greateft danger, from the inroads of troublefome neighbours.

But, befides the reafons already taken notice of, there was this to recommend the obfervance of thefe feftivals,—that there was not the leaft danger from it, notwithftanding the frequent return of the feafons for this purpofe. They were under a theocratic government, and God, who was their King, by requiring this fervice, became engaged for their fafety during their attendance upon it, and their abfence from their houfes for this purpofe. Accordingly, it deferves to be remarked, that, in a long feries of ages, during which this œconomy fubfifted, there does not occur a fingle inftance in which their tranquillity was difturbed, during thefe facred feftivals:—A circumftance this which cannot be accounted for, without calling in the interpofition of Providence for the folution of it, and fuch as, duly attended to, fhould have ferved to encourage their confidence in, and obedience of, God. And here permit me to add, that, admitting the nature of their religion might carry fome difadvantages along with it, and did, in fome meafure, feclude them from a commerce with others, it had the moft happy tendency to unite them among themfelves, in the pleafing exercife of all the focial affections, than which, fcarce any thing could more contribute to their happinefs,

confidered

confidered either as a people, or as individuals.

From the confideration of the times devoted to the fervices of religion, let us direct our attention to the places of their worſhip.

SECT. IV.

Of the Places of Public Worſhip.

OUR inquiry leads us no farther back upon this part of our fubject, than to the commencement of the Jewiſh commonwealth, which we confider as coeval with the delivery of the law at Sinai. And, from that time, we find the worſhip of God, reſtricted, firſt to the tabernacle, and afterwards to the temple.

God having eſtabliſhed a facred polity among the Iſraelites, took care to provide for the regular adminiſtration of that worſhip which he required of them. And that it might be conducted with as much decorum and eafe, as their unfettled fituation in the wilderneſs would admit, he gives orders to Mofes for conſtructing a tabernacle or tent, which might be a kind of portable temple, the archetype, or model of which, he had himſelf given him.—A defcription of it, with all its furniture, you have Exod. xxv. 10, &c.

From this defcription it is evident to every perfon, that the plan upon which it was formed, ed, and the high finishing which was given to it, were calculated to produce a noble elevation of sentiment with respect to the glorious Being, to whom its service was devoted. The whole apparatus made use of in the service to be performed in it, and the pompous ritual that attended it, were equally calculated to inspire the worshippers with sentiments of piety and devotion, and of the necessity of purity in all their intercourses with the Deity, if they would hope to be accepted in them.

To inquire into the particular reasons of the appointment of every part of this sacred tent, and of every circumstance of the service that was to be performed in it, would be unnecessary. It is sufficient to observe in the general,—that every thing in the construction, apparatus, and service of it, has this uniform tendency. One thing, however, in the description of it, merits our particular attention, and that is—the apartment called, *The Holy of Holies*, and the furniture of it. Of this, the most remarkable was, *The Ark of the Covenant*, so called, because in it were deposited (together with Aaron's rod and the pot of manna, which were preserved as memorials of very illustrious events) *The Tables of the Law*, which God gave unto Moses, when he made the covenant with Israel at Horeb. 1 Kings viii. 9.

The cover of the ark was called, *The Propitiatory* or *Mercy-seat*, and was overshadowed with a bright cloud, the visible symbol of the Divine

Divine Presence*, from which God was wont to give audible responses to the High-Priest, as often as he consulted him, upon any important emergence connected with the interest of the state.

During

---

* Mr Toland (in his *Hodegus, or the Pillar of Fire and Cloud, that guarded Israel, not miraculous*) maintains, that the cloud which rested on the mercy-seat, in the most holy place of the tabernacle and temple, had nothing miraculous in it, and could, with no propriety, be considered as a symbol of the Divine presence. According to him, it was no more than artificial, and excited by the incense burnt by the high-priest, when he entered into it. In proof of this he appeals to Levit. xvi. 12, 13. where the high-priest is directed to take a censer full of burning coals, &c. And from thence he infers, that the cloud which covered the *Mercy-Seat*, was no more than a cloud of smoke of the high-priest's making. And afterwards he adds—" If any be desirous to know what that
" odoriferous incense was, whereof we read in the receipt
" for making the *smoke* or *cloud*, there is a particular descrip-
" tion of it, according to the art of the apothecary, for the
" service of the temple, Exod. xxx. 34—38."

What might have been Mr Toland's design in this attempt, may be difficult to determine. But if we may judge from the manner in which he manages it, we should be apt to imagine, that it was not the most favourable for the Mosaic institution of religion, notwithstanding his profession to the contrary. But, whatever it might have been, his reasoning in support of his favourite scheme, is not so solid, as it may appear plausible.

It is very true, the high-priest was required to bring a censer full of incense with him into the most holy place, and to burn it there, that *the cloud of the incense might cover the Mercy-Seat*. But pray, what is there in this, incompatible with the residence of a visible symbol of the Divine presence? If this was the cloud, which is represented as hovering above the mercy-seat, and no other, then it is evident that it should be found here, only when incense was burnt in it, and yet we find it was otherwise.

Thus,

During the sojourning of Israel in the wilderness, the residence of the ark was determined by the several marches they were appointed to make. It accompanied them wherever they went, as containing the symbol

Thus, Exod. xl. 34. at the erection and consecration of the tabernacle, we find that *the cloud* covered the *tent of the congregation*, and *that the glory of the Lord filled the tabernacle*, before any incense appears to have been burnt, or service performed in it.

In like manner we find that, upon the introduction of the ark into the temple, built by Solomon, the house was filled with a cloud, 2 Chron. v. 13. and this cloud is called, verse 14, *The glory of the Lord*. And here it deserves to be remarked, that the house of God was filled with this cloud, not after the oblation of sacrifice (for as yet there was none offered in it), but during the celebration of the Divine praises, and immediately after depositing the ark in its proper place.

Nay, not only does it appear that, immediately upon lodging the ark in the most holy place, those who carried it retired before there was time for burning incense, but we have no mention at all of the presence of the high-priest, who alone was authorised to officiate at this service. And we may well believe, that neither Solomon nor any of the inferior priests, would have dared to profane the temple, by the irregular performance of any of its services, at the very time they were assembled to consecrate it.

To this let me add, that we find no mention of this symbol of the Divine presence in the second temple; and yet, if it had consisted only of a cloud, raised by the smoke of incense, burnt by the high-priest upon his entrance into the most holy place, it must necessarily have been there, as well as in the first.

What he says, with so much confidence, concerning the receipt for making this odoriferous incense, is an unpardonable attempt to impose upon his readers, by making them believe that the receipt he refers to had a connection with the cloud that covered the mercy-seat. Let any one read Levit. xvi. 12, 13. and compare it with Exod. xxx. 34—36. to

which

bol of the Divine prefence with them, their marches being directed by that *Pillar of Cloud*, which conftantly hovered above it. And as it always took up its place in the centre of their camp, for the accommodation of all who attended it, fo to it they were obliged to repair for the performance of every part of the Divine fervice required of them. And during their fo long ftay in a vaft and howling wildernefs, what could be better calculated to fupport their fpirits, and keep them, from either peevifhly turning back to Egypt, or impatiently rufhing forward to Canaan, than the refidence of fuch a fymbol of the Divine prefence among them?

Was

which he fends us for the compofition of this pleafant perfume, and he will be convinced that they have no relation to one another.

In Levit. xvi. 12, 13. we find nothing prefcribed to be burnt in the moft holy place, but incenfe. In Exod. xxx. 34. the perfume fpoken of, is a compofition of various, odoriferous, fpices. In the one cafe, the incenfe is required to be burnt. In the other, the perfume is to be placed, fome of it, before the teftimony, in the tabernacle of the congregation And, if I might venture a conjecture, it might have been placed there, as the name given to it feems to indicate, to diffufe a pleafing odor through this facred place. And this might be the more neceffary, becaufe, by the rare accefs to it, as well as the clofenefs of the room itfelf which had no windows, there would be no free circulation of air in it.

Upon the whole, from any thing that has been advanced by Mr Toland, I humbly think, the commonly received opinion with refpect to the fymbol of the Divine prefence, deferves to be admitted, and carries nothing improbable in it. Nay, in the thing itfelf, there appears a great propriety on many accounts. In proof of this, fee Part I. Chap. ii. § 1.

Was not the motion of the *Pillar of Cloud and fire**, that constantly attended them, a proof that God undertook the direction of every thing which concerned them? But of this more afterwards.

During

---

* I know Mr Toland, in his *Hodegus*, already mentioned, gives an account of this matter, which, were it admitted, would entirely invalidate the force of our remark. He maintains that there was nothing miraculous in the whole transaction. The manner in which he attempts to explain it, is shortly this. He observes that, in travelling through such vast deserts as Israel was obliged to pass, and where there was no remarkable objects to direct their course, but all was one continued waste, caravans had need of some visible guide:—That, as the magnetic compass was not then discovered, those who conducted armies or large bodies, through such immense deserts, were obliged to kindle a fire and erect it upon a large pole:—and that this, according to the signals concerted, would serve to direct their motions, in the day time, by its smoke, and, in the night time, by the brightness of its flame. In proof of this, he quotes an instance or two from history, and shows that Alexander the Great, in his war with the Persians, and—that Cyrus and Cyaxares, in theirs with the Babylonians, Lydians, and Egyptians, were obliged to use such a method in conducting their vast armies, through the unknown and uncultivated countries they had to pass. And from thence, with the help of some forced criticisms on the historical narrative of Israel's march, he infers that it was, in a similar manner, they were conducted through all the mazes and windings of their long and tedious journey to Canaan,— even by a fire kindled in some pot or vase, erected upon a high pole, and placed upon the tabernacle, as the general's tent.

It is not denied that there are several things abundantly ingenious alleged by Mr Toland, in defence of his hypothesis. But, after all that has been said by him, they appear to me to be more ingenious, than solid.

I readily allow that it would be improper to plead for a miraculous interposition of Providence, where the ends of it would

During the continuance of Israel in the wilderness, the ark must have been ambulatory and unsettled, as their own situation was. —Upon their settlement in the land of Canaan, though it was not entirely stationary, it was

could be effected equally without it. *Nec Deus intersit, nisi dignus vindice*, &c. is a position that reason very readily assents to. But, as such an extraordinary appearance in favour of Israel, was calculated to produce the most happy effects to them, and to subserve the ends of Providence, I can see no impropriety in supposing it.

Besides, allow me to observe that the scheme, which Mr Toland has adopted, will not account for the direction of Israel through the wilderness,—for this plain reason. The country, through which they had to pass, was a mountainous one; and therefore it cannot be imagined that they had it always in their power to pitch upon such a spot of ground, as would afford them a sight, either of the smoke by day, or of the flame by night, sufficient to direct the motions of such a vast body as composed their camp.

To this led me add, that, supposing it to be no more than an artificial fire, (the use of which was well known) it would have been very improper for Israel to have used it. Though now the Egyptian army which pursued them, was destroyed, yet they could not be ignorant, nay they had reason to fear, that, in the course of their marches through the vast tract of country they had to pass, some new enemy might oppose their progress, and therefore, in all good policy, they should have chose some other plan of conduct. The reason is plain; because they could not but know, that the same signal which informed the distant parts of their own camp, when the centre was to move or stop, or whether they were to direct their course, would have conveyed the same intelligence to their enemies. And to infer, that, because such a practice was usual several ages after, therefore it obtained *then*, is not at all logical, or good reasoning. Nay, what I think much more probable is,—that after ages, hearing of this wonderful phenomenon, might from thence have taken the hint of the practice for which Mr Toland so warmly contends. And if the

pro-

was not so often moved. For a considerable time, we know, it was fixed first at Mispah, and afterwards at Shiloh. In the neighbourhood of this place it was, that the illustrious Joshua assembled the tribes of Israel, and made them renew

probability of this conjecture is admitted, it becomes no small presumption for this historical fact, as related by Moses.

Here it likewise deserves to be taken notice of, that the *sole* design of the pillar of cloud and fire, was not to conduct Israel through the wilderness. It answered other valuable purposes (see Part I. chap. 2, §. 1.) And therefore an artificial pillar would have been insufficient.

Mr Toland seems to lay great stress upon the words of Moses to Hobab, Numb. x. 29. and, because the word *Angel* signifies *Messenger*, contends that Hobab was to be understood by the angel, whom God told Israel he was to send before them in the way, Exod. xxiii. 20. But it requires no more than an ordinary degree of attention to the history, to be able to confute this hypothesis.

It is readily acknowledged that the word *Angel* does signify Messenger, whether it be a heavenly being that is spoken of, or an earthly. And therefore, in which of these senses it is, at any time, to be understood, must be determined by the context. Let us apply this observation to the present case, and it will be easy to see how forced his interpretation is.

At the same time that God told Israel that he was to send his Angel before him, he told them that *his Name was in him;* that is (according to the very lowest sense that can be given to the words) that he acted by his authority. Whereas, when Moses presses Hobab to go along with him, there is not the most distant hint, that he acted by any delegated power from God, as their guide. And indeed, if he had, his so determined resolution of leaving Israel and returning to his own country, would have been not only indecent, but equally criminal, without the Divine permission. And we may well believe that Moses would not have failed to have made use of such an argument to detain him: But we find not so much as a word to this purpose from him. But what puts it beyond all doubt, that the angel spoken of was some other than Hobab,

renew their covenant with God, of which he erected a monument or memorial, under an oak, that was by the sanctuary of God. A more settled residence of the ark became neceſſary after their settlement in Canaan, not only to encourage a happy union among themſelves, by bringing them often together for the exerciſes of public and ſocial worſhip, but

is what God ſays of him, Exod. xxiii. 21. " Beware of him " and obey his voice,—provoke him not: for he will not par- " don your tranſgreſſions, for my name is in him." Theſe words evidently ſuppoſe him inveſted, by a commiſſion from God, with power to puniſh them, if they did not follow his inſtructions.

It is true, Moſes ſays Numb. x. 31. " Leave us not, I pray " thee," &c. From thence Mr Toland infers the ſervices he had done them in conducting them hitherto, and the neceſſity of his continued directions in the wilderneſs. But, in anſwer to this, let me obſerve, that ſome learned men of conſiderable note have (without the leaſt view to this opinion of Mr Toland) given another turn to the words, and one which, I humbly think, they will very well bear. They conſider this addreſs of Moſes to Hobab, as an expreſſion of his gratitude to him, for the ſhare he had taken in their troubles, and the aſſiſtance he had given them in their marches, through the wilderneſs, and—an acknowledgment that, that if he did not go along with them, they were at a loſs to make him a proper requital for all his ſervices: Whereas, if he would accompany them to the promiſed land, he aſſures him v. 32, that " what good- " neſs the Lord ſhould do unto them, the ſame they would do " unto him."

To all this let me add, that there can ſcarcely be conceived a good reaſon why they ſhould, from the imagined neceſſity of his ſervices, urge Hobab to go along with them. For might not Moſes, who had reſided a long time in Median, tending his father-in-law's flocks, be as well acquainted with this wilderneſs as Hobab was? This circumſtance like- wiſe tends to overthrow Mr Toland's conjecture.

but also to prevent those corruptions in religion which might be apt to arise from every one's being allowed to worship at a private altar. It had besides a particular fitness to draw them off from worshipping God in groves and high places, as the inhabitants of the country, whom they destroyed or expelled, had done. This, God was at the greatest pains to guard them against: Not from any impropriety there could be in these places of worship abstractly considered, (for in such places the Patriarchs were wont to worship in early times, Gen. xxi. 33.) but because, had they been allowed to worship in these places, which, among the inhabitants of that country, were devoted to idolatry, and polluted by the impure ceremonies and practices that attended it, they were in no small danger of being corrupted *.

* However, in the more early ages of the world, groves might have been consecrated to the purposes of pure devotion, certain it is, that, in the progress of idolatry, they were employed in a manner that does sufficiently justify the prohibition of them. Many reasons (of which we are now ignorant) may have concurred to vindicate this measure. But still we know enough to evince the reasonableness of it.

Some, grossly ignorant of the nature of the Deity, may have pitched upon such places from a foolish conceit, that the nearer the place of their worship was to heaven, the more easy would be their access to him.

When the practice of Hero-worship began, some think mankind might have been induced to pay it in groves and high places, where the remains of their heroes may have been deposited, from an opinion that their departed souls delighted to hover about these places, and would be more attentive to the devotions that were offered to them there, than any where else. Thus, they may be considered as places consecrated to the manes

And having already too strong a propensity to the idolatrous services, which prevailed in this and the neighbouring countries, it was not improbable but they might have been soon led into the imitation of them, which would have defeated the original design of their separation from them. Whereas, by requiring Israel to cut down the groves, and to desert the high places frequented by the former inhabitants of the country, a very strong abhorrence of their manner of worship was excited and kept up. And what could be a more powerful preservative than this, against the infection to which they were exposed, or engage them more closely to adhere to the worship of the God of their fathers? The most nervous and pathetic dissuasives that could be made use of against it, might have had a temporary effect, but they could have had no more. They would have been soon forgotten, and, even while remembered, would have made but a slight impression upon the mind, compared with this manner of procedure,—

the

manes of their heroes, and thither they were wont frequently to repair, not only for the purposes of devotion, but also to consult them as oracles, with respect to future events.

How far these and the like opinions may have contributed to the rise of this practice, I will not take upon me to say. But one thing I am fully persuaded of,—that the abominable vices to which they became at last prostituted, under the pretence of religion, was a principal reason for the prohibition concerning them, and is such as must satisfy every impartial person, of the wisdom and propriety of it. See on this subject Dr Jenning's Jewish Antiq. and the Ancient Universal History. Vol. III. 8vo.

the cutting down and deſtroying the inſignia of idolatry. But ſuch a teſtimony as this of the Divine diſpleaſure againſt it, conſtantly exhibited to their very ſenſes, could not fail to ſtrengthen their abhorrence of it, and ſo wean them gradually from it.

For a long courſe of years after their obtaining poſſeſſion of the land of Canaan, Iſrael remained in a very unſettled ſtate. The frequent diſturbances they received from the old inhabitants of it and the neighbouring countries, kept them almoſt conſtantly engaged in wars. During ſuch a ſtate of things, it was ſcarce to be expected that they ſhould have much time, to turn their attention to any thing not connected with the ſecurity of the poſſeſſions they had already acquired, or the conqueſt of thoſe parts of the country that ſtill ſtood out againſt them. The times of peace, are the moſt proper for ſetting about what relates either to reformation or improvement, whether in the civil or religious departments of a kingdom.

At length, God having bleſſed them with peace and opulence, the illuſtrious David, King of Iſrael, from the overflowing gratitude of his heart for both, meditates the building a temple to God, aſhamed that, while he himſelf dwelt in an elegant palace, a manſion no better than a tent ſhould be provided for his Creator. This, however adapted to the unſettled ſtate of Iſrael, when it was firſt conſtructed, ſeemed altogether unſuited to the grandeur to which their nation was now raiſed,

fed, or the gratitude which it became him to show to that God, who had, from the smallest beginnings, and through a series of miracles as well as years, brought him to such a happy and flourishing state.

David must have allowed, that the tabernacle which God had planned for himself,— for his *Schechinah* *, was the most proper residence

---

* The word *Schechinah* is a technical term, used among divines, to denote the visible symbol of the Divine presence. It needs not be observed, that, considering the immensity and spirituality of the Divine nature, it could not, properly speaking, be either confined to place, or represented under any particular form or shape. However, as the Deity saw meet, in some of the earlier ages of the world, to discover himself to mankind, by one appointed to personate and represent him, it was necessary he should do it in some visible manner. And accordingly, it deserves to be taken notice of, that he chose to manifest himself under the appearance, very often, of a bright, resplendent, cloud, which was hence called a *Glory*. The brightness or glory sometimes assumed the shape or similitude of a man, and sometimes appeared without any particular shape or similitude at all. In the first of these ways, the Deity was wont to appear in the more early ages of the world; and to this there is a manifest allusion in the several modes of phraseology, in which the sacred writers speak of him. But when, in after times, mankind became greatly addicted to idolatry, the Deity chose the latter mode of appearance, that he might not seem to give the least encouragement to it, which perhaps that of a human shape or form might have been construed into.

Those bright and luminous appearances, by which the presence of the Deity was notified, might, very properly, be denominated, according to the etymology of the word, the *Schechinah*, that is (according to the Hebrew root, *Schachan*, from which it is derived) *the habitation of the Divinity;* though generally, among divines, it is restricted to that visible and resplendent cloud, which conducted the Israelites through the wilderness to Canaan, and afterwards took up its residence, in the

dence of his glory in time paſt. But now, imagining that their ideas of the Divine grandeur, ſo far as they could be affected by any external appearance, ſhould keep pace with the improvements they had made in taſte and elegance, he began to revolve in his mind the ſcheme of a temple for God, that might ſerve as a monument at once of his and the nation's gratitude and veneration for him. What David projected, having received the approbation of God, his ſon Solomon executed. And, with a great profuſion of expence, oranment, and elegance, he reared up a fabric, which juſtly became the object of admiration to all, who either ſaw or heard of it.

It would be needleſs to enter into a minute deſcription of it. What was properly called *The Temple*, was but a ſmall edifice. The reſt of the huge pile that went under this name, conſiſted of many courts or cloiſters, for the accommodation of the Prieſts and others, who were obliged to attend there, in the way of their office, or the diſcharge of the duties of religion reſtricted to it. That part of the temple, which properly reſpected the ſervices

---

the moſt holy place of the tabernacle and temple, above the propitiatory, from which the oracles were given to the High-Prieſt.

The muſſelmen have entertained a great many ridiculous conceits upon this ſubject. See Calmet's dictionary, under the article, *Samuel*. But what is related above, is the ſubſtance of what we are authorized to ſay concerning the ſchechinah from the ſacred hiſtory. See Differt. 2. in the Miſcellan. Sacra, on God's viſible preſence. See alſo Lowman's Rational of the Ritual, &c. Part ii. chap. 2.

of religion, was built upon the model of the tabernacle, and therefore it is unneceſſary to enlarge in an account of it. This, in the ſucceeding periods of their commonwealth, like the tabernacle in the infancy of it, was the place at which their public aſſemblies for devotion were held, in ſo much that their ſacrifices, and ſome of their moſt ſolemn feſtivals, could be ſolemnized no where elſe.

This part of the inſtitution was highly proper, and admirably fitted, by ſuch an union of their religious ſervices, to promote the moſt happy concord among themſelves.

The deſignation of a court for the Gentiles, had an excellent tendency to prepare Iſrael gradually for the abrogation of the Moſaic form of religion, however fond they might be of it, by hinting to them, that the duration of it could only be temporary. It is true, the diviſion of it from the court of the Iſraelites, was a plain intimation, that, while the Gentiles did not, in all reſpects, conform to the religion of Iſrael, they were not to be admitted into a full communion of privileges with them. But, in the meantime, the admiſſion that was granted them even into the outer court, ſerved to make them ſtill better acquainted with that religion, and gave them the hopes that a thorough knowledge of it, would, in due time, pave the way for pulling down the wall that divided betwixt them, and ſo form them into one religious ſociety, or church.

From

From the above account of the tabernacle and temple, and the purposes to which they were intended to be subservient, the reader may judge how far it is probable, that the first hint of both was borrowed from those temples that so early obtained in Egypt.

Dr Spencer* warmly contends, that the Jewish tabernacle and temple were no more than imitations of the Egyptian. In support of this opinion, he pleads the authority of Herodotus and Lucian, who ascribe the first erection of temples to the Egyptians. But it is evident this can, by no means, be admitted as decisive upon the point. Considering how late these historians lived, and that their information could not lead them far back, every one must see that no great regard is to be paid to it. A much more probable reason for the great antiquity of temples, may be derived from the supposed original intention of building them.

It is the opinion of some, that, when the worship of deified heroes was introduced, and images were made to be memorials of them, mankind would soon find it necessary to build temples for the reception and preservation of these. And as afterwards they fancied, that by certain forms of incantation, they could charm down their souls to inhabit them, they might choose to build temples for their residence, that they might have the more easy access to them, in cases either of devotion or danger.

* See Dr Spencer de Legib. Ritual, &c. lib. iii. Dissert. 6.

danger. But what if all this should be admitted, and that, upon this principle, the Egyptians had temples long before the tabernacle was constructed by Moses, or the temple built by Solomon, it will, by no means, follow that they afforded the hint or model for either. Betwixt their respective designs, there seems to have been no correspondence. A much more rational account may be given of the matter.

Neither Moses nor Solomon considered the God they worshipped, as no more than a local deity, nor ever entertained a thought that he could be confined within the walls of the place consecrated to his worship. This is evident from the form used at the consecration of the temple. The reason for it seems to have been very different.

In the more early ages of the world, it is not improbable but the Schechinah, or visible symbol of the Divine presence, was generally to be met with in the places sacred to worship; and therefore, in that unsettled state of mankind, any one fixed place of residence would have been improper. It is more likely that it shifted as they did.

But when God had established his church among Israel, and meant to give them and the world, the most convincing proof of his having done so, one can easily see the propriety of such an appointment, first of the tabernacle, in their ambulatory, and afterwards of the temple, in their more settled, state. And what makes it probable that, from some such views as these, the tabernacle and temple were built,—is that, till the erection of the Jewish polity, we hear nothing of either among the ancient Patriarchs. And yet it cannot be doubted, but they were as well acquainted as Moses could be, with the practice of the nations around them in this point, and, if they had inclined, might have copied it much more early. But it is unnecessary to spend more time in an inquiry of this nature, as it can be of no great importance, whichever way it may be determined.

The magnificent temple built by Solomon, continued to be the place of the public worship of the true God, till Jerusalem was sacked by Nebuchadnezzar, and then it was rased to the ground.

It is highly probable that there were no Synagogues among the Jews, till after the Babylonish captivity. The first hint of them, they may perhaps have received from Ezra's assembling them in the streets of Jerusalem to hear the law read to them, which, during the captivity, had, very probably, been discontinued: From thence, I say, may have arisen their public assemblies for religious instruction, and afterwards the erection of synagogues, for their better accommodation, in attending on it.

Some have imagined that their Synagogues and Proseuchæ were the same; and that the place of meeting for the purposes of religion, received different names, according to the different lights in which it was viewed:—That it it was called a Synagogue, from its being the place of rendezvous for worship;—a Proseucha, from the prayers that were performed in it. But the more general, and, I humbly think, the more probable, opinion is,—that they were different. The synagogues were commonly situated in towns: The proseuchæ, in some retired place, very often at the side of the sea or some river, for the accommodation of washing before they addressed themselves to their devotions: The one, covered; the other, open: The one, for public; the other, for private, devotion. And to this let me add, that, as they differed in these respects, so also in point—of antiquity; it being highly probable that the Jews had their proseuchæ, not only long before the captivity, but as early as the days of the patriarchs themselves, for such seem to have been those retired groves, in which they paid their devotions to God. But not to enter farther into this inquiry. As these assemblies seem to have been established, rather by concert among themselves, than by an express commandment of God concerning them, a more minute consideration of them does not fall within our present design.

After the return of Israel from the Babylonish captivity, an unlucky schism obtained, by erecting another place of worship, in opposition to the temple at Jerusalem. Nehemiah, in execution of the scheme of reformation which he had set on foot, required that such of his countrymen as had married

wives

wives out of idolatrous families, should instantly dismiss them, in order to prevent the bad consequences that were justly to be dreaded from such alliances. *Manasseh*, the son of *Joiada*, the high-priest, had formed such a connection, but refused to submit to this appointment. Being, upon this, expelled his own country, he fled to Samaria, and put himself under the protection of *Sanballat*, his father-in-law, who was governor of it. *Sanballat*, from views very probably of interest to his own country, as well as resentment against the Jews, formed the scheme of setting up a temple upon Mount Gerizzim, in rivalship to that at Jerusalem. And having obtained a licence to this purpose from *Darius Nothus*, he constituted *Manasseh* high-priest, and afforded an asylum to all refractory Jews, many of whom came and settled in Samaria. But the authority of this institution was never acknowledged by the Jews: Nay, for this and several other reasons, the Samaritans were had in the highest abhorrence by them. And as, notwithstanding all that has been said in favour of it by the Samaritans, it must evidently appear to derive its authority from the appointment of a Heathen prince, we have no farther concern with it.

Long after the erection of the temple of Gerizzim, we find another built, by permission of *Ptolemy Philometer*, in Egypt. This temple was procured by the artful management of one *Onias*, who had himself been a candidate for the High-Priest's office, but, disappointed

appointed of this, fled into Egypt. By his diſtinguiſhed abilities and fine addreſs, he ſoon infinuated himſelf into the good graces of the reigning prince, and found it no difficult matter to perſuade him, that the permiſſion granted to the Egyptian Jews, to attend ſome of the feſtivals of their religion annually at Jeruſalem, might be productive of many inconveniences to them, and of great hurt to his intereſt. To prevent theſe, he propoſed that a temple, upon the ſame plan as that at Jeruſalem, ſhould be built in Egypt, where all the ſervices of their religion might be performed. Leave was accordingly granted to him for this purpoſe. The only obſtacle now to the execution of his ſcheme was,—the opinion that prevailed among the Jews, that Jeruſalem was the only place in which, according to their religion, it was lawful to perform certain parts of public worſhip. To remove this difficulty, he refers them to the prophecy of Iſaiah chap. xix. 19. and had art enough to explain it in ſuch manner as removed their ſcruples. Upon this, he ſet about building his new temple, and choſe a ſpot of ground at a little diſtance from *Heliopolis*, upon which ſtood formerly the temple of *Bubaſtis* or *Iſis*, as the moſt proper place for it*.

From the above account of this temple, as well as that of Gerizzim, the reader will eaſily ſee that a larger account of either, does

not

---

* See Prid. Connect. &c. Vol. II. p. 264. edit. 8.

not fall within the design, or plan, of this treatise.

In the Jewish history, we find mention made of another institution, closely connected with religion, that went under the name of, *The School of the Prophets*. At what time these schools first obtained, is uncertain. *Samuel* is by some thought to have been the founder of them, though others make the institution of a much earlier date. It is not improbable but such schools were planted in different places, and that they were intended, not only for the religious instruction of those, who might be afterwards employed in the immediate services of religion, or in the execution of any commands from God to his people, in the character of prophets, but also as seminaries of religion to all who chose to repair to them, either for the purposes of instruction or devotion. But as these colleges seem to have derived their institution, so far as appears, not from any appointment of God, we shall not enter into a more particular account of them.

Now, from the cursory view we have taken of the several places of worship under the Mosaic dispensation, and the Divine appointment concerning them, it is humbly submitted to the candid and impartial, if there appears any thing from it, to justify the imputation of *absurd and unphilosophical*, thrown upon that institution of religion, the offices of which were to be performed in them.

We

We are often apt to form our notions of propriety from narrow and contracted views, and,—from a comparison of the several peculiarities of this religion with the circumstances in which we are ourselves placed, to tax it as *absurd and unphilosophical*, because, forsooth, it does not correspond with these, or the sentiments we may have entertained of propriety. Whereas, did we allow ourselves to think seriously, all that could be required in this, or any other, mode of religion, is no more, than that the nature, constitution, and tendency of it, should be such as is worthy of its Author,—suited to the genius and circumstances of the people for whom it was principally intended,—to the great ends proposed by it, and—those ages of the world, through which it was to continue in force. And from aught has appeared hitherto, there is nothing in this repugnant to any of these.

Let us carry on our inquiry to the consideration, in the next place,

SECT. V.

Of the Officers of Religion.

IN the public offices of religion, it is necessary, for very obvious reasons, that some person should preside; and, for the same reasons, that there should be some appointed to do so. So much does this appear to have its foundation

foundation in nature, that we have never heard of a public inſtitution of religion, that wanted ſuch.

Under the Moſaic œconomy, there was ſuch an order of men. But, what was indeed peculiar to it, that order was reſtricted to a certain family; none of any other, according to the original plan, being allowed to be adopted into it. It became hereditary in the family of Levi. And, in ſuch a commonwealth as that of Iſrael, in which the miniſtrations of religion were ſo operoſe, and ſo much depended upon the punctuality and exactneſs of all its ſervices, and every the minuteſt circumſtance that attended them, there appears an evident propriety in ſuch a deſignation.

During the patriarchal ages, to preſide in the offices of religion had been the privilege of primogeniture. It is eaſy to ſee how, from thence, might ariſe the greateſt corruptions in religion. To remedy this inconvenience, which was the almoſt unavoidable conſequence of ſuch a ſtate of things, might have been one reaſon (and a very wiſe one it would have been too) for the inſtitution of the Moſaic œconomy, and the reſtriction of the pontifical order to one particular family, who, in all their miniſtrations, ſhould be obliged to conform to the directions they had received.

Beſides this advantage, ſuch a meaſure would be attended with another very great one. Thoſe who were to officiate in the ſervices of religion, would probably be better educated for them, than otherwiſe they would have

have been. They would alſo be hereby engaged to give a due attendance upon them, as their ſubſiſtence depended entirely upon the emoluments ariſing from their reſpective offices; for, in the general diviſion of the land, there was no proviſion made for them.

The ſervants of God, who officiated in the ſacred functions of religion, conſiſted of different claſſes or orders. Each of them,—the High-Prieſt, Prieſts, and Levites, had their ſeveral parts aſſigned to them.

The High-Prieſthood was made hereditary in the family of Aaron, and generally deſcended to the eldeſt ſon of the line of Eleazer, after the death of Nadab and Abihu, who left no iſſue, if no legal imperfection did diſqualify them, for holding it.

As the High-Prieſt was at the head of the ſacerdotal order, no doubt he might, if he choſe it, or any particular exigence required, officiate in the functions of the inferior Prieſts. But there were two very great privileges which belonged to him alone, and which it would have been highly impious, and equally dangerous, in any of the ſubordinate prieſts to have uſurped. The one was the privilege of officiating before God in the moſt holy place, upon the anniverſary of the atonement or great expiation. The other was,—the conſulting God in important matters, relating to religion, or the ſtate, by *Urim and Thummim**.

What

---

* Nothing can be more various, or leſs ſatisfying, than the opinions of learned men, concerning the Urim and Thummim. For

What the original opinions were concerning this kind of oracular confultation, may be feen below. But one thing we muft obferve there was, that difcovered the greateft wifdom and goodnefs in the appointment of it.

Mankind,

For gratifying the reader's curiofity, more than for his information, I fhall fubjoin the moft remarkable that have occurred to me.—The words *Urim* and *Thummim*, according to their original meaning, fignify *lights and perfections*. This, fome think, refers to the precious ftones in the High-prieft's breaftplate; and that when God fays (Exod. xxviii. 30.) " Thou " fhalt give to the breaftplate of judgment, lights and perfec-" tions," &c. he meant no more, than that they fhould pitch upon ftones of the higheft value, and of the moft brilliant quality, and give them the higheft polifh, in order to adorn it.—Others make the words to have a refpect to the refponfe that was to be given, and to denote the perfpicuity, accuracy, and perfection of it. The LXX tranflate thefe words δηλωσιν και αληθειαν, thus, *manifeftation and truth*. But this cafts little light upon the matter.

Upon a fubject of this nature, as the fcriptures are not explicit, little more than conjecture can be looked for. Accordingly, a great deal of this has been offered. Some think that the Urim and Thummim was no other than the Tetragrammaton, or facred name, engraved upon the breaftplate, from which the High-prieft received the refponfe.—Others have maintained that the refponfe was collected, by the uncommon luftre, and fome, from the prominence, of the ftones of the pectoral, and a combination of the letters engraved on it, for the feveral tribes. And becaufe all the letters of the alphabet are not to be found in it, the Rabbins, who are never wanting in fancy, where the indulgence of it could ferve a turn, fell upon an eafy device to fupply that defect. They tell us that the names of Abraham, Ifaac, and Jacob were engraven over the name of Reuben, and the words *Shibleh-Jah*, that is, *The Tribes of the Lord*, under the name of Benjamin, in order to make up the whole alphabet. Some are of opinion, that the Urim and Thummim were the names

Mankind, very probably from the easy access they had to the visible symbol of the Divine presence in the first ages of the world, had greatly abused this privilege. God, therefore, to preserve a proper veneration in the minds of men, in after ages, was pleased, for this among other wise reasons, to take up his special residence, upon the erection of the church of Israel, in that apartment of the tabernacle, that was called, *The Holy of Holies;* and

of two precious stones, set in a gold collar, that was hung about the High-priest's neck, in imitation of a golden chain, which the chief officer of justice among the Egyptians wore, and to which were suspended the emblematical figures of *Truth and Justice*, to keep him in mind of the regard he ought to have for both, in all his decisions. And there have not been wanting some, who have maintained that the pectoral had two golden figures, or little images, inclosed in the duplicature of it, and that from thence the response was audibly given. A writer of great learning gives it as his opinion, that the Urim and Thummim, were not only different in themselves, but applied to quite different purposes:—That the Urim was that part of the oracle that gave the response in doubtful cases, and was a little image from which an answer was audibly given, and—that it was much the same with the *Teraphim*, which had been used with the same view, from the earliest times, and were (as is generally agreed) little images, formed under certain constellations, and supposed capable of advising in doubtful cases, from the heavenly influences thus received:—And that the Thummim was that, by which the High-priest judged whether the sacrifices offered to God, were accepted or not. But, not to enlarge on this subject, on which it is impossible to arrive at satisfaction,

Whoever would wish to see more on it, may consult Calmet's Dictionary, under the words Urim and Thummim—The Ancient Universal History, Vol. III. p. 76. *et seq.*—Dr Jennings's Jewish Antiq. Vol. I. p. 233.—Dr Spencer de Ritualib. Judæor. de origine Urim & Thummim, and Mede on Deut. xxxiii. 8.

and to this the high-prieſt alone was to have acceſs, and that but once a-year, let the neceſſities of the ſtate be ever ſo urgent.

While the theocracy continued, ſome other method of conſulting him, ſeems to have been neceſſary, in extraordinary caſes. I know it has been ſaid, that if, in the interval, any thing occurred that required the Divine oracle, the High-Prieſt might, by repairing to the tabernacle, and conſulting God, with his face directed towards the place where the Ark of the Covenant was depoſited in the holy of holies, receive an anſwer. But what if this ſhould be granted? Who does not ſee that there might occur caſes, and theſe frequently too, in which it might have been impracticable to have acceſs even to the tabernacle itſelf? Such were the caſes mentioned, 1 Sam. xxiii. 9—11. and chap. xxx. 7, 8. In ſuch, or ſimilar, caſes, where they could have no acceſs to the tabernacle, God ſeems to have provided againſt any inconvenience that might have ariſen from thence, by enabling the High-Prieſt to collect his anſwer with certainty, in ſome other way, which, though unknown to us, might have been abundantly determinate to him *.

---

* However unwilling the enemies of revealed religion may be to own the Divine origin and authority of it, do not the many ſtriking inſtances in which the Pagan religions mimic it, give a very high degree of credibility to it? One inſtance to this purpoſe, which I beg leave to mention, is that of the heathen oracles, which, upon inquiry, will be found to be no more

Subordinate to the High Priest, and devoted to the service of the tabernacle and temple, were the *Priests*. These also belonged to that branch of the family of Levi, who descended from Aaron. We have seen which of them

more than crafty inventions introduced into the system of their religion, to procure a regard to it, similar to what the oracles, in the Mosaic, had procured to it.

I know a very different account is given of the matter, but it is such as can satisfy none but the most credulous.

We know that when mankind came to advance departed heroes to the rank of inferior deities, they were taught by their designing priests (who well knew how to make their advantage of their credulity) that oracular responses could be obtained from them, by certain religious rites devised for this purpose. We know likewise, that, the people being once got to believe that the heavenly bodies were inhabited by these divine intelligences, their priests found it no difficult matter to persuade them next, that they did, by certain elementary influences, communicate a power of delivering oracles to those, who, by a proper discipline, were prepared to receive the prophetic influence. Such as this is the account which Diodorus Siculus gives us of the origin of the Delphic oracle, in the life of Philip. He says that a shepherd, tending some goats, at a place where now the temple of Apollo at Delphi stands, observed one of these animals begin to dance, in a very extraordinary manner, upon his approaching a den or cavity, of great length and dark winding; That, astonished by this phenomenon, he went up to it, and immediately found himself seized with the prophetic furor and began to prophecy: That, upon discovering this, the inhabitants of Delphi erected a temple, upon that spot, to their god Apollo, who, by communicating the afflatus to his priest or priestess, seated upon a tripod, that it might be the more easily received, enabled them to give responses to those who consulted them.

It is not at all improbable, but, in those ages of ignorance, this tale, ridiculous as it is, and none can be more so, might have gained credit among a superstitious people. But who may not see, that this heathen practice might very probably have

them were appointed to the office of the High Priest. All the other sons of the family, were consecrated to the service of the altar, in the station of inferior priests.

It is easy to observe that, in process of time, the number of Priests must become too great to be able to attend, all of them, at once, at the national altar. Therefore, in the reign of David, they were divided, into twenty four companies. The commencement of each company's service was to be determined by lot, and this order ever after to be observed, all beginning their course upon Sabbath, and continuing it only for a week, at a time. And as each course received its denomination from the head or chief of the family

have taken its rise from the Jewish one under consideration; and that all this account of the miraculous manner of its discovery, was artfully framed to procure the greatest respect to it, and profit to the priests? And what is a strong presumption of this, is—that when, in ages of greater improvement, it could not bear examination, the pretended deity thought fit to retire from his temple, or keep silence in it. And when his votaries were pressed to account for this, the manner in which they attempted to do it, must make us stand amazed at their weakness, or rather at their assurance (for we cannot suspect them of so much weakness), and at the credulity of the people they had to do with.

Plutarch, who was himself a priest of Apollo, in his treatise concerning the cause of the ceasing of oracles, is not ashamed to ascribe it to the decay of the prophetical exhalations, which he supposed to spring from the earth, occasioned by floods of rains, which, he says, might extinguish,—or peals of thunder, which might dissipate, them. Does not such an account from a man of his learning, give reason to suspect his ingenuity, and that he did not himself believe it? See more on this subject in Gale's Court of the Gentiles, Part III. p. 60. and in Shuckford's Connection, &c. Vol. II. p. 394.

ly, from which they were defcended,—thefe were called, *the Chiefs* of the *Priefts*. The bufinefs of the Priefts in waiting, was not only to offer the victims proper for every particular fervice, but alfo to attend to the other offices of the tabernacle,—to inftruct the people *,— to fanctify the moft holy things,—to burn incenfe before the Lord,—to minifter unto him, and—to blefs in his name for ever †.

A third clafs of Ecclefiaftics were the *Levites*. When we talk of the Levites as a fet of men employed in the offices of religion, we mean only that part of the tribe of Levi, who were defcended from the families of *Gerfhon* and *Merari*,—were fubordinate to the Priefts, and defigned to affift them in the more laborious parts of the tabernacle fervice.

From a confideration of the ftate of Ifrael in the wildernefs and that after their fettlement in Canaan, it is evident, that the fervice of the Levites muft have been very different in the one of thefe periods from what it was in the other. When the tabernacle obtained a fixed refidence, their labour became greatly abridged. And therefore, as the conftant attendance of them all was not neceffary, they were, like the Priefts, divided into twenty four courfes. And during their abfence from the fervice of the tabernacle, it deferves to be remarked, that they were difpofed of in fuch manner, as contributed not a little to fpread the

---

* Levit. x. 11. Deut. xvii. 9. 10. Deut xxxiii. 10.
† Levit. ix. 22. Numb vi. 23. Deut. xxi. 5.

the knowledge and influence of religion. They had no less than 48 cities assigned to them among the several tribes:—An institution this truly admirable, as it converted these cities into so many seminaries of religion, and afforded the people, whose situation would not allow their frequent attendance at the tabernacle or temple, the opportunities of receiving instruction from their intercourse with the Levites who resided among them *.

I know the account we have given of these sacred orders, is far from being full and complete. Neither was it necessary to our design that it should. If it can convey the idea of the propriety of such an institution, it is all that was intended by it.

Some may perhaps allege, that there was a vain and ostentatious display of pomp, in the selection of such a vast number to the service of the tabernacle and temple, and—in that external splendor that attended every thing which respected, at least, the two higher orders, and particularly in the manner of their designation to their respective offices,—their qualifications for them, and—the costly vestments, in which they were required to officiate. But in this, as well as in many other things relating to this religion, those who make the objection, discover their ignorance of human nature, and of the design of the things they find fault with.—That simplicity which they so much applaud, and which may not

* Nehem. viii. 7, 8.

not be unsuited to the present dispensation, would have been altogether unsuited to that, under which Israel lived.

Mankind were then to be taught (if I may use the phrase) by a visible language:—A service exhibited before their eyes, and intended, by these means, to affect their hearts. And indeed it had an admirable tendency this way. Divested of this external show, religion, in those early days, would have made but little impression upon the minds or lives of mankind. Whereas, the care that was taken, by the ritual that respected the Priests,— in the restriction of the public offices of religion to one family,—the alliances which they were allowed to contract by marriage,—the solemn forms by which they were to be inaugurated,—the various rites they were required to use, previous to an address to any of the services of religion, and—the splendid garments in which they were to appear at the performance of them: All these, I say, were calculated to have the most happy effects, both upon the Priests themselves, and the whole body of the people. They had a tendency to beget in the minds of the Priests, a due sense of the sacred nature of their office,—the importance of their character,—an ambition to support it with becoming dignity, and—to guard them against the indulgence of a wanton imagination in the services of religion, or any unnecessary conformity to the rites made use of, in the idol or dæmon worship of their neighbours. They, at the same time, served

to

to give the people the most exalted sentiments of that God they were called to worship, and afforded the most instructive hints, many of them, of that purity of heart and manners, which it became all to cultivate, who would reasonably hope to be accepted by him.

As the service of the temple required the attendance of the sacerdotal tribe, God raised up, when any particular exigence made it necessary, some who were called *Prophets;* and these, by virtue of the commission they received from God, may be justly enough reckoned among the ministers of religion. These were commonly, though not always, taken out of the *Schools of the Prophets;* having there, by a proper novitiate, discipline, and education, been prepared for appearing with greater advantage in this character.

All who have read the sacred history with attention, must have observed, that inspiration was not always supposed necessary, in the character of a prophet. When he was to foretell future events for the confirmation of the faith of God's people, then, it is evident, it was indispensably necessary. But very often this character implies no more, than that of a preacher of righteousness, or of one who took upon him the religious instruction of the people *, or presided in the praises of God †.

The occasion of their appearance was generally extraordinary. And if we will consider

---

* 1 Cor. xi. 4, 5.—and 1 Cor. xiv. 1, 3, 4.
† 1 Sam. x. 5, 6. 1 Chron. xxv. 1.

sider the manner and circumstances of it, we shall find them admirably suited to the ends proposed by it; which were, the establishment of the faith of Israel, and their encouragement from thence to adhere to the religion of the true God, to revolt from which they had discovered but too often a sad and shameful propensity.

They are often represented, by the modern enemies of revealed religion, in a light designedly the most unfavourable, in order to prejudice mankind against every thing that may have come from them. Thus *Lord Bolingbroke* represents inspiration as proceeding, according to the notions of Pagan antiquity, from an intoxicating vapour which blew into the inspired persons,—or from the action of dæmons, or genii, upon their bodies. He tells us, that the general effect of such inspiration was,—that the persons so inspired, uttered their vaticinations in fits of madness, that made their bodies to swell and become distorted by convulsive motions*, so that one should be tempted to believe that the ancient prophets answered the description given by the poet of the Sybil.

> —— Subito non vultus, non color unus,
> Non comptæ manfere comæ, sed pectus anhelum
> Et rabie fera corda tument; majorque videri
> Nec mortale sonans, afflata est numine quando
> Jam propriori Dei.   *Virg. Æneid.* 6.

Had

---

* Bolingbroke's Philosoph. Works, Essay i. p. 145. 8vo edit.

Had he rested here, we should have considered him as intending no more, than to give an account of the absurd notions entertained by the Heathens, of their Vates or Prophets. But, afraid that his design might not be perceived by some, and to put it beyond all doubt with any, he adds—" Now, nothing could
" more resemble a Heathen, than a Jewish
" vaticination; and no wonder that it should
" be so. Egypt and the East were the great
" schools of such philosophy and theology as
" I have mentioned. They abounded with
" Seers of visions and Dreamers of dreams,
" with Prophets and Diviners, with Wizzards
" and cunning men, with theurgic, as well
" as natural, magic, and all the occult sciences.
" ces. The Greeks borrowed from hence
" almost all the knowledge, real and imaginary,
" ginary, that they had, and so did the Jews
" too *."

The words need no commentary. They are plain enough, and lead us, without danger of mistake, to infer the opinion he entertained of the Jewish prophets, by that which he had of the Egyptian, and the respectable band with whom he classes them.

Tindal affects not the least disguise, but plainly tells us, in so many words, that some of them acted (if the command of God to them was to be understood literally) like madmen or idiots †.

Now

---

* Bolingbroke's Philosoph. Works, Essay i. p. 146.
† Christianity as old as the Creation, Vol. I. p. 129.

Now, whence can such representations of the conduct and characters of the Jewish prophets proceed? Whence, but from either a malevolence of heart, or an ignorance of the customs of those early times? It is very true, the manner of their life and dress, joined with the uncommon freedoms they used with those in high life, gave offence sometimes to them, and brought no small reproaches upon themselves: But they served, at the same time, to attract attention, convey instruction, and bring about reformation. And, accordingly, we find many of them highly honoured and respected by the most distinguished personages of those times*;—a plain evidence that there was nothing in their appearance or manners, that was *then* thought so ridiculous as the prejudices of our modern infidels, or the fancy of our fastidious wits, would represent them.

After prophecy had ceased, and none appeared any more in the character of prophets, strictly so called, there sprung up, in the latter periods of the Jewish state, others who were employed in the offices of religious instruction. Such were the *Scribes* and *Rabbins*. The *Scribes* were a learned profession or body of men among the Jews, so called for their knowledge of the Jewish divinity,—for their accuracy in transcribing, and—their skill in interpreting the law, both oral and written. We hear of no such denomination

of

---

* 2 Kings v. and viii. chap.—Jerem. xxxix. 11. and xl. 1, &c.

of teachers before the days of Ezra, who is himself called a Scribe, and therefore it is probable that it was an office unknown before that period.

Rabbins were another set of teachers in great vogue among the Jews, from the character they had acquired for theological knowledge, and had schools in which they read lectures upon the law, to those who choosed to attend them. Their schools soon procured them great fame. Then it was that they affected to be called *Rabbi*, for they were not so from the beginning: a title in high esteem among themselves, and veneration among their countrymen.

But however honoured these professions, and they who occupied them, might have been among the Jews, yet as neither of them were of Divine institution, or in sacred orders, it does not fall within the design of our plan, to treat more fully of them.

The services of religion, considered as so many acts of homage to the Deity, must be allowed by all to be of a nature too sacred, to admit their being rashly and precipitately undertaken. A previous preparation for them is highly proper. To show wherein it consisted under the Mosaic œconomy, is the design of the following section.

SECT

SECT. VI.

Of the Preparation required for the Services of Religion.

THE privilege which most distinguishes the man from the brute, is the capacity of worshipping, serving, and enjoying God. Hence arise the obligations upon him to religion; and these are, at once, so strong and natural, that we find them universally acknowledged. For, however mankind may have differed in the manner of worshipping God (and in nothing have they differed more widely) yet all have agreed that some worship is due to him, and accordingly have paid it, each in that manner that appeared best.

And if we will consider the sacred nature of that most glorious Being who is the object of worship, nothing can be more reasonable than a solicitous concern to perform it in such a manner, as may be most acceptable to him. This, in the issue, will always be profitable to the performer. It would serve at once to guard him against those indulgences, however agreeable to himself, which, he had reason to think, would be unsuited to the nature of the Deity, and—to make him embrace what appeared most rational and consistent.

It is abundantly evident, that any intercourse that can subsist betwixt God and man, in the present state, can only be in a way suited to the spirituality of their respective natures, that is, in a moral and spiritual way, —in the communication of the most benign influences upon God's part, and the exercise of suitable affections upon ours.

It is true, God, who knows our frame, has, in condescension to the infirmities of it, been pleased to institute certain external ordinances, suited to this our embodied state, in which we receive our strongest impressions from sensible objects:—Ordinances, which, by the scope they afford for the exercise of our several graces, in the objects they present to us, and not by any physical influence they can have, must tend to promote the improvement of the devout worshipper.

But, admirably adapted as the ordinances of religion may be for this purpose, a careful preparation upon our part for an attendance upon them, is necessary to insure the wished-for success. And so sensible have mankind been of this, in all ages of the world, and under all dispensations of religion, that we find them generally very observant of the previous preparation for the services of it:— an acknowledgment this, that God is greatly to be feared and had in reverence by all that draw near to him.

The preparation required under the Mosaic œconomy, previous to an engagement in any of the sacred services of religion, was multiform and various, and extended both to the Priests and to the people. It required in the

M

first,

firſt, that, beſides ſeveral qualifications that reſpected their family, perſon, and character, they ſhould, in the moſt ſolemn manner, be conſecrated to the ſervice of the altar, and that, ever after, they ſhould pay the cloſeſt attention to the rules preſcribed for their approaches to it. And of the people, it required an equally careful preparation, according to the ritual enjoined.

Almoſt every particular ſervice of religion under this diſpenſation, required a certain form of preparation for itſelf: But there were ſome things in which they all agreed. Thus, for inſtance, it was required, that all who were to addreſs God in any of the duties of religion, ſhould carefully abſtain from every thing that could infer the leaſt ceremonial taint:—from every thing, whether in itſelf, or in the opinion of mankind, foul and unclean:—and if, by any means, ſuch taint was contracted, that it ſhould be removed by certain waſhings and purgations. Now, what could be the deſign of all this ceremonial pomp? Few could have been ſo ignorant, even under that dark diſpenſation, as to imagine that it was inſtituted for its own ſake, or from any intrinſic value or efficacy it could have to ſanctify the worſhippers. It muſt have had a moral couched under it. It was intended as emblematical of that purity that was requiſite to render their approaches to the Deity acceptable,—and of the obligations upon them to impreſs their hearts with a ſenſe of the glory and majeſty, the purity

and

and holiness, of the God they worshipped,—to disengage their hearts from all foreign cares,—to raise and elevate their devotion, and—to put them into a temper and disposition the most fit for offering a dutiful service to God, and for receiving the largest communications of love and favour from him.

At the same time that this ritual had a direct tendency to promote the valuable ends just now taken notice of, the simplicity of it might be also intended, and was admirably calculated, to guard Israel against the use of those superstitious, and, some of them, barbarous rites, that obtained, by way of lustration, in the worship of their Heathen neighbours.

The methods practised by these for purgation, were various. The invention of man, encouraged by superstition, knows no bounds. They were particularly fond of purgations by wind, fire, and water, considering these elements as of a purifying nature. To this the poet seems to allude, when he says,

Quin, et supremo cum lumine vita reliquit,
Non tamen omne malum miseris, nec funditus omnes
Corporeæ exedunt pestes, penitusque necesse est
Multa diu concreta modis inolesere miris.
Ergo exercentur pænis, veterumque malorum
Supplicia expendunt. Aliæ pendantur inanes
Suspensæ ad ventos: aliis sub gurgite vasto
Infectum eluitur scelus, auf exuritur igni.
Virg. Æn. lib. vi. lin. 735, &c.

It may be alledged that these words of the poet could only have a reference to later times

times. But should this be allowed to be the case, there are not wanting hints in the sacred history, that seem to point to these and some other methods of purification practised among the Heathens, before the institution of the law.

It is generally thought, that, at first, no more was intended by the practice of some Heathens, in making their children to pass through the fire to Moloch, than to purify and consecrate them to the sun, whom some of them worshipped under the name of *Moloch,* that is, The King, as they meant, of the Heavenly Hosts. And indeed this is not improbable, though afterwards, by an easy transition, they came to adopt the more barbarous practice of actually burning them, as a sacrifice to this idol.

To put a stop, therefore, to this gross superstition, and the ablutions by water mixed with salt, sulphur, spittle, and I do not know how many other things, which were very frequent among the Heathen nations, God enjoins the use of pure water.

Some have thought that this appointment carried an allusion in it to the flood, which has been considered by many as a kind of lustration, by which the earth, polluted with vice, became, as it were, purified.

This was the opinion of some philosophers, and of many Jews and Christians *. But I humbly think, there was no necessity for concluding

---

* Spencer de Legib. Ritualib. Hebræor. Dissert. iii.

cluding that the appointment either took its rife from, or had any original reference to, this. It might have been practifed, by way of luftration, not only as a thing they had eafy accefs to, and that could be attended with no expence, but alfo as a rite abundantly fignificant of that purity, which they ought to cultivate in all their religious fervices.

It is well known that the Heathens ufed blood, and fometimes even human blood, by way of luftration. They imagined that the blood of their facrifices, was the favourite food of their demons. For this reafon they were at the greateft pains to preferve it for them in fome veffel, or, when this was not at hand, in fome hole in the ground. And then, while they ate the flefh, and the demon, as they imagined, drank the blood, they hereby not only declared themfelves his votaries, and profeffed to hold communion with him, but confidered themfelves as become purified*.

This opinion and practice fo frequent among the Heathens, very probably gave rife to the appointment of, what is fometimes called *The water of feparation*, and fometimes, *The water of purification*. It was fo called, becaufe thofe who, by the touch of a dead body, had contracted a ceremonial taint, and fo were excluded, while under fuch taint, from the fanctuary of the Lord, became, by being fprinkled with this water, purified, and had free accefs to it again. An account of the manner

---

* Spencer de Ritualib. Hebræor. lib. ii. cap. 11. fect. 1.

manner in which it was prepared, and the ingredients with which it was mixed, you have Numb. xix. What the true reasons of the appointment of this rite were, and particularly, why it should not be a *Bullock*, but a *Cow*, and one too of a *red* colour, whose ashes should be used on this occasion, may be impossible, at this distance of time, to determine. Some, not improbable, conjectures might be formed. But they can be no more than conjectures. Those who wish to be informed of them, may consult Spencer de Legib. Ritualib. Hebræor. lib. ii. cap. 15. and Lowman's Rational of the Ritual of the Hebrew Worship, p. 236.

It is, it must be acknowledged, difficult, if not impossible, to offer such an account of the mode of instruction used under this œconomy, as will satisfy all. Some who are disposed to object to it at all hazards, will be apt to allege that it is, at least, doubtful, whether the meaning of it, as we have interpreted it, could be then well understood: And, even if it could, that another mode, better accommodated to the circumstances of mankind, might have been devised.

To the one or other of these conclusions, the cavillers against this dispensation are necessarily reduced upon this head. And indeed, could either of these be made appear, the objection could not be denied to have great weight. But if it can be evinced, that this mode of preparation for the service of religion, carried neither of these alleged improprieties

proprieties in it, nothing can be more unfair than to object to the œconomy, under which it obtained, on this account.

That the intention of this symbolical ritual was well enough understood by those who were to be regulated by it, I cannot allow myself to doubt. It is very true, the connection betwixt signs and the things signified, must be allowed to be, in most cases, arbitrary. But, at the same time, must it not be admitted, that, in many cases, the connection is so far from being distant and remote, that it may be called, *natural*. Of this kind were most of the rites used for purgation, such as aspersion and washing with water, &c. In these instances, it is abundantly evident; and I doubt not but, were we well acquainted with the usages of those times and the ideas affixed to them, it would appear equally evident in the rest. For, as I observed already, p.   it is not to be imagined that God, who appointed the rites, would leave the interpretation of them to uncertain conjecture. Nothing can be more probable than that, at their original institution, certain and determinate ideas would be affixed to them.

Neither is it any argument against this, that we find the intention afterwards forgot, and the mere literal observance of them rested in. This, indeed, is not to be wondered at. Many reasons might contribute to it. Men of a pragmatic turn and lively imagination might, were it only to display their talents,

lents, offer a meaning of them very different from the original, and might have influence enough with fome to adopt it. While others, unwilling to fubmit to that perfection of purity which they recommended, might be content even to deceive themfelves into a belief, that a fcrupulous obfervance of the latter was all that was required.

Nay, the growing obfcurity of the original meaning of a fervice expreffed by fymbolical rites, was the almoft unavoidable confequence of their being continued in religion, after the ufe of fuch fymbolical language had, by a more general knowledge of letters, begun to ceafe in the commerce of life. But, does it not deferve to be taken notice of, that, to remove all ambiguity that might arife from this or any other fource, the prophets of God, raifed up in a long and continued fucceffion, not only pointed out the abfurdity of a literal, but alfo the propriety of the original, meaning of them?

It is not more certain, that the defign of this pompous ritual was originally well underftood by thofe for whom it was intended, than it is that there was an admirable propriety in it, at the time of its inftitution.

Let it be remembered that, in thofe early and remote ages, a fymbolical language was that alone in which knowledge could be communicated to the prefent, or tranfmitted to fucceeding ages; and this confideration will be fufficient to juftify the original inftitution

tion complained of, through ignorance, by many.

But, if to this we add the tendency which such a ritual had, we shall be forced to own the injustice done to this œconomy of religion, by all such objections. Let it be considered, that, by its address to their senses, it was calculated to make a deep impression upon the minds of the worshippers, and, by the variety of which it consisted, to show them the necessity of a constant fitness for the services of religion, when called to them: And must it not be owned, that the very ritual, which, at first sight, seemed to represent it in an unfavourable point of light, does really place it in one rather beautiful and agreeable?

But of this the reader will find more in the sequel.

SECT VII.

Of the Style and Manner, in which every thing relating to Religion, under this Oeconomy, was expressed.

THIS, I know, has been matter of offence to many, who, because they did not themselves understand it, rashly concluded that as little did those whom it principally concerned. But that, in this, they mistake, will, I think, be no difficult matter to show.

For

For this purpose it may not be improper to observe, that the progress in the manner of communicating knowledge must have been slow, and different methods must have been used, the succeeding method being always considered as an improvement upon what went before.

From a variety of causes that might be assigned, it cannot be denied, but we must be at a loss concerning the nature and manner of the first writing, and the time of its invention. However, from the remains of ancient learning that have come down to us, we may be able to deduce reasons sufficient to vindicate the method used for the communication of religious knowledge, under the Mosaic œconomy, from the imputation of impropriety, with which it is charged by some.

Here, in the entry on our design, let me observe, that nothing has more contributed to the unfavourable sentiments that have been entertained by some, concerning the manner of conveying religious knowledge, under this dispensation, than an inattention to the circumstances of the time and place in which it first obtained. Judging of it by the sentiments or circumstances of the present times, no wonder it should appear uncouth and improper. But who may not see this to be an unfair standard of judgment; and such as has a tendency to mislead those who are to be determined by it?

To what time or nation, the invention of letters

letters shall be ascribed, it is very difficult, if it be at all possible, to say. Many nations have claimed the honour of the invention, without being able, any of them, to prove their title to it. It is as difficult to ascertain the time, as the original author, of this invention. It is certainly of a very early date. And hence very probably it is, that, for want of proper information upon the point, it has been ascribed to the gods. But the truth seems to be,—that the invention of writing; by the use of alphabetic letters, is not to be ascribed to any particular age. The advance from the first method of communicating knowledge, till that by alphabetic characters or letters, was probably gradual and progressive.

The first, because the most simple, method, it is highly probable, notwithstanding all that has been said against it by a learned divine of our own country*, was a kind of *picture-writing*. By tracing out the natural images of things, mankind endeavoured to communicate their ideas of them to one another. Thus, when they would express the idea of a bird or horse, they painted or engraved the figures of these animals. And because these writings, were probably at first employed in the service of religion, they might have received the name of *Hieroglyphics*.

It

---

* Dr Shuckford's Connex. of Sacred and Proph. Hist. Vol. I. p. 246. and Vol. II. p. 334.

It is eafy to fee, that this method of communicating knowledge, muft have been attended with many inconveniences. One, in a particular manner, is obvious,—that, as their fcientific learning was, for a long time, conveyed down, from one generation to another, by a kind of picture-engraving upon obelifks or pillars, this method muft have been attended with great expence and labour.

This circumftance neceffarily fet their invention at work, to find out fome more compendious method, and one that might, at the fame time, in fome meafure, not only exprefs thofe things which were the objects of fenfe, but alfo their abftract ideas, or mental conceptions. And the method they are thought to have chofen for this purpofe, was the ufe of certain analogic or fymbolic characters, of which, were it neceffary, many inftances might be given.

The obfcurity, which was the neceffary confequence of the imperfection of all thefe methods of communicating knowledge, obliged them to feek after one ftill more perfect, and feems, at laft, by an eafy tranfition, to have led them to thofe arbitrary marks, which afterwards came to be called *Letters*, or alphabetic characters. And as thefe could not be fuppofed to arrive at a high degree of perfection all at once, it is generally fuppofed that, in the formation of fome of the earlieft alphabets, they adopted fome of the hieroglyphic figures of the analogic or fymbolic kind,

kind, which they had been accustomed to use before *.

From this short account of these early ages of the world, while we see the admirable propriety of the hieroglyphic method of instruction,—the various improvements which it received, and—its aptitude to those times in which it obtained, we may, at the same time, see the great imperfection of it.

But had it been incomparably more perfect than it was, there were very good reasons for a change from this to what may be called, The *ritual* method of instruction, made use under the dispensation of Moses.

In those early ages, they had no access to religious knowledge, but from their columns and pillars, the repositories of their learning. And therefore it is evident, that the diffusion of knowledge, by means of these, could be neither extensive nor quick.

Besides, there might be another reason for the alteration of the method of instruction at this time. It is the opinion of some, and not an improbable one, that their hieroglyphics, or the analogic and symbolic sculptures upon their pillars, which were, at first, intended for instruction, came, at length, to be abused to the purposes of idolatry, and proved the occasion of the use of idols or images in the worship of their gods. And, if there be any ground for this conjecture, may we not see

---

* See a great deal on this subject, in Dr Warburton's Div. Legation of Moses, Vol. III. p. 70, &c.

see a very good reason for laying aside this, and beginning the ritual, method of instruction?

It is true, it may be alleged, that, before this time, the alphabetic method of writing had come into use; and that this was not liable to the objection just now mentioned, against the hieroglyphic manner. But, let it be remembered, that, in the first periods of alphabetic writing, (and it is uncertain if they were so early as this) there was a great mixture of the hieroglyphic kind; and still the propriety of the ritual method of instruction will be apparent, as a guard against the danger that might arise from a passion for the other.

With the same view, some have thought that Moses, agreeably to the spirit of the second commandment, did alter the form of many of the Egyptian letters, which still retained a strong resemblance to the hieroglyphic characters from which they were borrowed. And, if this be admitted, it becomes another reason for the introduction of the ritual institution at this time. Being forbidden the use of hieroglyphic characters, and little acquainted with the new alphabet which Moses had formed, what other mean had Israel of religious instruction?

It is not improbable, that Moses, about this time, began to teach them the use of letters; and it is no unnatural conjecture that what are called, *The Lettered Mountains*, in the neighbourhood of Sinai, were engraven by the

the Israelites, as a kind of practice for acquiring a knowledge of letters, and a facility of reading, while they were encamped in the plains round that mountain.

I know this conjecture is exploded by some learned men, and their opinion is,—that the writing found on these mountains, is no more than the names of those travellers who have visited them. But this opinion, I humbly think, is still more improbable than the former, and that for two reasons. The one is,—that the extent of the writing is incomparably greater than can be supposed to have been done by travellers, whose stay in such a desart could be but short. The other is,—that the characters are such as are entirely unknown,—unlike any ancient character that has come down to us, and not understood even by the Arabs, who live in the neighbourhood. And when we consider, that the practice of travelling to and visiting these mountains is no more than modern, it may justly appear strange that the characters should so soon become unintelligible, had they, according to the supposition under consideration, been so lately engraved.

But though the discovery of such a method of communicating knowledge, as we have been speaking of, must have been attended with many and great advantages, yet the progress of knowledge by means of it could, at first, be but slow. For, let it be considered, that Moses, having received the hint of this manner of writing from God, very probably

bably in the Mount and by the writing upon the tables of ſtone, muſt, for a long time, have been the only perſon among the many thouſands of Iſrael, who was capable of teaching this uſeful art. And the people muſt have been the longer of underſtanding it, that neither the improvements of the time, nor their ſituation in the wilderneſs, afforded them any conſiderable advantages for the acquiſition of it.

I am aware that a good deal of what has been obſerved above, concerning the early uſe of hieroglyphics,—the prohibition of them among the Iſraelites, and the introduction of a new character by Moſes, may to many appear hypothetical; and I acknowledge that, in ſome meaſure, it is ſo. Neither needs this be wondered at, conſidering the little information we have concerning thoſe early ages. But, though no poſitive evidence can be adduced for every thing that has been advanced on this part of the ſubject, yet it muſt, at the ſame time, be owned, that there is nothing improbable in the conjecture: Nay that, from the fragments of ancient learning that have come down to us, there are ſeveral things that make it more than probable, that ſome ſuch, as we have ſuppoſed, was the matter of fact.

We who know a more eaſy and expreſſive way of communicating our ſentiments, are apt to think and ſpeak of this, with a certain degree of contempt. But they only can indulge in this, who do not allow themſelves to think of the ſmall progreſs that had then been made

made in the improvement of the writing art. No wonder the eſſays in it, ſhould have been yet but rude. It is a long time, before, in any art, a tolerable degree of perfection can be acquired. At firſt, nothing can appear more uncouth and enigmatical, than the meaning of a great part of the Jewiſh ritual; yet it is not to be doubted but it was abundantly well underſtood, ideas preciſe and determinate being affixed to every part of it.

It may be alleged, that though, for the reaſons aſſigned, the ritual method of inſtruction, might, at the firſt inſtitution of it, have been admitted,—it ought to have ceaſed, when greater improvements had diſcovered a better. But there are not wanting reaſons, all of which juſtify the continuance, as well as the firſt uſe, of it.

Let it be remembered, that the people for whom it was firſt intended, retained very much of the ſame national character (owing, no doubt, in a great meaſure, to their little commerce with the nations around them); and what elſe could be expected, but that there ſhould remain the ſame, or, at leaſt, many of the ſame reaſons for the continuance, that there were for the original inſtitution, of it?

Beſides, does it not deſerve to be taken notice of, that an alteration in this, would, upon the whole, have been equal to a repeal of their inſtitution of religion? For this old mode had become ſo wrought into the forms of teaching it, that it was, in ſome meaſure, eſſential to it, and could not be ſeperated from it,

it, without modelling it anew. But any improvement of this nature, was not of importance sufficient to bring about such a change.

By continuing the original platform of their religion and the manner of explaining it, another advantage was gained. They became hereby reminded of the rude and uncultivated state in which their ancestors were; and so,— by observing the progress of improvement to which they were themselves advanced, were naturally led to a proportionable gratitude to God for it.

And to this let me add, that any obscurity that might be gradually superinduced upon the ritual method of teaching, was, in some measure, compensated for, by the teaching of a succession of prophets, who appeared to carry on, together with the original usages of religion, the important interests of it, by the particular instructions they were charged with from God.

I know it will be objected, that the style in which they delivered themselves, was often as dark and enigmatical, as that of symbols which obtained at the first institution, and of rites which took place in the succeeding periods, of their commonwealth.

Perhaps this objection may appear with more strength, than it is really possessed of, from an inattention to the genius of the language in which they wrote. It was indeed a language highly figurative; but, though, on this account, it may appear obscure to us, it will not follow that it did so to them.

A

A learned author has ingeniously observed, that the pompous and figurative style of the ancient Asiatics, had probably been fashioned to the mode of hieroglyphic writing, to which they had been early accustomed. Thus, he observes, that the expressions of *spotted garments* were used, in the prophetic language of the sacred writers, to denote iniquity:— *the sword and bow*, a warrior:—*balance, weights, and measures*, a Judge or Magistrate:—*The sun, moon, and stars*, Emperors, Kings, and Nobles: *Stars falling from the firmament*, the destruction of the nobility:—In a word, that the prophetic style seems to be no more than a *speaking hieroglyphic*. And from this remark, he observes, we may be enabled to vindicate the character of the Old Testament writings, from the illiberal cavils of modern libertines, who have foolishly mistaken the colouring complained of, for the peculiar workmanship of the prophet's heated imagination, while it was no more than the sober, established, language of their times *.

But though what has been just now observed may convince the candid, that the obscurity charged upon the sacred style of the Old Testament was not so great as the conceited Sciolist of modern times may imagine, it is not denied that a certain degree of it, hung upon almost all the writings of the prophets. Neither in this was there any impropriety. It was what necessarily arose, not only from the

* See the Divine Legat. of Moses, Vol. III. p. 163.

the nature of the writings themselves, which, in many places, looked forward to times and events *then* future, and therefore such as could not, in many cases, be well understood;—but also from the design of them, which was not intended to be *then* fully developed. And the reason is very plain. A full discovery of it, in some instances, would have made the Jews at less pains to preserve writings, in which they were made to see that the character of their long wished for Messiah did not correspond with the notions they had formed of him, and so would, in a great measure, have defeated the very intention of the prophecy, by preventing the accomplishment of it *.

Prophecy

---

* Many are the instances which the sacred history furnishes, in proof of the justness of this observation. Thus every one who is acquainted with the history of Israel, must see how closely connected with the fate of Joseph, was that wonderful series of events that concerned the church of God. And is it not *now* abundantly evident, that, if the prediction concerning his elevation had been fully understood by his envious brethren, some of them would, in a surly mood, have prevented the accomplishment of it, by cutting him off?

Who can read the surprising manner of the preservation and advancement of Moses, so connected with the deliverance of Israel, and either doubt of a Providence, or the propriety of the manner in which its operations were conducted in this matter? Some time before his birth, Pharoah issued out a decree, enjoining the slaughter of all the males of Israel, as soon as they were born. This barbarous order took its rise from his own guilty fears, and was, no doubt, intended to remove them, by removing the dreaded causes of them. But God, who sees from heaven, laughs to scorn the designs of the wicked, when they would oppose those of his Providence, and—in this instance, makes the very scheme intended for the destruction, turn out for the deliverance, of Israel. By this

Prophecy had a double intention. The one refpected the prefent: The other, future times. So far as regarded the times that *then* were, it muft be owned, it was abundantly intelligible. And with refpect to that part, which looked forward to future times, it was enough that the arrival of thefe afforded a key, by which to open and explain it

It is very common to allege, as a farther apology for the fymbolical and ritual fervice of the Jews, and the highly figurative writings of the prophets, that there was fcarce any thing in either, but was to be confidered as a type * of fomething correfponding to it under

this means Pharoah's daughter becomes the inftrument of faving the life of Mofes, when he was in the utmoft danger of lofing it, and nourifhed and educated him who was to be the deliverer of Ifrael, from the bondage to which they were fubjected in Egypt. But this, it is probable, fhe would not have done, had fhe known that he was the perfon deftined to be employed in the accomplifhment of fuch a defign.

Another ftriking illuftration of this remark, we have in the cafe of our Saviour's nativity. Who may not fee that it was the Roman cenfus, or taxing appointed by Auguftus, that brought up Mary to Bethlehem, and at that critical time that was fixed, by ancient prophecy, for the birth of our Lord? But muft it not, at the fame time, be owned, that, had the Jews imagined, that a Son to be born of Mary, and at this place, was to lay claim to the honour of Meffiah, and to plead prophecy as an evidence of his title to it, they would (confidering their expectations of a temporal prince, and the little hopes they could have of finding fuch in him) have done every thing in their power to prevent the accomplifhment of it, by either altogether hindering, or retarding, her journey to Bethlehem?

*There is, I humbly imagine, fcarce any doctrine that has been explained, with lefs accuracy, than that of types. And there
are

under the gospel dispensation. But they stand in need of no such apology. Nor do I think, that their most zealous friends ought to use it. There is no small danger in pushing this too far. I am disposed to believe, and do readily acknowledge, that some of them were to be con-

are few, a mistake in which has been attended with worse consequences.

The word Τυπος occurs frequently in the New Testament, and under very different meanings. In its original and primary meaning, it properly signifies the mark or impression made by one thing upon another; and sometimes, in a more lax sense, that general likeness or resemblance, which one thing may bear to another. And hence, because a lively and inventive imagination has discovered a very striking likeness betwixt many of the persons, rites, and usages under the law, and those under the gospel, they were early fancied to be types, the one of the other. A conceit of this kind, pleasing the first authors of it, as a valuable discovery, or a proof of genius, it gained credit with others; so that, at last, having obtained the sanction of those who honoured themselves with the character of orthodox, scarce any, till this enlightened age, have ventured to find fault with it. And, even in it, such an attempt is beheld with an evil eye,—by some.

The general doctrine concerning types is,—that Christ was prefigured by almost every thing under the law. Under the influence of this principle, did not many of the primitive Fathers give into the most mystical and allegorical comments upon the Jewish scriptures? It is true, many of the moderns allow, that they carried this allegorizing humour too far, and yet some of themselves have fallen into it. Let me single out only one. Let any one consult Witsius de Œconom. Fœder. in his chapter, De Typis, and there he will find a pretty large specimen of types, which he divides into three classes, —what he calls, *Natural*, *Historical*, and *Legal*. Thus he tells us, that Abel, Noah, the Ark, Moses, Aaron, &c. were all types of Christ. We may admire his fancy and piety:— the one in the connections he traces;—the other, in the application he makes of them. But surely we cannot admire his talents as an interpreter or commentator. We may, in

the

considered, in this light. But I am humbly of opinion, that they were thus to be considered, only in so far as a hint was given of such intention. Thus much the gospel history seems to admit. But to attempt to stretch the matter

the instances he takes notice of, trace a striking analogy and resemblance in many things, betwixt, what is called, the Type and the Antitype. But, upon what authority, are we thence warranted to consider them as thus related? To this let us take his answer in his own words.—" Quando in anti-
" typo aliquod reperitur, in quo cum typo similitudinem ha-
" bet, merito asseritur, Deum, qui omnia ab initio novit,
" typum ita disposuisse, ut eam, quæ in antitypo est, verita-
" tem præsignificaret. Nisi quis statuere mallet, similitudi-
" nem, quæ inter artificiosam picturam et rem depictam in-
" tercedit, casu potius, quem ex artificis in en ione, esse:
" quod ab omni ratione alienum."—But who that is in the least acquainted with the nature of just reasoning, may not discern the grossest paralogism in this? Though the point which he endeavours to establish is the existence of types, yet here he takes it for granted, from the fancied resemblance which certain things and persons bore to one another, that they stood in the relation of correlates,—and that, because he is pleased to make the one, the antitype, the other must be the type.

In the chapter concerning types, he lays down certain canons for the interpretation of them. But, let the improvement he has made of them, be a proof of their importance.

That this humour of discovering types in almost every thing in the Old Testament, took its rise, in some measure, from the indulgence of a lively fancy, I have already observed. To this, another cause may have also contributed,—a mistake of the meaning of the sacred writers in many places, and particularly of the Apostle Paul, in his Epistle to the Hebrews.

The young converts to Christianity to whom it is addressed, retained a strong passion for the laws of Moses, on account of the splendor that attended its ritual and service, and were for blending its institutions with those of Jesus. One part of the

ter farther, may be, nay, I am afraid, has already been, productive of hurtful consequences to religion.

It is easy for a lively and inventive imagination to trace a resemblance in many things

be-

---

the Apostle's design was to show them, that there was no reason for a superior esteem of the law, on this account. In execution of this part of his design, he runs a parallel, in many instances, betwixt these two dispensations of religion, and evinces that the superior excellence belonged to the gospel. This he does by showing them, that the great things they so much admired under the law, were no more than *shadows* of still greater things that were *then* to come, and had since *actually* come under the gospel; that is—that they were of a far inferior value, and could no more compare with them, than empty shadows can with the most important realities. If those who lived under the dispensation of Moses, had a temple, sacrifices, an altar, High-Priest, &c. to boast of, so had the Christian, that is, something similar to these, which, therefore, in condescension and compliment to their dialect, he calls by these names.

Thus his figurative language, or rather the argument contained in it (which, by being misunderstood, has given rise to a misconstruction of the doctrine of types) was, properly speaking, no more than an *argumentum ad hominem*, and an accommodation of his phraseology to that, for which they had a preconceived fondness. And, therefore, till this excellent epistle is more studied and better understood, than, I am afraid, it generally is, a correction of the prevailing mistake in the doctrine of types is not to be looked for.

That there are types in the Old Testament, is not denied. But these are much more rare, than is generally imagined. To constitute any thing a type of another, I humbly imagine it is necessary, that it be not only well calculated, but *really* intended, to prefigure or presignify something *future;* else, with what propriety, could it, in the common acceptation of the word, be considered as a type of it? Nay, if the obscurity of the type was such as to obstruct the view of the thing prefigured, what was the use of its appointment? would it not seem to

reflect

betwixt the law and the gospel.—But, to infer from thence, that the one was intended to be a type of the other, leaves it to every one to give that interpretation he pleases of the scripture, and of the design of the Mosaic institution, and— at the same time to insist that the interpretation he gives is a just one *.

From

reflect both upon the author and institution of it, were the word type to be understood in the common sense of it? For a type, not to be understood, till the thing prefigured takes place, is almost the same thing as no type at all.

But should those things that are called types, be denied to be such in the common acceptation of the word, this will by no means destroy their usefulness or importance in religion. Besides the original intention of the institution to those among whom it obtained, *they would, from the coincidence in resemblance and design, serve to show that they were but parts of one great dispensation, and that both proceeded from the same Divine original.* I am sensible that, in this opinion, I differ from some, for whose judgment, upon subjects of this nature, I have the highest respect; but I can see no bad tendency to be dreaded from it, unless that be reckoned bad, that it strikes at the favourite and admired system of some. But, if what has been advanced on the subject, be the truth, no matter. Let every system fall, that cannot stand in consistence with it. All the author aims at, in so short a note, is no more than to excite an inquiry into a subject, but yet very imperfectly understood, in hopes of doing thereby an essential service to the cause of rational religion. And if he is in a mistake, he will be equally glad to be set right. Any attempt to this purpose, conducted with temper, and upon the principles of solid criticism, he will listen to with candour and gratitude. See a good deal on this subject of types, in Dr Tykes's Paraphrase on the Hebrews, Introd. p. 43. and his notes on chap. ix. 24.

* A striking instance of this humour for allegorizing, we are furnished with in Josephus. Speaking of the tabernacle and its furniture, he says (I give you a translation, to save the trouble of transcribing the original)—" If any man will con-
" sider the structure of the tabernacle, the sacerdotal vestments,
" and

From this conceit, and the unlimited indulgence of it, have sprung those many figurative and allegorical commentaries, disquisitions and sermons that made their appearance in the last century, and some, much earlier.—
A

" and the vessels that are made use of in sacrifice, he will find
" reason to call our lawgiver a pious man. In these he will
" find an image or representation of the universe. The ta-
" bernacle of thirty cubits is divided into three parts, two of
" which are for the Priests, and to these all have access. The
" third is reserved for God himself. By the twelve loaves of
" shew-bread placed upon the table, he would intimate to us
" that the year is divided into twelve months. The seventy
" pieces of which the candlestick is made up, refer to the
" twelve signs, through which the seven planets move in their
" course. The curtains, with the four colours wrought into
" them, represent the nature of the elements. The fine linen
" signifies the earth, out of which the flax grows. By the
" purple we are to understand the sea, from the blood of the
" fish, which gives it the tincture. The hyancinth is the
" symbol of the air, and the scarlet of the fire. The linen gar-
" ment of the High-Priest, is also intended to represent the
" earth —the violet colour, the heavens. The pomgranates
" answer to the lightening,—and the noise of the bells, to the
" thunder. The four-coloured ephod, bears a resemblance
" to the nature of the universe and the interweaving it with
" gold, seems to me to have a regard to the rays that give us
" light. The pectoral, placed in the middle of it, intimates
" the position of the earth, in the centre of the world. The
" girdle, about the Priests body, is as the sea about the globe
" of the earth. The two sandonyx stones, are a kind of figure
" of the sun and moon. The twelve other stones, may be
" understood either of the twelve months or the twelve signs of
" the Zodiac. The violet-coloured tiara speaks a resemblance
" of heaven, and it would have been an irreverence to have
" written the sacred name of God, upon any other colour.
" This is a plain illustration of these matters." Antiq. lib. iii.
cap. 8. A strange specimen this, of the wild flights in which one may bewilder himself, if he will allow fancy to direct.

These

A strain of piety and devotion must be generally allowed them: but it must be, at the same time, admitted, that they discover little, if any critical, acuteness; and that, in place of casting any light upon the sacred text, they have generally obscured it, at least, left it involved in the same darkness, in which they found it. This will always be the consequence of the indulgence of such an humour, and happy it is for the interests of rational religion that it begins to decrease.

Though it must be, and readily is, allowed that the institution of Moses looked forward to that of Jesus, we cannot imagine that it was *principally* intended to elucidate it.—No. It was primarly designed to answer the purposes of religion to those who lived under it, so far as was suited to their age of the world, and the opportunities they enjoyed. To them, it had an immediate: To us, only a remote respect. And therefore I am humbly of opinion, that, to understand properly the meaning of what are now called *types* and *figures*, it would be proper to suppose ourselves

in

These (besides the ignorance of Astronomy, or the system of the universe, which they betray) are so wild, that one can scarce bring himself to imagine that Josephus was in earnest. But the truth is—there is all the appearance of his being in earnest in what he says; and the occasion upon which he introduces it, will not allow us to suspect otherwise. And if we will consider that he was himself a Priest, I think we may be warranted to say, that, if he so egregiously mistook in decyphering the meaning of the several things relating to the tabernacle, the vulgar would be still more liable to err, by indulging the same humour.

in the situation in which the Jews were, in the several ages in which any of them took place: And, from the writings of those ages, and not from the ideas of this, we are most likely to derive the real meaning of them.

It is true, there are but few writings upon the subject of religion, extant, of great antiquity. There are none of near so great antiquity as the very latest of the books of the Old Testament.—Some of the books of the Apocrypha are the oldest: I say some of them; for others of them are not Jewish, but a Christian forgery. Their next oldest writers are Philo and Josephus, who were cotemporaries with the Apostles. There are also extant, what are called, the Jerusalem and Babylonish Talmuds:—The first compiled about the close of the fourth, and the latter about the beginning of the sixth, century. Dr Lightfoot has availed himself of these Jewish writings, and from them cast considerable light upon the scriptures. Were others to pursue the same tract, some more, useful, discoveries might be yet made, though indeed, it must be owned, the labour necessary for making them, would be great and disagreeable.

Perhaps the New Testament is the best commentary that can be applied to, for rightly understanding the Old. The writers of the New, it may be supposed, would be well acquainted with the phraseology of the Old.—The long use in which it had been had, and the connection of it with the rites of the Jewish religion, necessarily introduced a great deal of it into their writings, especially such of them as were addresdreſſed to the Jews, and, at the ſame time, rendered an illuſtration of them leſs needed.

There is, however, illuſtration enough, had it been attended to, to have prevented many of the miſtakes into which ſome divines have fallen. But the misfortune with many of them has been, that, in place of looking into ſcripture, that, from thence, they might deduce their ſyſtems, they have ſearched into it for a confirmation of thoſe they had previouſly adopted, and, in the interpretation they have offered of it, did not ſcruple to bend it to their favourite opinions.

Thus ſome, having embraced the opinion, that a great deal of the religious ſervice which obtained under the Moſaic diſpenſation, was intended to be typical of that which was to be required under the goſpel, have found out a thouſand fanciful likeneſſes betwixt them. Into this error ſome have been led, and in it others have been confirmed, by the frequent uſe that is made in the New Teſtament, of thoſe modes of ſpeech which were ſo common in the Old. But, had they duly attended to the occaſion and manner in which they are introduced, they might have eaſily perceived that the deſign of the ſacred writers never was, to offer a proof of their beloved hypotheſis by the highly figured language in which they expreſſed themſelves. Nay, they might have found that they adopted this, becauſe particularly accommodated to the genius of the Jewiſh nation, which, from its very infancy, had been accuſtomed to it. And with this obfervation (which might be illuftrated by many inftances) conftantly in their view, they might have efcaped the violent paffion they have contracted for the doctrine of types and figures.

In the above account we have caft together, what may fuffice to give a tolerably full view of what is diftinctive and characteriftic in the Jewifh religion. We have alfo endeavoured to fhow, that the rites and ufages of it, were not mere arbitrary appointments, but all of them admirably adapted to the age of the world and genius of the people, for whom they were principally intended.

Here I might reft the proof of the injuftice done to this religion, by reprefenting it as an *abfurd and unphilofophical fuperftition.* Were there no more to be offered in vindication of it, enough, it is hoped, has been faid to fatisfy the candid and impartial. But, before we proceed to the conclufion which we mean to draw from the inquiry, in which we are engaged in favour of this religion, it may not be improper to take a more comprehenfive view of it, and of fome things in the adminiftration of their government, that feem to be connected with it.

PART

CHAP. II.

Of the political State of Israel, as interwoven or connected with their Religion.

IT is well known to all who are in the least acquainted with the history of Israel, that, from the time they can be denominated a nation or people, God may be considered as their King, Ruler, or Supreme Magistrate. Viewed in this light, it will be pleasant to observe the correspondence which there is betwixt the religious and the civil part of their constitution,—how each supports the other, and—both unite in forwarding the grand designs of God's providence and grace to mankind.

My design does not require, that I should give a regular, historical, account of the nature of that government under which Israel lived, in the several periods of their existence as a state: Nor that I should inquire into the several departments of their government, and the manner in which the administration of it was conducted. It leads me no farther than to point out the wisdom of its constitution, and of some of the *seemingly* most exceptionable

tionable parts of its adminiſtration; and—to
ſhow how admirably adapted the one was to
the genius and circumſtances of the people
who were to be the ſubjects of it, and—the
other, to promote the intereſts of that religion, which God had eſtabliſhed among them.
And of theſe I ſhall treat in the following
ſections.

SECT. I.

*Of the propriety of the Reſidence of the viſible Symbol
of the Divine Preſence among the Iſraelites, for the
Purpoſes both of Religion and Government.*

THIS ſtate was evidently founded on religion, and was to ſtand or fall by the regards that were to be ſhown to it.

The ſcheme of religion which God taught
Iſrael by the miniſtry of Moſes, differed ſo
widely in its nature and tendency from every
other that had obtained in the world, and
particularly from that of the Egyptians, of
which they were paſſionately fond, that it
required ſomething extraordinary to reconcile them to the thoughts of embracing it, at
the expence of renouncing all attachment to
any other. And yet this was indiſpenſably
neceſſary to the ſucceſs of it. To this end,
the perſonal reſidence (as it were) of God,
in a viſible, glorious, appearance, among them,
had an excellent tendency.

In

In that early age of the world, neither the nature of evidence, nor the manner of investigating it, nor the art of judging of the weight of it, were well understood. A visible proof,—one palpable to sense, became, therefore, necessary to overcome the prejudices they might entertain in favour of a religion, of which they seem to have been fond, and which, it is probable, laid them under less restraints, than that to which God called them by his servant Moses.

Without some such thing as this, it would have been no easy matter to have persuaded Israel, notwithstanding the high veneration they had for Moses, that the religion he taught them was from the supreme God, when so different from, nay, subversive of, that which, in Egypt, they had always heard represented as true. They would have been apt to suspect, that all the affectionate regard he showed for them, was only intended to cover some design he had upon them; and that the extraordinary talents of which he was possessed, improved by an education in Egypt, (then one of the most celebrated schools of learning in the world) had suggested the plan for their deception, and eminently qualified him for the execution of it. But when God, from whom, as he informed them, he had received it, continued to reside among them, and thus to give them the most incontestable evidence of his presence with them, there could be no room for a doubt concerning it.

This

This circumftance, which tended fo much to confirm their faith in this new religion, tended equally to fupport *their* fpirits under the difadvantages of their fituation, and *Mofes* in the adminiftration of government over them.

Imagine with yourfelves fuch a vaft body of people upon their march through a pathlefs defert, to a country (as they were informed) flowing with milk and honey, that is, the moft pleafant and fertile that could be imagined,—inceffantly expofed to dangers, and haraffed with fatigue, and—to appearance, often in danger of perifhing for want, and you will be fatisfied that nothing but a feries of miracles could fupport them.

Nay, it had been no wonder, had their dangers and wants preffing upon them, proved even too ftrong for all the miracles that were wrought among them, and made them, in fome of the pangs of their diftrefs, fufpect, that, however God had hitherto been with them, he had now feparated from them, and left them to perifh, unlamented, in the wildernefs. Such a thought as this, would naturally arife in minds alarmed with conftant fears of danger, nay, broken with a long feries of repeated diftreffes. In fuch a fituation, fome conftant and vifible fymbol of the aufpicious prefence of God with them, feemed neceffary. Without this, it had been no wonder had they deemed their fituation forlorn. Now, fuch a fymbol as this was the Schechina.

Neither was it more neceffary to encourage
the

the hopes of the people, than it was to give Mofes the due management of them. In a multitude confifting of fo many thoufands, it is not to be doubted that there muft have been many of a refractory fpirit,—many who, from jarring paffions and interfering interefts, would be difpofed to raife commotions, and ftir up a people, not at all indifpofed to it, to mutiny and rebellion.

In fuch circumftances, how great muft be the tendency of the vifible fymbol of the Divinity to keep them in awe, and procure their dutiful obedience? Tender as the concern of Mofes was for them,—great as the facrifice was which he had made, in renouncing all hopes of increafing honour at the court of Pharoah, by the favour of his daughter, who had taken care of him in his early years, and charged herfelf with his education,—refolute as his appearance was in working their deliverance, and—affiduous as his care was in conducting them through the wildernefs,—this, all this, would not have fufficed to fecure their allegiance. And, in fact, we find it did not. Often they grumbled, and fometimes they rebelled; and what lefs than an immediate interpofition of the Deity refiding among them, could have reduced them to order? Confidering the complexion of the people,—the many hardfhips they had to pafs through,—and the many arduous exploits they had to achieve, for the accomplifhment of his defign in their felection from the nations around them, it was neceffary he fhould take

take them under his immediate government.
Any other guardian, they would never have
submitted to. But, when he vouchsafed to
take them under his special tutelage and protection, what stronger, and, at the same
time, sweeter, inducement could they have,
to a faithful subjection and allegiance? How
would this naturally inspire them with a resolution, that might render them superior to
every danger or enemy to which they could
be exposed? And, in circumstances such as
theirs, what could be more necessary?

By their long residence in Egypt, they
were not only never called to the exercise of
courage, which is necessary to strengthen it, but
their spirits were so broken by the cruel and inhuman usage they received in that country, that
it were no wonder if the very mention of an
enemy or danger should have intimidated
them. But what undertaking could appear
so arduous, that they should think of decli-
ning it, when they considered themselves as
conducted to it, under the auspices of such a
Leader? And if a degree of courage was necessary to secure the possession of the country
after they had obtained it, equal to that
which was at first necessary to the conquest of
it, surely nothing could be better calculated
to inspire that courage, than the choice God
made of them,—his residence which he had
established among them, and—the characters
under which he was pleased to make himself
known to them, so suited to their circumstances,

stances, and encouraging to their confidence in him.

SECT. II.

Of the happy Correspondence betwixt the Civil and Religious Government.

IN the first period of their government, Moses, who was, under God, the Founder, was also the Administrator of it, or their chief Magistrate. In the management of the complicated task assigned to him, he came to feel the weight of government too heavy for his shoulders alone to support. For his relief, therefore, in the executive part of it, God desired that he might gather unto him "Se-
" venty men of the elders of Israel, whom
" he knew to be the elders of the people, and
" officers over them, and bring them unto
" the tabernacle of the congregation, that
" they may stand there with him. And, says
" he, I will come down and talk with thee
" there; and I will take of the spirit which is
" upon thee, and will put it upon them; and
" they shall bear the burden of the people
" with thee, that thou bear it not thyself
" alone." Numb. xi. 16, 17 *. These were intended

---

* Most of the Rabbinical, and some Christian, writers, who have treated of the Jewish Sanhedrim, have pretended

intended to be so many coadjutors, or assistant-counsellors to him, during their unsettled state in the wilderness.

After their settlement in Canaan, it became necessary that government should be established upon some certain and settled foundation. And as then the business of the state became more various, extensive, and complicated, certain officers were appointed under the name of *Judges*.

But, in all the different modifications of their government, one thing deserves to be taken notice of,—that the High-Priest, Priests, and Levites, bore a considerable share in the administration, and were employed in matters of a forensic nature*. And what could be

more

---

to trace the institution of it, as far back as the time of Moses; — to found the erection of it upon this command of God to him; and—to allege that it continued to subsist, through all the intermediate periods of their state, till a full stop was put to its jurisdiction by Titus, upon the reduction of the city of Jerusalem.

The pride of the Jews made them fond of ascribing to it so high an original. But, besides that this command to Moses, seems only to refer to the institution of a temporary relief to him, there are many things that will not allow us to carry it so far back, and some things that would induce us to carry it no higher than the government of the Asmodean family, or the time of the Maccabees.

See the Author's Dissertation on the conduct of the Jewish Sanhedrim, and the advice offered by Gamaliel, in the famous trial of the Apostles, Acts v. 17—41. considered as an argument for the truth of Christianity.

* I know there are some who consider the office of the several orders of the sacerdotal tribe, as restricted to the services of religion, and who allege that any jurisdiction allowed them,

extended

more wife, than thus to raife the reputation and influence of thofe who were to prefide in the exercifes of religion, upon the obfervance of which the very being of their ftate may be faid to have depended, becaufe it was the foundation upon which the fabric was reared?

Many of the political laws may, to a fuperficial reader, appear nugatory, but, carefully examined, they will be found to have a quite different appearance. They were all of them fuch as tended to promote a flourifhing ftate of their commonwealth. But ftill religion was their principal aim, and their fubferviency to this end far from being obfcure.

Thus, let us look into their code of laws, and we fhall find one law which forbids the hufbandman to muzzle the ox that trode out the corn: Another, that requires to bring back the ox into the way, that had ftrayed out of it; A third requires, that, in harveft

---

extended no farther than to things relating to religion. But nothing can be more evident, from many parts of the Jewifh hiftory, than that there were fome of them appointed to act in the character of Judges. To this purpofe fee Deut. xvii. 8, 9. Deut. xix. 17. Deut. xxi. 10.—1 Chron. xxiii. 4. —2 Chron. xix. 8. And though there may be many wife reafons, why, under a civil eftablifhment of religion, its minifters fhould, as little as poffible, interfere in the adminiftration of matters relating to the policy of the ftate, yet, when it is confidered that the Jewifh ftate was, in a particular manner, founded in religion, and had its civil interefts connected with the regard fhown to it, one may eafily difcern the propriety of the facerdotal order having a fhare in the adminiftration.

vest or vintage, the fields should not be too narrowly cleared of all that grew upon them.

Were we to consider these laws separately by themselves, and independently of the moral design of them, we should be apt to tax an attention to them, as too little even for an ordinary legislator. But who does not see, that the design of God in enacting these, extended far beyond the letter of them; and that he meant by these, and laws of a similar nature, to recommend the exercise of humanity, charity, and benevolence, in their intercourse with one another, wherever the proper opportunities offered? And here it may not be unworthy of notice, that the subjects of this state are taught the exercise of these virtues, by the injunction of acts of mercy to the brute creation.

This manner of instruction the Divine Legislator might pitch upon, not only to restrain those acts of cruelty and violence to them, in which they were but too apt to indulge themselves, but also with a higher view:—Even to guard them against an insensibility to the miseries and distresses of one another, which he well foresaw would be the consequence of a total want of compassion, even to creatures of an inferior order.

In some of the laws given to the people of Israel, the design is abundantly obvious.—Of this sort are those just now taken notice of. In others, the design is more obscure, for want of an acquaintance with those rites or usages to which they had a reference. Thus,

for

for inftance, God forbad the rounding the corners of their heads, or marring the corners of their beards*? He alfo prohibited in garments the ufe of ftuff made of lint and wool †. Confidered abftractedly, neither of thefe could be faid to deferve the attention of a wife legiflator. But, as things in themfelves indifferent, and even trifling, may fometimes derive importance from the circumftances that attend them, fuch was the cafe with refpect to thofe things which were the fubjects of the laws under confideration.

Among many of the ancient idolaters, it was a cuftom to cut off fome of the hair of their heads and beards, and to ftrow this upon the bodies of their deceafed friends, when they were about to confign them to the grave, in hopes that the infernal deities, to whom this was devoted, would be thereby rendered more propitious to them ‡.

No conceit can be fo abfurd and ridiculous, but it may gain credit with a people given up to fuperftition. Accordingly we are told, that fome of the idolaters of ancient time, imagined that the increafe of their wool and flax was owing to certain, lucky, fiderial influences; and therefore that they were wont to wear garments into which both had been wrought, and thus to exprefs their regard and gratitude to the ftars, to whom they confidered themfelves indebted for them.

It

---

* Levit. xix. 27.—and xxi. 5.   † Levit. xix. 19.
‡ Spencer de Legib. Hebræor. lib. ii. cap. 12. § 2.

It is easy to see how incompatible with a pure and rational religion, such doctrines as these were: Nay, that, in proportion as they gained credit, they must necessarily have a most baneful influence upon its votaries. And therefore, what could be more worthy of the Deity than to forbid, in a religion of which he was the Author, the use of rites which were accounted sacred among idolaters, and which, if once allowed to mingle with his, would directly lead to principles and practices, neither of which he could approve?

I might take notice of many other of their laws, and show you that the tendency of them all, was to form the minds of this people to the love, and their lives to the practice, of virtue. But these already taken notice of, may suffice for this purpose.

The multitude and minuteness of their political or judicial laws, may, with some, be an objection against the wisdom of the Legislator, and seem calculated to distract the attention of the subjects. But those who think so should consider, that the same code of laws will not answer for all; and—that these must be varied, according to the temper, situation, and circumstances of those who are to be governed by them. And if this is but properly attended to, I am humbly of opinion, that the wisdom of the Jewish Legislator will be very readily admitted. For, considering how gross the understanding of this people was, such a minute particularity was necessary. And the weight of that yoke, which would have been
galling

galling to those of a more gentle disposition, was necessary to keep them in proper subjection.

SECT. III.

Of some of the most exceptionable Parts (as they are commonly reckoned) of the Administration of the Theocracy, under which Israel lived.

A SUPERFICIAL view of any subject, seldom fails to lead to a wrong judgment concerning it. Never perhaps did the justness of this observation appear more glaring, than in the positive and dogmatic decisions that have been given upon the Divine conduct, in the administration of the government exercised over Israel.

Many have presumed to take it under their cognisance, and have as decisively determined upon it, as if they were, in every respect, competent judges.

The theocracy of the Jews has afforded ample scope for the humour of Sceptics and Infidels to display itself.

Some, more disposed to blame than to commend, have affected to find fault with the selection of Israel, and the gift of such extraordinary privileges bestowed on them. This conduct they represent as incompatible with that philanthropy, which is ever one of the distinguishing characteristics of the Deity,

and

and as favouring more of the partiality of a
local Deity, than of the benignity of him,
who lays claim to the character of the Parent,
as well as Lord, of all.

Could we even suppose the privileges which
distinguished the nation and people of Israel,
to have been bestowed upon them solely for
their own sakes, there could be no just ground
of blame, on this account. It might be easily
vindicated on the principles of reason.

Is not life itself the gift of God? Are not
all the comforts with which it is enriched,
derived also from the same source? And is he
not at liberty to bestow them in what proportion and measure he pleases? We may observe, in the scale of being, a vast and beautiful gradation,—one order and rank of creatures rising above another, from the meanest
reptile upon earth, to the brightest Seraph in
heaven. We may observe a great difference
in natural and intellectual abilities,—in local
connections and advantages. But, who that
pretends to the least degree of wisdom, ever
took it into his head to arraign the goodness
of God, because he made not the whole creation, Angels? Or because, if such a species as
man must have a place in it, he did not endue
every one of the species with all the abilities
of a Sir *Isaac Newton*,—the riches of a *Crœsus*,
or the dominion of an *Alexander?* No better
reason have they to complain who find fault
with the larger distribution of the Divine
blessings, which, in those early ages, fell to
the lot of Israel or the Jews. The differences

just

just now mentioned, are so far from being an evidence of a defect of goodness in the Author of them, that they are a proof of the diffusive nature of his goodness, and become the means of producing a greater sum of happiness upon the whole, than there could have been without them.

In like manner, no more ground was there to complain of the distinction which was made betwixt the Jews and the Gentiles, the two classes into which the world was, in early times, divided.

It was not any particular attachment to the Jews, that influenced God in the choice of them. Such fondnesses are generally the indications of weakness, and therefore not to be ascribed to God. Every part of his conduct is connected with the ends of his moral government, and intended to be subservient to them. And so was this, in an eminent manner, though it has not been so much attended to, as it ought.

This very choice of Israel, which has given so much offence to some, as favouring of partiality and bias, was intended as the means of the most diffusive beneficence, in due time, to the very nations from whom they were separated, and of accelerating, instead of retarding, the spread of the true religion among them.

Did those who are so apt to cavil, consider the matter in this point of light, they would have the greatest reason to admire what before they were so ready to censure, and would
be

be furnifhed with the means of vindicating,— the ways of God to man.

At the time when God fet up the Jewifh commonwealth, and took the people who compofed it under his fpecial tutelage and protection, vice had grown to an enormous fize, and religion, which fhould have been the means of reformation, had become ftrangely corrupted. A fignal interpofition of Providence became neceffary to provide for its fupport in the world, in a way honourable to God and ufeful to man. And if God fhould choofe the method complained of, as the moft fubfervient to this end, who that allows himfelf to judge with candour, but muft admit the propriety of it?

How their feparation from the nations around them, conduced to the purpofes of the intended reformation, will be the fubject of inquiry in Part II. § 2. I fhall therefore content myfelf with obferving at prefent, that, but for the diftinction now under confideration, Ifrael would probably, according to the ordinary courfe of things, have been involved in the fpreading corruption of religion. Whereas, by being made the depofitories of certain facred oracles delivered to them, they became, in a variety of ways, as I fhall fhow afterwards, the happy inftruments of preparing the nations around them for receiving the knowledge of the gofpel, and fo of communicating it, till it fhould become univerfal. And if this can be made appear, the formidable

dable objection above-mentioned vanishes all at once.

If the objection from the particular choice of Israel, is not admitted against the goodness of the Divine administration, their *slow marches* towards Canaán, and—their *long stay* in the wilderness, will, they think, surely be conclusive against the wisdom of it.

" Why (they ask) keep such a vast body, so long in a howling desert, and, instead of conducting them by a direct course, lead them, by so many windings and traverses, to the land of promise? Has this, say they with an air of triumph, the appearance of Divine conduct?" Yes. It undoubtedly has.

No doubt it had been easy for Moses to have conducted Israel into Canaan by a much shorter course than that he took. But that he did not, is of itself no small presumption of his acting under a Divine agency. For, what else but a consciousness of this, could have prompted him to the course he followed, so opposite to the measures which human prudence can be supposed to dictate? Or, how could he otherwise have flattered himself with so much as the hopes of being able to support such a vast body of people, in such a desert country,—through such tedious marches, and —for so long a time?

Besides the argument in favour of the measure complained of, drawn from the consideration of its uncommonness, allow me, that you may the better discern the propriety of
it,

it, to take notice of another circumstance of no small weight.

Israel had, by their long stay in Egypt, contracted a strong passion for the mode of religion professed in that country; and therefore had God led them directly to, and set them in possession of, the land of Canaan, with such an attachment in them to idolatry, they would have run ten thousand risks of being immediately seduced by the religion of that country, which, in its principal features, bore a very strong resemblance to that of the country which they left. In such circumstances, the wilderness became a very proper school, in which they were to be trained up in the new religion which Moses taught them. Here they had no intercourse with other nations, and therefore had not the influence of their example to struggle with. They were so entirely at leisure to attend to the instructions they might receive with respect to religion, that, were it only to avoid the weariness that must have arisen from the want of occupation, it must of necessity, if not choice, have become their business. While, in the mean time, every thing in the Divine administration towards them, and particularly the manner of their subsistence, and the series of miracles which were wrought to provide for it, served to confirm them in their attachment to this religion, and the Divine Author of it.

Nothing could be more difficult than to get the better of prejudices in favour of a system of of religion which probably dazzled the imagination,—gratified the taste for external splendor, and laid little or no restraint upon the passions and appetites of its votaries. To effect this, required no inconsiderable time. Every check which Israel received from the purity of this new religion, would, in a peevish mood, make them think of falling in with the religion of the country they had come from, which left them more at liberty. It must be time and patience that could get the better of such propensities, and enable them so coolly and deliberately to consider the nature, and weigh the evidence, of the religion offered to them, as to make them not only embrace, but also adhere to it, in the sharp trials they had to pass through.

Besides, let it be considered that the Israelites were a headstrong and obstinate people,—impatient of controul,—violently addicted to idolatry, and—prone to rebellion. And who but must see that there would have been the greatest impropriety in leading a people, under the influence of such passions, immediately into the land of Canaan? How far must such a measure as this have gone to defeat the very design of their settlement in it, or, at least, to retard the execution of the Divine plan? Much farther, surely, than all their journeyings in the wilderness. Their possession of it, therefore, was put off till that race should die out. At least, none of them, who came out of Egypt, remained but two, Joshua and Caleb, who, in honour and reward

ward of their fidelity, were preserved to conduct their countrymen into Canaan.

All those who were allowed to settle there, not only received their birth in the wilderness, but, being educated and disciplined in this school, were happily prepared to encounter the many hardships they had to undergo, before they could obtain the peaceable possession of the land destined for them. And, in the mean time, the visible presence of God among them,—the remembrance of his just severity to their fathers, and—his indulgent kindness to themselves, served to invigorate their spirits under all the difficulties of their service, and to attach them with the warmest gratitude to him.

These reasons, were there none other, would be sufficient to vindicate the Divine conduct, from every imputation of the want either of wisdom or goodness, that could be thrown upon it, for the so long time that Israel spent in the wilderness; and might show how vain, as well as rash, are the censures of ignorance and prejudice. But they stop not here. Both show themselves again in the severe strictures they make upon the conduct of Israel towards the inhabitants of Canaan, after their settlement in it; or rather upon the administration of God, their supreme magistrate, who, they allege, authorised it.—" To destroy and slay,
" without mercy, the inhabitants of a coun-
" try, who had provoked them in no other
" way, but that they did not tamely yield to
" them the possession of it, when they inva-
" ded

" ded it, is a conduct too shocking for any
" policy, that makes the least pretensions to
" humanity. What then shall we say (to use
" the words of a much admired writer*) of
" the order of God to the Jews, when they
" were fugitives from Egypt, to immolate
" seven or eight small nations, whom they
" did not know, and to destroy all the wo-
" men, all the old men, and even the children
" at the breast, reserving none but the little
" girls."

In this objection, the rashness, to say no more, of those who make it, discovers itself. No doubt, God is both merciful and just; and therefore we may be sure there can be nothing, in the commission which he gave to Israel with respect to the inhabitants of Canaan, incompatible with this character. Nay, duly attended to, it will be found to be perfectly consistent with both parts of it.

From the history we have of this country it evidently appears, that its inhabitants were addicted to the most abominable crimes †, these mixing themselves with their religious services; so that, as one emphatically expresses it, *" It was become piety with them, to be exceedingly wicked."* To this excess of vice they had given themselves up for more than 400 years; for we find they were remarkable for it, even when the promise of their country was made

---

* Voltaire's Philosophy of Hist. chap. xxxvi.

† We are told, Wisd. xii. 4, 5. what some of their vices were.

to Abraham*. And therefore what ground could there be to complain, if God, after so long a space given them for repentance and reformation, but neglected by them, should punish them with an awful severty, and so not only put a stop to their abounding wickedness, but thus make others, and particularly the Israelites, who were to occupy their country, stand in awe, and dread the danger of imitating them?

Considered in this light, the havock made among them, must appear to be no more than a just expression of the Divine displeasure, against their atrocious wickedness.

Those who start the objection against the Divine administration, paint it too strongly, when they represent the conduct of Israel, as not only cruel but unjust. The Israelites were to be considered, in this matter, as no more than the instruments of the Divine vengeance, not of their own private resentments.

If the earth is the Lord's and the fullness thereof; if the portion allotted to any nation or people is the gift of God; upon what principle can it be denied that he may recall it when he pleases? or deprive those of it, who, by the most ungrateful abuse, have forfeited it, and rendered themselves unworthy of the continuance of it? Had God seen meet to destroy them, as he did the old world, by water; or, as he did Sodom and Gomorrah, by fire from heaven; we would have revered,

without

---

* Gen. xv. 13, 16.

without daring to blame, such a tremendous display of juſtice and power. But if, in this caſe, he ſhall chooſe to employ any of his rational, inſtead of his inanimate, creation, to execute the purpoſes of his providence, where is the material difference? In both caſes, his conduct is equally juſtifiable.

Nor can it lie as an objection againſt this mode of procedure, that it has a tendency to encourage the moſt licentious and barbarous ravages in thoſe, who, prompted by avarice, ambition, or a luſt of power, ſhall wiſh to poſſeſs the property of others, and have but ability to do ſo.

In this caſe there was evidently ſomething very ſingular, that muſt for ever prevent its being pleaded as a precedent. A ſpecial commiſſion is received from God for this purpoſe; and the execution of it becomes not only admirably ſubſervient, but even neceſſary, to the accompliſhment of his deſign, in the ſettlement of this land. And, with reſpect to the warrant under which they acted, they could be in no doubt, becauſe they had this, not only in commiſſion from the ſervant of God, who, under his auſpices, had been their deliverer from Egypt, and their conductor through the wilderneſs, but they had even ſenſible evidence for it, in the countenance and aſſiſtance which God all along gave them. So that, till others can plead the ſame, or a like licenſe, it would be moſt impious, as well as inhuman, to venture upon the like courſe.

Thus far we have argued the matter upon the

the fuppofition that a real excifion of the Canaanites was enjoined, and have fhown that this meafure might have been juftified, in their circumftances, upon the principles of reafon and religion. But I humbly imagine we are under no neceffity, from the facred hiftory, of adopting an interpretation that would oblige us to underftand it, in its utmoft latitude.

It is true, Mofes, by commiffion from God, gives it in charge to Ifrael, that, "when the "Lord, their God, fhould deliver thefe na- "tions to them, they fhould fmite them and "*utterly* deftroy them:—that they fhould make "*no covenant* with them, nor fhow *mercy* unto "them, neither make *marriages* with them *." In another place, he fays—"Of the cities of "thefe people which the Lord, thy God, doth "give thee for an inheritance, thou fhalt fave "alive nothing that breatheth: But thou "fhalt *utterly* deftroy the Hittites, and Amo- "rites, and Canaanites, and Perizzites, the "Hevites, and the Jebufites, as the Lord, thy "God, hath commanded thee, that they "teach you not to do after all their abomina- "tions which they have done unto their "gods, fo fhould ye fin againft the Lord, "your God †."

Let us take the whole of the charge together, and I humbly imagine, it will be evident to the candid reader, that the words which contain it, were not to be underftood in their utmoft extent. And, if one part of the

---

* Deut. vii. 2, 3.   † Deut. xx. 16, 17, 18,

the commission is allowed to explain the other, (which it is but reasonable it should) are we not led to conclude, that it could mean no more, than to destroy them from being a *nation*, or a separate people by themselves, that so, by thus reducing them into a state of contempt, they might not be hurt, either by the force of their arms, or the influence of their example? And what makes this construction the more probable and just is,—that, with the very same breath, with which he charges Israel to destroy them *utterly*, he tells them that they were not to allow them to dwell in the land,—nor were they to make any covenant with them, nor enter into any marriages with them.—And would not all these have been unnecessary cautions, if the command to destroy them, admitted of no softening?

It is true, the words of the command are very express and peremptory: " Thou shalt " save alive nothing that breatheth, but shalt " utterly destroy them." But, besides what has already been offered to show that they ought to be understood in a restricted sense, allow me to observe, that, if they are considered, as they ought to be, as making a part of the instructions given to Israel for their conduct towards those they might have occasion to be engaged in war with, the edge of the objection is, all at once, blunted.

One general instruction given them was, ver. 10.—that, before they commenced hostilities against any city, whether of the country in which they were to settle or any other, they

they should make them overtures of peace, upon reasonable terms. After laying down this general rule of conduct, the sacred historian proceeds to inform them, how they ought to behave to those cities that might be at a distance from the place where they were to settle:—that, if they accepted the terms offered to them, they might enter into alliance with them, because, from their distance, there was little danger to be dreaded from it: but that, even in this case, though they were to take them under their protection, they were to treat them as tributaries. In this manner were they to behave to them, in case of a submission. But if they stood on their defence, and put the issue of the siege upon their conduct and valour; in that event, they were to smite every male thereof with the edge of the sword; but the women and little ones, and the cattle, and all that was in the city, even all the spoil thereof, says he, thou shalt take unto thyself.

With respect to the cities which belonged to the seven petty states, whose country they were to possess, he tells them, they were to behave in a very different manner, if they listened not to the terms proposed to them. To these they were to give no quarter. All, without exception, were to be cut off. And the reason seems to be,—Because, discovering by such conduct (I mean a refusal of the overtures of peace) the most hostile disposition to Israel, they had the greatest reason to dread every possible hurt from them; and
therefore

therefore were called upon, by a principle of self-prefervation, as well as of religion and found policy, to provide for their own fafety, by deftroying thofe, who were implacable enemies to it.

From this account of the matter it is evident, that it was only in cafe of an abfolute refufal of the terms offered to them, and the reduction of their cities by ftorm, that the Ifraelites were required to deftroy them *utterly*. And as the command was reftricted folely to this cafe, would it not feem to intimate that there were other cafes, in which their prefervation was perfectly compatible with the regard they owed to the Divine command? The danger which Ifrael had to dread from incorporating with the inhabitants of thefe feven nations, or allowing them to dwell among them, while they remained obftinately attached to idolatry, was—that they might be foon infected with it. But if they renounced their idolatry, and the abominable practices into which it led, as the danger from them would then ceafe, fo there is nothing in the Divine command that made an excifion, in that cafe, neceffary.

And now, if we receive this comment, who but muft admit the lenity of the meafure to the Canaanites, as well as the wifdom of it, to the Ifraelites? If the Canaanites met with deftruction from the victorious fword of Ifrael, they had themfelves only to blame. By complying with the reafonable terms propofed to them, it was in their power to have prevented

vented it. Less than what was appointed to be done to the inhabitants of this country, could not have secured Israel against danger from them, and more was unnecessary.

By thus degrading them into a servile state, (for it is probable they still lived tributaries to the Israelites) God secured Israel against all corruption from their example, not only by the contempt in which they would necessarily hold them, but also from a constant exhibition before their eyes, of the danger to which they would expose themselves by an imitation of it.

Upon the whole, let this objection against the Divine administration be but considered in a proper light, and, formidable as it may, at first sight, appear, it dwindles into nothing.

From what has been offered above, the reader is left to judge of the candor of M. Voltaire, in the representation he has given of this matter. What a pity is it, that one of abilities so distinguished as his were, should not have made a better use of them. Lucky in one respect for the cause of revelation, has been the zeal which the friends of infidelity have shown against it. It has seldom failed to discover, and thereby to defeat, their design in it.

M. Voltaire is not more unfair in the construction he puts upon the commission, above mentioned, given to Israel, than he is in the alleged reservation, with respect to the *young girls,* said to be contained in it.

It requires no great penetration to see his design

design in this remark. But he ought to have been ashamed of having made it, without so much as the least apparent ground for it, in the charge given to Israel, as must be evident to every one who takes the trouble to read it. Such a strange freedom as this in the representation of an historical fact, especially when the tendency of it is to beget the most unfavourable sentiments of the Deity, is inexcusable in a writer of any character. To ascribe it to inattention, is but a poor apology for him. And yet could we suppose this to be the case, it would be the best that could be offered.

The objections already taken notice of, against the Divine administration in the management of this people, are not all that have been made. When a captious humour is once indulged, it is hard to say where it will stop.

The long and miserable captivity, to which this people of God were subjected in Babylon; and, at last, the destruction of their nation, city, temple, polity, and government; have been represented as incompatible with those auspices, under which the foundations of their church and state were laid, and that particular care which God was said to have taken of both. But, in this, there will be found to be as little force as in any of the former. Nay, the conduct complained of, becomes at once a proof and illustration of God's design in the original choice of this people, and an excellent mean of accomplishing it.

In support of this opinion, it may not be improper

improper to remind the reader, that the eſtabliſhment of this ſtate was founded in religion, and deſigned to be ſubſervient to the purpoſes of its honour and intereſt. And therefore, whenever this people, forgetting the original deſign of its inſtitution, indulged in practices incompatible with it, their governor was called upon to interpoſe for its ſupport, as long as its ſubſiſtence was neceſſary. And if, in the mode of his adminiſtration, he ſhould chooſe to employ any of the neighbouring nations as inſtruments for correcting them, may we not be able to trace ſome reaſons more than ſufficient, to vindicate his conduct?

He had, at the firſt erection of their ſtate, and often afterwards, told them, that, while they continued a virtuous, they ſhould continue a proſperous and happy, people,—the envy of all around them. But that, as ſoon as they degenerated from piety and religion, and indulged themſelves in courſes inconſiſtent with theſe, they ſhould become ſubjected to the very people they ſo much deſpiſed. The firſt they had experienced, in the long and proſperous ſucceſſes they enjoyed. And when, elated with theſe, they forgot or diſregarded their God, what could be more reaſonable, than that, for the puniſhment of their folly and ingratitude, they ſhould feel the effects of his diſpleaſure, in the latter? Beſides, let it be conſidered, that their puniſhment had a tendency to bring about their reformation, and an accompliſhment of the plan of the Divine Providence: The one, by convincing them,

them, from their own sad experience, of the danger of a departure from God, and a daring opposition to his government: The other, by carrying the knowledge of their religion into those countries, whither they were themselves carried captive; and so, by diffusing it, preparing the world, in due time, for the reception of that religion, which was to become universal.

Such reasons as these, show that the very captivity of the Jews was nowise incongruous to the original design of God, in the choice of this people. And it cannot but be agreeable to observe, that, as the plan of Providence, which required the separation of this people, was not yet accomplished, he, once and again, brought about their return to their own country, and the restoration of their religion and liberty:—And that both continued to subsist, though with evident marks of decline, till the destruction of their city, which was the seat of their government, and of their temple, which was the centre of their public worship. Thus the one became an evidence that a period was put to their polity: The other, to their religion: And both, to the distinction that had long subsisted betwixt them and other nations, neither of them being any longer necessary.

At first indeed, upon reading the history of the many miseries and calamities, in which this people were involved through a series of ages, and particularly by the long siege of their city, and the dreadful carnage that followed

lowed the reduction of it, the tender and feeling heart becomes very fenfibly affected, and we are apt to lament their unhappy fate. But, when we confider the acount, which Jofephus*, an hiftorian of their own nation, and a Prieft of their own religion, gives of their enormous wickednefs, (not to fay any thing of what we have in the facred record concerning them) we muft pronounce them a people ripe for deftruction, and fuch as the vengeance of God could not allow to pafs any longer unpunifhed.

From the view we have taken of the Divine adminiftration towards this people, I hope it is evident, that nothing but ignorance or prejudice can make any entertain an unfavourable opinion of it :—Nay, that it appears to have been conducted by the moft confummate wifdom,—with the ftricteft regard to the true intereft of this people in particular, and of mankind in general; and—that it was, in the whole of its tendency, moft admirably fubfervient to both.

It would argue an unpardonable levity and inattention, after fuch a minute review of the Divine conduct to the church and people of Ifrael, to difmifs the fubject, without any ferious reflections upon it. If the importance of

---

* De Bel. Jud. lib vi. cap. 16. " I am perfuaded, fays he, " that, if the Romans had delayed the punifhment of this " wicked people, their city would either have been drowned, " or fwallowed up with an earthquake, or have been deftroy- " ed with thunder and lightning, like Sodom; for, of the " two, the Jews were the much more wicked people."

of any subject can render it deserving of such, this may. But, rather than enter upon these at present, it may not be improper to delay a little, till, by taking a more comprehensive view of the subject, in the following Parts, we are enabled to make the proper observations upon the whole, and then they will appear with greater advantage.

PART

PART II.

Of the DURATION *of the* MOSAIC *Oeconomy.*

THE Mosaic institution of religion, may be considered as comprehending laws, moral, political, and commercial. And all these, during the subsistence of the Jewish commonwealth, had a very close and natural connection, and did unite in the great design of their promulgation, which was to promote the interests of religion, upon which their very state was founded.

It is almost unnecessary to observe, that, when we inquire into the duration of this œconomy, there can be no question made about the obligation and continuance of that part of it, which was of a moral nature. The laws with respect to it, must be allowed to be of eternal obligation, because equally binding upon all, and not intended for certain, peculiar, situations and circumstances.

With

With respect to their political and municipal laws, it cannot be alleged that these remain in force any longer than the state subsists, for which they were originally designed. Our inquiry, therefore, is reduced into a very narrow compass, and relates only to the ceremonial of their religion. And of this under the following sections.

SECT I.

That the Duration of it was never intended to be more than temporary.

THE position which is to be the subject of this section, the Jews are necessarily obliged to impugn. And arguments, more plausible than solid, have been made use of by them, in support of their opinion. From the Divine origin of the Mosaic law, and the immutable perfections of its great Author, they argue in favour of the continued force and duration of it. They insist, that, had he ever entertained a design of superseding that sacred ritual, which was the distinguishing characteristic of this religion, the intended repeal of it would have been clearly mentioned, and mankind not left to gather it from obscure hints, or forced interpretations, of the Divine oracles.

In this manner the Jews reason in defence of the perpetuity of their religion. But I humbly

humbly imagine, a more than abundant proof of the contrary, may be easily brought from a consideration of the nature of this dispensation of religion,—the plainest hints of the sacred oracles, and the conduct of the Divine providence, with respect to it.

The Jews themselves admit, (and indeed it is evident from the whole structure of their religion) that, so far as it was ritual, it had an immediate reference to them, and those, who, by being proselyted to it, should conform to all its precepts †. And must not every

---

† Though the Mosaic religion prohibited its votaries from having any unnecessary intercourse with their heathen neighbours, while they continued such, it, at the same time, provided for their reception into the Jewish church; and, in consequence of this, their admission to all the privileges of native Jews. The terms required of such as were candidates for admission into the church of Israel, were—that they should submit to circumcision, which implied in it a virtual subjection to the precepts, doctrines, and rites of this religion. And when we consider the danger that attended a compliance with this rite to adult persons, we cannot but see the propriety of its appointment in this case, as it must have excluded all who had not a high value for this religion, and a thorough conviction of the purity, both of its doctrines and precepts.

The Rabbins have made the form of admission very tedious and solemn: But, as this seems to have no foundation in scripture, I have nothing to do with it.

Those who were proselyted to this religion, were called *Proselytes of the Covenant or of Righteousness, and Proselytes of the Gate.*—The first were so called, because they became bound to the observance of the whole law.—The other, by way of distinction from them, have been called Proselytes of the Gate, because they were allowed to dwell within their gates, upon their submission to, what are commonly called, the seven precepts of Noah, and their abstinence from every thing that

might

every one, who does not entertain the most narrow and contracted notions of the Deity, see that a religion of such a texture as this, was never intended to be of universal obligation, or of perpetual duration? For, are there not many things in it, which indicate its incompatibility with either? For instance, do we not find that, in the reign of Solomon, a temple was built at Jerusalem, and, by the special command of God, appointed to be the centre of the public services of their religion, —the place to which the tribes of God were appointed to go up, at least, three times a year, and where alone it was lawful for them to perform some of the most sacred and solemn parts of their worship? Duly attended to,

might appear affronting or injurious to the religion of those they lived among.

It must be owned, there is not the least evidence, from the sacred history, for the appointment of what is called, *the Noahic precepts* *; still less for the necessity of a submission to them, in order to the privilege of a residence among the Israelites. And even if there was any evidence for this, they could, with no propriety, be called Proselytes, who submitted to this and no more; because such submission had little more connection with the religion of Israel, than with that of any other nation. So that, upon the whole, it is presumable, that the distinction of *Proselytes of the Gate,* is only the invention of later times, and of Rabbinical fancy.

---

* The Rabbins teach, that God gave Noah seven commandments to be observed by his posterity. These are called the law of the Noahides.
 I. The first enjoins the worship of God alone, and forbids idolatry and superstition. II. The second forbids the profanation of the name of God. III. The effusion of human blood. IV. All criminal and incestuous conjunctions. V. Theft and fraud. VI. Respects the establishment of magistrates and judges. VII. Forbids the eating of flesh with the blood, or while the animal was alive.

to, what could be a stronger hint than this,—
that such an institution of religion, was never
intended to be of perpetual, no more than
of universal, obligation? One reason for such
an interpretation of this part of their ritual,
is very obvious. For, should the nation of
the Jews have increased, in a course of ages,
as might have been expected, and so been
obliged to remove from Judea into other
countries, in quest of settlements, who might
not see, that they could not, without the most
manifest inconvenience, attend at Jerusalem,
during the most solemn festivals of their religion, which they were required to celebrate
annually, and yet could celebrate no where
else?

It is true, it may be alleged, that this does
not conclude against the perpetuity of this
religion. For, though in the case supposed,
—the increase of the nation of the Jews, the
obligations of it ceased with regard to those
to whom the observance of its ritual became
impracticable, yet they might still continue
in force with respect to those who were not
in such a situation.

It is readily granted, that *Nemo tenetur ad
impossibile*. This is a maxim of common sense.
And is it not from thence presumable, that
this religion was never intended to remain
longer in force, than while its votaries were,
from their local situation, capable of performing the services of it, and that, when
this ceased to be the case, by their dispersion
into different and remote countries, it was to
give

give place to another mode of religion, that required no such restrictions as these imposed?

Besides, let me observe, that, could we suppose this religion to become universal, by a continual accession of proselytes from all nations, the duration of its obligation would carry another evident impropriety in it. It would require of many nations, in the observance of these festivals, an acknowledgment incompatible with truth,—an acknowledgment of the most signal interposition of Providence in behalf of their ancestors, who yet had no connection with them. And if, to avoid this difficulty, it should be alleged, that this religion was intended only for the people of the Jews, exclusive of all others, I submit to every impartial person, if such an opinion (however flattering it might be to the pride of the Jews) would not carry in it a charge of partiality, highly affronting to the Deity. Would not this be to suppose, that he took a most tender care of this people, while he seemed to neglect the rest of mankind, and so have a tendency to sour their tempers, beget in their minds the most unfavourable sentiments of him, and make them throw off all religious regards to him? These, and such as these, are the reflections, which the Jews and others were naturally led to make, from an attention to the constitution of this religion.

But, that they might not remain ignorant of his design, through perhaps an inattention to these hints, God was pleased to speak to them in a manner, which, while it guarded them

them againſt an indifference for this mode of religion from the temporary duration of it, was too plain to be miſunderſtood, had it been duly attended to,—plain enough to check their violent paſſion for it, from its imagined perfection and the perpetuity of its obligations. Thus ſaid he, by a ſucceſſion of Prophets—" To what purpoſe is the multitude
" of your ſacrifices? Behold, to obey is bet-
" ter than ſacrifice, and to hearken, than
" the fat of rams:—That, when the Moun-
" tain of the Lord's houſe ſhall be eſtabliſhed,
" all nations ſhall flow into it:—That, when
" the ſceptre ſhould depart from Judah, the
" *Shiloh* ſhould come, and that to him ſhould
" the gathering of the people be:—That his
" houſe ſhould be called a Houſe of Prayer
" for *all* people:—That he would give the
" Meſſiah, the *Heathen* for his inheritance,
" and the *uttermoſt part* of the earth for his
" poſſeſſion:—That, from the riſing of the
" ſun, even to the going down of the ſame,
" his name ſhould be great among the *Gen-*
" *tiles*:—That he would give him to be a
" light to the *Gentiles*, that he might be his
" ſalvation to the ends of the earth." And a great deal more to the ſame purpoſe.

Here indeed I might reſt the proof of our propoſition. The places referred to are all ſo much in point, that they muſt be allowed, by every candid reader, to be deciſive. But it may not be unpleaſant to behold how the events of Providence, connected with this ſcheme of religion, all ſeem to indicate its

temporary

temporary duration likewise. I shall take notice only of a few, which can be accounted for, upon no other supposition.

We find, from the history of this people, that their temple was early reduced into the hands of their enemies. Was not this of itself a plain hint to them, that the obligation of the ceremonial of their religion, which was to be performed there, could not be of perpetual force, else the observance of it would never have been made to depend upon a circumstance, so extremely precarious as the possession of a temple consecrated to it?

It is true, as the ends of this dispensation were not yet answered, God allowed the temple to be rebuilt, after it had been seventy years in ruins. But, does it not deserve to be remarked, that this new temple was not honoured with the symbol of the Divine Presence, which was the glory of the first? And, in what light could this be considered, but as an intimation, that this œconomy, like a constitution gradually worn out by age, was fast decaying, and would, at last, die away?

This temple, after it was rebuilt, remained 600 years, because the ends of erecting it, and of that institution of religion to which it belonged, were not yet accomplished. But, as soon as they were, did not God then bring about the final destruction of it, as a demonstration that their polity, religious as well as civil, was now come to an end? For surely, had God intended that the obligation of the Mosaic

Mosaic œconomy should continue to bind, he would not have permitted any human power, by destroying the one, to put a period to the other.

It is very remarkable, that, a considerable time after the destruction of the temple by *Titus,* an attempt was made by *Julian* to rebuild it. But the awful manner in which it was defeated, we know. Than this there could scarce be given to the Jews a stronger intimation, that the manner of worship there wont to be performed, was not to be restored, and, by consequence, that it had given place to another mode, which, though less splendid, was better calculated to become universal. And to this, may I not add, (what indeed seems to be a corroboration of the remark) that, as long as this institution of religion continued in force, so long the Jews continued to reside in Judea and the countries adjacent to it, which made their attendance on the service of the temple, not only practicable, but practicable without great difficulty. But no sooner did the obligations of it cease, than they were dispersed through the different nations of the world. This was not merely in punishment of their extraordinary wickedness. It was also intended as a gracious notice of the abolition of that œconomy of which they were so fond, and—perhaps as a happy mean of preventing their final ruin, by engaging them to adopt that scheme of religion, which had succeeded it.

From what has been offered above, we are furnished with the most unequivocal marks, that this institution of religion, was never intended, by the Divine Author of it, to be either of universal or perpetual obligation.

Nor does all this, or any part of it, if but rightly understood, carry the imputation of a defect, either in the wisdom or steadiness of the Divine counsels. A wrong conception of the nature of the Divine dispensations to mankind, could alone give rise to such an idea.

Some are apt to figure out every branch of the Divine administration, as a distinct dispensation of God's providence and grace to mankind. In this view, they consider every alleged repeal of any of them, as an affront to the Deity, because, say they, an imputation upon his wisdom, as if he had been unable, at first, to have devised the schemes most proper for the execution of his purposes, and therefore was obliged to patch and alter his plan, as after occurrences seemed to require. Could we be made to believe every dispensation of the Divine grace, to be independent of, and unconnected with, the other, there might be some appearance of justness in the reasoning. But, even in this case, it would be no more than the *appearance* of it. Because, upon this supposition, the perfection which it would be necessary to ascribe to it, would be relative rather than absolute:—No more than was necessary to answer the particular ends intended by it. And consequently, ly, if, at any period, we can suppose these to be attained, it can be no reflection upon the Divine wisdom, to suppose the obligation of it to cease. Nay, it would be an imputation upon it (and a very just one too) to suppose the continuance of it, when it is no longer necessary. Such a notion as this of the Divine administration, which supposes, at different periods, so many distinct œconomies or dispensations, is loaded with many difficulties, from which it is not easy to relieve it. It has also been the source of many illiberal reflections, which have been thrown out against it by those, who, to justify their own conduct, are obliged to find fault with the Divine. Whereas, did we, unwarped by the doctrines of ancient systems, accustom ourselves to think more freely, we should, I apprehend, think more justly, on the subject. We should consider each of, what we call, the Dispensations of God to mankind, rather as connected with, than independent of, one another;—rather as so many parts of one grand scheme or dispensation, than so many distinct ones by themselves. And indeed, if we will but attend to the history of the Divine administration to mankind, from the earliest hint given of it to the original Pair in Paradise, to the completion of its design in the life, death, resurrection, and ascension of our Lord, we shall find the several parts of it connected:— so connected, that they may be resolved into and considered as so many under-parts of one grand

grand defign, which required fuch a fucceffion of ages to unfold it.

Now let us confider the matter in this light, and it will be eafy to fee how this part of the Divine fcheme is, all at once, freed from the difficulties, which, upon the other hypothefis, feemed to encumber it.

In this view, the Mofaic œconomy is no more than a fingle branch of a vaft and complicated fcheme, for the redemption of mankind. However proper, therefore, it muft be allowed to be, during the period affigned for its continuance, yet, being intended to be no more than a preparation for another more perfect, the abolition of the one becomes the natural confequence of the commencement of the other. And fo, what was, at firft, thought to be an objection to the Divine wifdom, becomes, in the iffue, a bright illuftration of it, and affords matter of the higheft wonder and praife in the contemplation of it.

SECT.

SECT. II.

That the Mosaic Dispensation of Religion, was intended to prepare the World for the Reception of the Christian.

WHEN I speak, in this section, of the Mosaic and Christian dispensations, I speak according to the ordinary and vulgar mode, though, in the preceding section, I have considered them, rather as so many parts of one great whole, than different dispensations. And this manner I choose to follow, though not quite accurate, to avoid the trouble of a frequent repetition of the distinction, that I may not be mistaken.

It has been the custom of many, and a custom authorised by long use, to represent the people of the Jews, as the favourite and peculiar people of God, as if they were such in contradistinction to others, with respect to whom he was comparatively indifferent. But this, to say the least, is a very vague way of speaking, and has a tendency to create very unfavourable sentiments of the Divine administration, in the minds of the weak and the ignorant.

It is very true, they are represented as a kingdom of Priests, and a holy nation *. But who

---

* Exod. xix. 6.

who does not fee that this character of them is not to be interpreted, so as to favour the notion of a partiality and bias, but was intended to express the choice which God made of them, and their consecration, in consequence, to the profession of religion, and—all for accomplishing the purposes of the Divine grace, to the rest of mankind, as well as to themselves?

For elucidating the design proposed in this section, it will be necessary to keep this remark in view. It will the better dispose us to listen to what may be offered in support of it.

Before we attempt a proof of the connection betwixt the Mosaic and Christian dispensations, or the subserviency of the one to the interests of the other, it may not be improper to carry our views a little higher, and show the connection of the Mosaic dispensation with what went before, as well as with what followed after it. Or, in other words, it may be proper to show, that, as the dispensation of Moses seems to have been necessary to usher in the dispensation of the Gospel, so there were other dispensations which were equally necessary to prepare the world for the reception of it, and—that all of them occupied, with the greatest propriety, the time and place assigned to them.

As this inquiry comprehends a large tract of time, it may not be improper, for the sake of order, to arrange what shall be thought necessary to observe upon it, under the following

lowing divisions, which point out to us so many remarkable epochs, as it were, in the history of mankind.

§ 1. THE first naturally includes that period of time, which passed from the creation, to the destruction of the old world.

If we will attentively consider the nature of man, we must own that the obligations of religion, or, if you will, his' obligations to the worship and service of God, considered as the fountain both of his life and happiness, were coeval with his creation. But if we will, at the same time, consider what must have been the situation of mankind, in some of the first and earliest ages of the world, we shall find that—" While the condition of
" mankind was simple and rude, his reason
" (as a celebrated writer of our own country
" observes) would be but little exercised. His
" intellectual powers are extremely limited.
" What among polished nations is called
" *speculative reasoning or research*, is altogether
" unknown in the rude state of society, and
" never becomes the occupation or employ-
" ment of the human faculties, until man be
" so far improved, as to have secured, with
" certainty, the means of subsistence, as well
" as the possession of leisure and tranquillity.
" The thoughts and attention of a Savage are
" confined within the small circle of ob-
" jects, immediately conducive to his pre-
" servation or enjoyment. Every thing be-
" yond that escapes his observation, or is
" perfectly

" perfectly indifferent to him. The first
" ideas of every human being, must be such
" as he receives by his senses. But, in the
" human mind, while in the savage state,
" there seem to be hardly any ideas but what
" enter by this avenue. His thoughts extend
" not beyond what relates to animal life.
" In situations where the extraordinary ef-
" fort either of imagination or labour is re-
" quisite, in order to satisfy the simple de-
" mands of nature, the powers of the mind
" are so seldom roused to an exertion, that
" the rational faculties continue almost dor-
" mant and unexercised*."

" Whoever has had any opportunity of
" examining into the religious opinions of
" persons in the inferior ranks of life, even
" in the most enlightened and civilized na-
" tions, will find that their system of belief
" is derived from instruction, not discovered
" by inquiry. That numerous part of the
" human species whose lot is labour,—whose
" principal, and almost sole, occupation is
" to secure subsistence, views the arrange-
" ment and operations of nature, with little
" reflection, and has neither leisure nor ca-
" pacity for entering into the path of refined
" and intricate speculation, which conducts
" to the knowledge of the principles of natu-
" ral religion. In the early and most rude
" periods of savage life, such disquisitions
" are altogether unknown. When the intel-
" lectual

---

* Dr Robertson's Hist. of America, Vol. I. p. 308.

"lectual powers are just beginning to unfold,
"and their feeble exertions are directed to a
"few objects of primary necessity and use:
"When the faculties of the mind are so li-
"mited, as not to have formed abstract, ori-
"ginal, ideas; it is preposterous to expect
"that man should be capable of tracing, with
"accuracy, the relation betwixt cause and
"effect, or to suppose that he should rise
"from the contemplation of the one to the
"knowledge of the other, and form just
"conceptions of a Deity, as the Creator or
"Governor of the universe. The idea of
"creation is so familiar, when the mind is
"enlarged by science and illuminated with
"revelation, that we seldom reflect how pro-
"found and abstruse this idea is, or consider
"what progress man must have made in ob-
"servation and research, before he could ar-
"rive at any knowledge of this elementary
"principle of religion. Accordingly several
"tribes have been discovered in America,
"which have no idea whatever of a Supreme
"Being, and no rites of religious worship.
"They have not in their language any name
"for the Deity. It is only among men, in
"the most uncultivated state of nature, and
"while their intellectual faculties are so
"feeble and limited, as hardly to elevate
"them above the irrational creation, that we
"discover this total insensibility to the im-
"pressions of an Invisible Power. The hu-
"man mind, formed for religion, seems open
"to the reception of ideas, which are desti-
"ned

" ned, when corrected and refined, to be the
" great fource of confolation, among the ca-
" lamities of life *."

The account given, by this author, of the ignorance of fome, and the wild notions of others, with refpect to religion, in thofe countries which are the fubject of his hiftory, exhibits a very juft picture of the human race, in their rude and uncultivated ftate :—A picture which fhows us, by the by, what a forry length mere reafon would carry mankind in matters of religion, and, by confequence, what need, however fome may difclaim it, they have of a revelation from God.

The mention of this remark brings to my view, the propriety of the Divine difpenfations to mankind, in the early ages of the world. The cares of life would neceffarily engrofs their attention, and the exercife of their faculties, for the fupply of their wants, and fo leave them but little leifure for religion, and—yet, even in this ftate, it was not proper they fhould be without it.

What God did, in fuch a fituation, for their inftruction, muft, in every point of view, be allowed to be the moft proper. He vouchfafed to communicate to them difcoveries of his will, as they were able to bear them, and in a manner the beft adapted to make a deep impreffion upon them. For this purpofe he was gracioufly pleafed to affume a vifible appearance, and under this to converfe with mankind, and give them

such

---

* Dr Robertfon's Hift of America, Vol. II. p. 380.

such directions for the conduct of their life and the service of religion, as were most proper for them to observe. And who does not see that, without some such method as this, it must not only have been a considerable time before man, by the exercise of his faculties, or the result of his observations, could have formed any tolerable directory for himself in either, but also that, could we suppose a revelation of the Divine will to have been any how communicated to him, some such method as this seems to have been necessary, to gain credit and regard to it? The revelation of the Divine will which claims *our* belief, stands in no need of a Divine appearance to prove the authenticity of it. It has abundance of evidence without this. But it is such evidence, as a revelation, in that early age of the world, was incapable of. Thus, for instance, miracles, if they are such as lie under no suspicion of fraud, must be admitted as a sufficient evidence that the person who performs them, acts under the agency of a power superior to his own, and so claim an attentive regard to them, and, by just consequence, to the doctrines which they were intended to support. But it must be evident to every one who allows himself to think, that they could have been of no service, as a proof of a Divine revelation, in that early period, in which we suppose it to have been made. He who would judge properly of the importance of miracles offered with this view, must be supposed to be pretty well acquainted with the great laws
of

of Nature: For it can only be by a knowledge of thefe he can take upon him to fay, how far an action that would be confidered as a miracle, is, or is not, agreeable to them. And yet this very degree of knowledge by which it muft be judged of, can only be the acquifition of confiderable time, labour, and obfervation; and therefore muft come too late to be of fervice in the fuppofed early appeal to miracles, in behalf of a revelation.

There is another argument in favour of a revelation offered to us, deduced from the evidence of prophecy. But this, it is evident, alfo, could be of no fervice in the firft offer of a revelation to mankind. The defign of prophecy is to lead forward the views of mankind to future times,—and, confidered as an argument for the truth of any fyftem of religion, it derives all its force from the completion of it, in the exact correfpondence betwixt the event and the prediction. Hence, therefore, it is evident, that, in the cafe under confideration, this could be of no avail either, becaufe, in the interval (and perhaps a long one too) betwixt the prophecy and the time fixed for the completion of it, mankind muft have been left in a very anxious and comfortlefs fituation. This inconvenience, which neither miracles nor prophecy could have prevented, is, all at once, obviated by the vifible prefence of the Deity.

It is true, it may be alleged that there was fomething miraculous in this.—True. There was fo. But this was fuch a miracle as mankind

kind were well qualified to judge of, without being poffeffed of an extenfive and minute experience. The very firſt thoughts they would beſtow upon the Author of their exiſtence, would naturally prefent him to their minds, as a being truly great and glorious; nay, the moſt glorious of all beings: And this very view which he is fuppofed to exhibit of himfelf to mankind, joined with the fublime and ufeful difcoveries which he would make to them, ferved to confirm them in this opinion.

It is not to be imagined that they could have exact ideas, if any at all, of the fpirituality of his nature. Neither were thefe the firſt which it was proper to give them. At firſt, all that was neceffary was no more,—than to teach them the dependence they had upon him, and the obligations they were under to his fervice. And what could be better fitted for thefe purpofes, than fuch a difplay of his awful greatnefs,—fuch a manner of Divine appearance? Of the effect this fhould have upon them, they were fufficiently qualified to judge. And fcarce, from any other mean that can be conceived, could they, in their fituation, have judged, with fuch certainty, of the authority and obligations of the revelations communicated to them.

Befides, as this manner feems to have been the moſt eafy for communicating the knowledge of thofe important truths, which were to be the bafis of their religious fervice, does it not deferve to be taken notice of, that it had

had a particular tendency, at the same time, to make the deepest impression upon their heart? And yet, without such impression, it is highly probable it would have had but very little influence upon their conduct in life.

It is not improbable, that, together with any instructions which God might have given them in religious truths, he would also appoint certain institutions, which, tho' simple, (because suited to that early period, when an operose service would have been highly improper) would admirably serve to recal them to their minds,—and, by the frequent observance, to feed and nourish those habits of devotion, which they were calculated to form.

The account we have of this early period, is but very short. It deserves the name of Annals, or a few Hints, rather than a History. But short as it is, have we not reason from it to think, that, of this nature, were the institutions of the Sabbath, sacrifice, and social worship; all which, it is highly probable, had their origin as early as mankind began to be formed into societies?

It is remarkable, that, though God chose, in this manner, to make the first discoveries of himself to mankind, yet he did not make them very frequent. This reserve seems to have been necessary, not only that he might not lessen the reverence for the Divine appearances by rendering them too familiar, but also that he might give room and leisure to mankind to improve upon the hints he had given

given them. These were never intended to supersede, but to assist, the exercise of their rational faculties. He always meant to deal with them agreeably to the nature he had given them.

The first discoveries deserved their regard, from the evidence they carried along with them of their authority. But, though this was ground sufficient to engage their attention to them, what an additional pleasure would it be, when, by the exercise of their reason, they found them to be, in their tendency, not only agreeable to, but perfective of, their nature?

The reality of a visible Divine appearance in early times, must be allowed by all who admit the authority of the sacred record. But learned men have run into different sentiments, as to the time when it first obtained. Dr Shuckford maintains, that, till the time of Abraham, there was no such thing as a visible appearance of the Deity ever heard of in the world, and that he was the first who was honoured with the sight of such appearance:—That, before this time, mankind worshipped the invisible God, whom no man had ever seen or could see; and that, though he often spoke to Adam, Cain, Noah, and others of the antediluvians, there is no intimation that he was ever seen by any of them:—That the illustrious Personage, who was afterwards made flesh, and who, personating the Deity, came to be called, " The God of Israel, and " the God of Abraham, Isaac, and Jacob,"

appeared

appeared to Abraham in visible form:—And that, after this, there were two distinct Persons known and worshipped by the faithful, namely, God whom no man had seen at any time, and the Lord, who appeared at divers times to them.

This is the substance of the Doctor's opinion upon this point. And all this he endeavours to support by some criticisms upon the sacred text, and by observing that it was not science, but a belief of facts, that had led the Heathens into the theology of visible appearances. For, till the faith of these appearances had spread and obtained in different countries, the doctrines concerning them had never been adopted into any of their systems *.

It is needless to enter into a minute examination of what Dr Shuckford has advanced upon this subject. A few passing observations are only necessary.

It would be strange if a man of his abilities should adopt an opinion, for which he could not advance something plausible. It must be owned he has done so for this. And yet, after all, I must confess, I am far from being satisfied of the justness of it.

We have seen already some very good reasons for a visible appearance, as early as we have supposed. And though indeed it must be owned, that we are not expressly informed of

---

* See Shuckford's Connection, &c. Vol. II. p. 446, and Vol. III. p. 47.

of any visible appearance, yet the interviews betwixt God and Adam, and Cain, and Enoch, &c. and the phrases and modes of speaking arising from thence, such as,—" His face," —" His presence,"—" Coming to him,"—and —" Walking with him," all evidently suppose it. And to interpret these without admitting it, would be to render the meaning of every historical narrative precarious. Besides, it must be difficult to assign a good reason, why, if it had been delayed so long, it should be made at this particular time. It is true, the notions of God that still prevailed were but very imperfect. But, imperfect as they were, there is reason to think that they were less so at this time, than they were more early, and consequently that the Divine appearances were *then* more needed.

Dr Shuckford seems to lay too much stress upon Gen. xii. 7. Because there it is said, that Abraham built an altar to the Lord, *who appeared to him*, he from thence infers that he was the *first* to whom he did appear. But might he not, with very great propriety, have done all this, even allowing former appearances? If this was the first appearance vouchsafed to him, was it not highly becoming, however frequent they might have been to others before him, to have paid this piece of respectful homage to him? In support of this opinion, Dr Shuckford alleges, that, though the Patriarchs before Abraham worshipped only the invisible God, those who succeeded him,

him, worshipped also the Lord who appeared to many of them.

I must own it does not, after all he has said, appear to me certain, that they were acquainted with any such distinction. This would be to suppose an advance in theological knowledge, which it is doubtful if ever they attained, and seems to have been too much for these early times. Whether they had, so early, any notions of the spirituality of the Divine nature, which would render the Deity invisible, is extremely doubtful. And therefore might they not, very probably, have considered the glory they beheld, as the real Divinity? Or, if they believed him to be, in his nature, invisible to sense, might they not, without supposing any extraordinary advance in science, consider the visible, resplendent, glory which they beheld, as that particular form, in which he chose to manifest himself to, and converse with, them? And so, in either of these cases, there is no necessity for supposing their knowledge of this second Person; and indeed it does not appear to me that they ever had it.

It is not improbable, that, for some of the first ages, this visible glory had a fixed residence, to which mankind might repair for the performance of their religious services. But, if this was the case, there is reason to think, that, when afterwards they became better acquainted with the nature of God, and consequently of religion, it did retire, and only appear occasionally, till the establishment

blifhment of the Jewifh church. And then it took up its refidence with them, as a ftanding evidence of their felection from the nations around them, and a happy mean of training them up, to be fubfervient to the purpofes of the Divine providence and grace, to the reft of mankind.

The progrefs of the human mind in intellectual improvement is but flow; and, confidering the ftate of the world in its early ages, muft have been flower in any fuppofed period of them, than in any following period of the fame length. The fituation of mankind afforded them but little time for fpeculation, and therefore it muft have been a confiderable while before they could make any great advance in the knowledge of abftract truths. For this reafon, not only did God, as we have obferved already, favour them with certain revelations and difcoveries by means of a vifible appearance among them, but he was pleafed alfo to lengthen out the life of man to fo great an age.

This, it is probable, might have been one reafon for this part of the Divine œconomy. For, had the life of man, in thofe early ages, been circumfcribed within fuch narrow bounds as it afterwards was, the improvements in religious, as in every other branch of knowledge, muft have been very flow. Had they, foon after any difcoveries were vouchfafed to them, been removed,—before, by their deductions from them, they had made any confiderable acquifition to their ftock of knowledge,

knowledge, it muſt have been tranſmitted to ſucceeding generations with very little, if any, increaſe, as they had no other method of preſerving it but by tradition. Whereas, by the longevity of mankind, and the conſiderable time which thoſe of one generation were cotemporary with thoſe of another, both the revelations made to them and their improvements in religious knowledge in conſequence of them, would be handed down, not only with greater certainty, but with an additional degree of brightneſs, proportioned to the periods they paſſed through.

A regard to the infantile ſtate (if I may uſe the phraſe) of the human mind, made it neceſſary to proportion the degrees of light and knowledge communicated to it, to the expanſion of its faculties, or their capacities to receive them. Accordingly it deſerves to be taken notice of, that both the nature and degrees of the diſcoveries made to mankind, were ſuited to their circumſtances, or the progreſs they had made in improvement.

The firſt hints given them of religious truths or doctrines, were not of the more abſtruſe kind, or of difficult conception. This would, all at once, have defeated the deſign of making them, by turning away their attention from them. They were ſuch as would, eſpecially from the manner of their communication, immediately ſtrike the mind, and ſo gain an eaſy admiſſion into it. Accordingly, may it not be obſerved, that, no ſooner do we hear of the creation of man, than we hear

hear of his Maker's intercourse with him? He appears to him, and gives him such evidence of his deriving his being from him, and depending upon him for the continuance of it, as could not fail to procure his dutiful regards, and, at the same time, he received the necessary hints of the proper manner of expressing them.

Soon after the sad and dismal catastrophe of the fall, with what admirable propriety does God manifest himself to man? Was it not in a manner suited to his unhappy situation? To give him time for reflecting upon the guilt and dangerous consequences of his conduct, he does not immediately appear to him. He allows the unhappy discoveries he made, and his own reflections upon them, to punish him in the first instance. But when a consciousness of guilt and apprehension of danger had so alarmed him, as almost to overwhelm his spirits, and sink him into despondency, then does he manifest himself to him. And after expostulating with him the reason of his extraordinary conduct,—Behold! while man stands trembling before him, in the most dreadful fear of the Divine vengeance, then does he drop the hint of his merciful intentions towards him:—I say, a hint of this; for who may not see, that this was all that he was then able to receive, or capable to understand? To have immediately communicated to him, the whole plan of his redemption through Jesus Christ, would have answered scarce any other purpose than to have

have aſtoniſhed. This is a ſcheme too deep in its contrivance, and too operoſe and difficult in its execution, to have been tolerably conceived by man, at this period. What was imparted of it, was ſufficient to ſooth his fears,—to revive his hopes,—to encourage his confidence, and—thereby the future ſervice of his God. Any more would have been unſuited to his ſituation, and therefore improper.

And as the nature, ſo alſo the degrees of the diſcoveries made to mankind, in thoſe early ages, were every way the moſt proper. They were made, not all at once, but in a gradual manner, the former always tending to prepare for the following. In this reſpect, the progreſs of moral or religious light or truth, reſembles that of natural. From a thick darkneſs it proceeds to an obſcure dawn, and from thence, by increaſing degrees, as the intellectual eye can bear it, to meridian ſplendor.

But not only was this gradual illumination of the world, ſuited to the weakneſs of its ſtate, but it was alſo the beſt method to fit it for ſtill greater communications of light and knowledge, by the ſcope it afforded for deliberate improvements.

In the manner we have already hinted, did God go on, inſtructing mankind in religion, as occaſion required, till, at length, their increaſing wickedneſs made it neceſſary, for the ends of his moral government, to give a check to it by an overflowing deluge, which ſwept off

off the inhabitants of the world at that time, Noah and his family alone excepted.

§ 2. By the preservation of Noah and his family, the earth was peopled again. He becomes the parent of the New, as Adam had been of the Old, world. And with him was preserved the knowledge of what related to it, so far as was necessary to be communicated to after ages.

Had not, by the Providence of God, Noah been so long a cotemporary of Methuselah, and he of Adam*, the revelations made to them and others in the Antediluvian world, must have been lost. But, by these means, they are preserved, and Noah serves as a depository, not only of the Divine revelations, but also of the knowledge and learning of the old world.

His family thus preserved, in so miraculous a manner, while the rest of mankind were swept off, could not fail to inform the world, as soon as it was peopled again,—of the signal interpositions of God to mankind before the flood, and the awful tokens of his displeasure to the Antediluvians for their disregard of them.

---

* It evidently appears, Gen. v. 5. that Adam did not die till the year of the world 930. From Gen. v. 22, it will appear, by a calculation formed upon the account given of the preceding generations, that Methuselah was born in the 687th year of Adam's life, and consequently was his cotemporary for 243 years. And as, upon the same principles of calculation, it must appear that Noah was born A. M. 1056, and that Methuselah did not die till A. M. 1656, he must have been cotemporary with Noah no less than 600 years.

them. For this purpofe they were the beft qualified, not only by their acquaintance with the hiftory and fate of the old world, but alfo by the communication of the new revelations made to them, in confequence of the remarkable alteration of circumftances which had been fuperinduced by the flood.

One would have thought that the account of the awful deftruction of the Old World and the caufe of it, which Noah would not fail to make the New acquainted with, would have fecured them againft a deviation from the prefcriptions of God in matters of religion, left they fhould be involved in a fimilar ruin. But we find, from the hiftory of thofe early times, that it was not long (not above 400 years), when, in place of the worfhip of the only true God, they gave into the worfhip of all the hoft of heaven. A temporary check was given to the prevalence of this fin, by the difperfion at the tower of Babel. But it foon gathered ftrength again.

§ 3. AND then it was, that Abraham was pitched upon, as the moft proper perfon for checking its progrefs, and laying the foundations of a church in his family, that might preferve the religion of the true God,—fpread the knowledge of it through the world, and—fo gradually prepare it for the reception of the religion of Jefus, to which, when it had anfwered the ends of its inftitution, it was to give place, as the laft mode or form which it was to affume.—And various, but all of them

indeed

indeed moſt wiſe, were the ways which God took to render this ſcheme ſubſervient to theſe ends.

We are apt, at firſt, to imagine that there was a rigour and ſeverity countenanced by this religion, that ſeemed inconſiſtent with an extenſive communication of it, or its doctrines.—True. There was no ſmall degree of rigour required by it:—Such a degree as admitted but little ſocial or commercial intercourſe with neighbouring nations,—no alliances with them by way of marriage, nor—any intercommunity of worſhip. But, though the ſtatutes which reſpected theſe, muſt be allowed to have, in appearance, an unfavourable aſpect upon the ſpread of their religion, let it be obſerved, that, while they ſeemed indiſpenſably neceſſary to prevent all infection from the corruption of their neighbours, they had not, ſo much as might be at firſt imagined, the effects of keeping other nations ignorant of their religion. Nay, I am not ſure, but they became the early and principal means of making them better acquainted with it, as they would naturally make them inquire into the genius, character, manners and religion of a people, who affected a ſuperiority over all their neighbours, and would ſcarce deign to treat them with that civility, to which their common nature intitled them.

But, if the circumſtance of their ſequeſtration was any bar to the diffuſion of the knowledge and influence of their religion, any inconvenience that could ariſe from this, was ſufficiently

sufficiently guarded against by the means, which seemed more immediately intended to promote both.

We have already shown that the duration of this institution of religion was never intended to be more than temporary; and hinted that it was, at last, to give place to one, that would be universal in its conquests, and lasting in its obligations. And now, to trace the methods by which this, so desirable an end, was to be effected, may be an employment, at once highly agreeable and useful.

At present I shall only observe (because I may have occasion to illustrate this remark afterwards) that this was an event, that could not, all at once, be accomplished. The attachment of mankind to any scheme of religion of which they have been fond, is too strong to be immediately dissolved. For, though, by means of an external force imposed upon them, their profession might be altered, their faith would probably still remain the same. Any change in this must be the consequence, not of compulsion, but of persuasion and conviction. And were not the methods which God made use of, the most proper for bringing these about?

What *all* the reasons were which induced God to the choice of Abraham, as the Founder of this new and visible church, it would be presumption in us positively to determine, since he has not seen meet to inform us. But, if I might venture a conjecture, I would beg
leave

leave to take notice of some, that seem abundantly to justify it.

If, as some allege, Abraham was expelled his own country, for his aversion to that gross idolatry which prevailed in it *, who may not discern the propriety of the choice of such a person, not only as the reward of his distinguished piety and unshaken steadiness in the religion of the true God, but also as the most effectual check to the growing evil for which he suffered so much?

Besides, let me observe that Abraham was a very proper person on another account. He seems to have been, not only of a distinguished rank in his own country, but also of a character well known in others †. And therefore these circumstances could not fail to make his religious sentiments be inquired into, especially as they differed so widely from those which seem to have almost universally prevailed.

From the whole of his character, he evidently appears to have been a person of the most

---

* Look back to the note p. 71. on this subject.

† Josephus informs us (Antiq. Lib. I. cap. 8, 9.) that, by the favour of Pharoah, Abraham had frequent opportunities of conversing with the Priests of that country;—that he was in high reputation among them for learning; and that he took that opportunity of setting them right, as to many of their rites, ceremonies, and opinions in religion.

Dr Shuckford informs us, (Vol. I. p. 308. of his Connection, &c.) that Persia and India were full of the fame of Abraham. See also a good deal collected, as to the fame of Abraham for learning, by Gale, in his Court of the Gentiles. Vol. II. p. 9, 10, 11.

most eminent piety, and as such would, no doubt, be zealous in diffusing the knowledge of the true God and his religion. The frequent intercourse with God, with which he was honoured,—the covenant entered into with him,—the distinguished promises made in it to him and his family, and—the prospect of the most extensive advantages from it, to the rest of mankind,—all these would, with united influence, operate in the most powerful manner upon him, and give life and spirit to his endeavours in behalf of religion.

§. 4. When his family had become numerous, some events happened, that not only determined their descent into Egypt, but their residence in it, for a long course of years,— no less than 215*. This was no accidental occur-

---

* It must be owned that there is, in appearance, some difficulty in reconciling the different accounts we have of the residence and distress of Israel, in a strange land. The first account we have is Gen. xv. 13. which runs thus:—" Know " that thy seed shall be a stranger in a land that is not theirs, " and shall serve them, and they shall afflict them 400 years." The next account we have of them is to this purpose, Exod. xii. 40, 41. " Now the sojourning of the children of Israel, " who dwelt in Egypt, was 430 years: And it came to pass, " at the end of the 430 years, even the self same day it came " to pass, that all the hosts of the Lord went out from the " land of Egypt."

From these accounts there arise two difficulties to be cleared up;—the one, respecting the duration of the residence: the other, the duration of the distress of Israel, in a strange land.

With respect to the first, there is an alleged contradiction charged upon the sacred record, the term of their residence being represented in the one place, as consisting of 400, and

in

occurrence in the history of this people. It was expressly foretold, and seems to have been connected with the great design of Providence, now under consideration. And it is easy to see how it became subservient to it. No

in the other of 430 years. But this difficulty appears formidable only at a distance. When narrowly examined, it immediately vanishes. For, let us attend to the æras of the commencement of these periods, and we shall find them very different; and from an attention to this single circumstance, these two accounts may be easily reconciled.

The account in Exodus seems to begin the computation of the 430 years, from the covenant made with Abraham (see Galat. iii. 17.), which, as appears from Gen. xii. 4. was when he was 75 years of age; from which to the giving of the law was 430. This account is confirmed by the Samaritan copy of this text, which runs thus—" Now the inhabi-
" ting of the children of Israel and *their fathers*, whereby they
" inhabited in the land of Canaan and in the land of Egypt,
" was 430 years." From this account two things are evident. The one is,—that what is here said, is not confined to the children of Israel, but extends to their fathers also, and so seems to lead back our view to the period from which we have begun the computation. The other is,—that it does not restrict their residence in a strange land (as some have imagined) to Egypt, but takes in the time of their first settlement in Canaan. Now, if these observations are but attended to, the residence in Egypt will be found, from the following calculation, to be no more than 215 years, as in the above account. Thus,

	Years.
From the covenant entered into with Abraham at the age of 75 years, to the birth of Isaac, when Abraham was 100 years old, Gen. xxi. 5.	25
From the birth of Isaac to that of Jacob. See Gen. xxv. 26.	60
From that to the descent into Egypt. See Gen. xlvii. 9.	130
	215

Deduct

No doubt, Abraham would be at all pains to inſtruct his ſon Iſaac, who was the darling of his ſoul and the hope of his family, as well as the church of God, in the knowledge of religion, and, at the ſame time, to guard him
                               againſt

Deduct this from the 430 years, the term of their reſidence in a ſtrange land (for to this it ſeems to be preciſely fixed by the account in Exod xii. 40, 41. and Galat. iii. 17.) and there remains 215 years for their reſidence in Egypt.

The other account which we have,—that in Gen. xv. 13. *ſeems* to limit the term of their reſidence in a ſtrange land to 400 years. It is true, it does ſo. But in this, there is nothing repugnant to the former account, if we will only conſider that the ſacred Hiſtorian reckons in this, from a different æra, even from the birth of Iſaac. What makes this probable is,—that what he here ſpeaks of, is made to have a particular reference to the *ſeed of Abraham*, that is, to his deſcendants by his ſon *Iſaac*. Now let it be conſidered,
                                                            Years.
That from the birth of Iſaac to that of Jacob was } 60
  (Gen. xxv. 26.)   }
From the birth of Jacob to his deſcent into Egypt,   130
                                                    ―――
                                                    190

This added to the 215 years, the time of their reſidence in Egypt (as appears from the preceding calculation) makes 405. And as we know that the ſacred Hiſtorians often omit the mention of broken numbers in their computation of time, the difference of 25 years will not affect the account.

The other difficulty,—that concerning the diſtreſs of Iſrael in a ſtrange land, ariſes from the words in Gen. xv. 13. From the want of a proper attention to them, ſome have extended their diſtreſs to 400 years. From the manner in which the account is given in our tranſlation, a curſory reading might ſuggeſt this idea; but a little attention is all that is neceſſary to correct it.

We are expreſsly told, upon the authority of an Apoſtle (Galat. iii. 17.) that, from the time of the covenant entered into with Abraham, to the giving of the law, was but 430
                                                            years.

againſt thoſe corruptions which ſo much prevailed in the nations around him. And it can be as little doubted that Iſaac would be at equal pains to inſtruct his children, and they theirs; ſo that, upon their deſcent into Egypt, they would carry their religion along with them. Their attachment to it appears in their application to the then reigning Prince, who was favourable to them, for a place in which they might worſhip God, according to their own mode, as their religion did not allow them to join in that of the Egyptians.

Oppoſite as *their* ſyſtem of religion and that of the Egyptians were to one another, it is not improbable, that, from the mutual intercourſe they muſt neceſſarily have had, they would become acquainted with the nature, doctrines, and rites of each other's religion. And as the Iſraelites ſeem to have contracted a taint from the religion of the Egyptians, it is equally probable that they, on the other hand,

years. Now of theſe, 215 were ſpent before the deſcent into Egypt, and, at leaſt, 80 years more under the auſpicious adminiſtration of Joſeph. For we find (Gen. xli. 46.) that he came into favour with Pharoah at the age of 30, and (Gen. l. 26.) that he died not till the age of 110. So that, ſuppoſing their ſervitude to have commenced immediately upon the death of Joſeph (which is ſcarcely to be imagined) it could have laſted no more than 135 at moſt.

But the truth is—there is nothing in the words that ſeem to fix the term of Iſrael's ſervitude, but only their reſidence in a ſtrange land. And if (as ſome have ſuggeſted) the words of Gen. xv. 13. are read as follows—" Know that thy ſeed " ſhall be a ſtranger in a land that is not theirs (and ſhall " ſerve them, and they ſhall afflict them) 400 years," the difficulty vaniſhes all at once.

hand, may have borrowed something from that of the Israelites. And to this they might be more easily induced from the influence which Joseph had acquired among them. For, during his administration (which, as I observed before, lasted 80 years) he had many happy opportunities of making the Egyptians acquainted with the religion of the true God; and we may well believe his zeal for it would prompt him, as far as prudence could allow, to make the proper use of them.

In this country, Israel continued, as had been taken notice of above, no less than 215 years. And though, soon after the death of Joseph, they seem to have been reduced to a miserable servitude, yet, all this time, they were preserved, by the good Providence of God, a distinct people, nowise incorporated with the Egyptians, that, after sowing the seeds of the true religion in this country, they might become the instruments of conveying the knowledge of it to others.

§ 5. ABOUT the 215th year of their residence in Egypt, an event happened which became admirably subservient to this end. Grievously oppressed by the King of Egypt, God heard the cries they put up to him; pitied their distress; and sent Moses, one of their countrymen, who had left them a considerable time before, and taken up his residence in Midian, to rescue them from it.

This was an event that gave birth to a series of the most extraordinary and stupenduous

ous miracles:—Such as seemed to call the attention not only of Egypt, but of all the countries about, which should hear of them.

Egypt was, even as early as this, become the seat of learning,—of the arts and sciences; and particularly was famed, all the world over, for its knowledge in Theology,—in so much that most other nations seem to have borrowed a great deal of their religious rites from them. What, therefore, could be a more proper scene for these miracles? What a fitter theatre upon which the God of Israel might display his superiority over all those others, who were called, and honoured by the Egyptians, as gods?

The fame the Egyptians had acquired in theological, as well as other, knowledge, had, no doubt, brought many to visit their country. They had been accustomed to return with a very high opinion of it. To keep up this opinion, it is not improbable that the Egyptians might pretend, that their gods had a pre-eminence above the gods of other countries. They evidently did so in the competition with the God of Israel, Exod. v. 2. "Who is the Lord that I should obey his "voice to let Israel go? I know not the "the Lord, neither will I let Israel go."—In this proud and haughty answer of Pharoah, the God of Israel received, as it were, a challenge to show, before the Heathen, that he was God, and that, besides him, there was properly none else. And this was the conclusion, to which the competition betwixt Moses

and

and the Egyptian magicians did naturally lead. Nay, this was the very inference which impartial reason prompted Jethro to make, when he had received from Moses an account of the great things God had done for Israel. " Now I know (says he) that the Lord is " greater than *all* gods, for, in the thing " wherein they dealt proudly, he was above " above them." Exod. xviii. 4. Now, let any one reflect upon the whole of this extraordinary scene, and must he not see the tendency it had to spread the knowledge of the true God?

Pharaoh himself, though he had a heart too proud and obstinate to acknowlege, seems to have been convinced of, the superiority of the God of Israel. Such miracles,—so extraordinary in themselves, and appealed to in a case so extraordinary, could not fail to make a deep impression upon the hearts of all who witnessed or heard of them, in that country;—nay, and to make a great noise in all the countries around. For, it is not improbable but an account of them would be carried to countries the most distant, by strangers who had come to this to be improved by the learning of it. And would not all this contribute to diffuse the knowledge of the God of Israel and his religion?

The miraculous interposition in favour of Israel, and of that religion of which they were the votaries, did not end with their deliverance from Egyptian bondage. It was continued in a manner admirably calculated to
spread

spread the knowledge of it, wider and wider.

Pharoah had been obliged to confess the superiority of the God of Israel, to the gods of Egypt, by consenting to the dismission of a people, for whom he had so signally appeared. But, deeply affected with the loss he had sustained;—or, perhaps desirous to recover his honour, which he might imagine affronted by the manner in which he was obliged to yield, he musters up an army that might have been formidable to any but Israel, and, with all expedition, he pursues them, in hopes of gaining an advantage over them, from the difficulties in which he foresaw they must necessarily be entangled. He overtakes them at the borders of the Red-sea. And, in that very place, where he thought their overthrow was inevitable, he himself receives one, equally dismal as it was unexpected. And was not the manner of it such, as could not fail to spread the report of it far and wide, and raise the character of the God of Israel, among all who should hear of it?

Relieved from the fears of so powerful an enemy, do the Israelites immediately march to take possession of the country promised to their Ancestors?—No. They are kept traversing the vast and rueful desart that lay in the way to it, for no less than 40 years. For this, their so long stay in the wilderness, some reasons have already been assigned, Part I. Ch. ii. § 3. But, though these might be sufficient to vindicate it from any imputation of impropriety, allow me to observe, that another very
wise

wife and good end was answered by it,—that the notice which must necessarily be taken of this extraordinary event, could not fail to make the neighbouring nations acquainted with the character of the true God, and the history of this people, whom he had taken under his special patronage and protection.

§ 6. The long interval of time betwixt their settlement in Canaan, and the ceasing of prophecy at the death of Malachi, was filled up with a variety of remarkable events, all of them conducive to the spreading of their religious tenets, or, at least, the knowledge of them.

When, in the course of the Divine providence, they are at last brought to the country destined for them, the manner in which they are ushered into it, and obtained the peaceable possession of it, was such as could not miss to be taken notice of, by all around it. And what else was the tendency of this, but to diffuse the knowledge of that God, who appeared so remarkably superior to any they were acquainted with?

After the establishment, and during the continuance, of the theocracy among them, almost every remarkable transaction that concerned them, had either an immediate, or remote, tendency this way. Thus, every change in the administration of their affairs,—every war in which they were engaged,—every defeat they received,—every victory they obtained,—their prosperity in their own country,

try, or their captivity among strangers,—their settlement at home, or—their dispersions abroad,—all contributed, though in different ways, to publish the knowledge of their religion, together with the knowledge of their national character.

The succession of Prophets raised up among them,—the countries to which they were sent, and—the commissions with which they were charged, had also the same tendency. This the judicious reader will readily admit.

§ 7. About 500 years before Christ, died *Malachi*, the last of the Jewish Prophets. To account for the length of the interval, betwixt the ceasing of prophecy and the appearance of the Messiah, in a manner satisfactory to all, may perhaps be no easy matter. And yet I humbly imagine, reasons may be assigned sufficient to vindicate this part of the Divine administration,—to show that God was not unconcerned about the interests of religion, during this period;—nay, that it was filled up with events that served admirably to prepare the world for the reception of the Messiah, and that religion which he was to publish.

Upon comparing the history of religion before the commencement, and after the close, of this period, some, without allowing themselves to think seriously, are apt to arraign the Divine conduct, or, at least, to think that this intermediate period might have been filled up in a manner more useful to the interests of religion

religion than it was. But it ought to be remembered, that, in every case, where the Divine conduct falls under our consideration, the greatest modesty becomes us in judging of it; and that, though the wisdom of it may not be always apparent, we ought never to suspect the want of it.

As God has not seen meet to inform us of the reasons of this part of his administration, we must, in all our inquiries after them, satisfy ourselves with the most probable conjectures. And, from the history of the Divine providence, we may be enabled to form some of no inconsiderable weight.

Those who plead for precipitating the full discovery of the Divine will to mankind, scruple not to call this interval too long. But I hope it will appear in the sequel, that it could not well have been shorter, whether we consider the reasons of it, with respect to the Jews in particular, or the world in general.

The revelations made to the Jews, had they been duly attended to, were sufficient for the direction of their religious conduct. But they had, from the frequency and long continuance of them, become, in some measure, cheap among them:—So cheap, that it is certain, they did not pay the proper regard to them. And what could be better calculated to recover their influence, than the manner in which the Jews were punished for the neglect of them?

During the continuance of prophecy among them, they were, for aught appears to the contrary,

contrary, happily united in their syftem of religious truth. Scarce any difference of fentiment could arife, but might be eafily determined by an appeal to fome Prophet, whofe authority they all agreed in acknowledging. When they had no longer any Prophet among them, to determine points of controverfy, fome pragmatic religionift had the vanity to fet up for the head of a new fect. Another, either difliking his principles, or influenced by fimilar vanity, feparates upon a different plan of faith and conduct. And each had influence enough to draw after them many followers. During this period, and upon fuch principles as thefe, it was that the *Sadducees, Pharifees, Effenes, Herodians, and Zealots*, fprung up in the Jewifh church.

It does not fall within my defign to inquire into the different tenets, or creeds, profeffed by them. I take notice of the exiftence of thefe fects, only to fhow the unhappy confequences of the ceafing of a fpirit of prophecy from among them, and confequently the reafon they had from thence to wifh for the return of it.

The Jews had, from the nature of their religion and the privileges conferred by it, become, even to a degree of fuperftition, fond of it :—So fond of it, that the moft diftant hint of its intended abolition, fometimes fired them with a rage againft thofe who dared to give it. Confidering, therefore, their genius, circumftances, and prejudices, it became neceffary, in a gradual manner, to reconcile

concile them to the exchange of it for the Christian, to which it was, in due time, to give place. And had not many things, which occurred in this period, such a tendency? What think you of the withdrawing of some of the tokens of God's favourable presence, with which they had been formerly honoured? What think you of the prostitution of the most sacred offices of Priest and High Priest, to the purposes of avarice and ambition,—these, in place of descending as they ought to have done, according to the Divine appointment, being disposed of, by the arts of policy and intrigue, to such of the family of Aaron, as were the favourites or minions of those in power? Were not these, and many other things that might be here taken notice of, so many hints to them, that the duration of that œconomy, of which they were so fond, was verging to a close;—that it had a farther view than to them; and—was only a kind of sacred apparatus for one still more grand, that was, in due time, to open to the world? In all this, is not the wisdom of the Divine providence very conspicuous? The better the conduct of it is understood, must it not be the more admired?— This much may suffice in vindication of the Divine conduct towards the Jews, in the delay of the Messiah's appearance.

But, let us take a larger view of it, and there will appear the greatest propriety in it, with respect to the Gentiles also.

It has been already shown, the the design of the separation of the Jews, was not confined

fined to themselves.—It was intended ultimately to extend its beneficial effects to the rest of mankind, and, by spreading the knowledge of the true God and his religion, gradually to prepare them for the reception of the most perfect discoveries of it, under the Christian dispensation. Now let this be but attended to, and you will easily see, that the so much wished-for event of the Son of God's appearance in the world, could not, with propriety, have taken place sooner.

It is highly proper, that any scheme of religion that lays claim to a Divine origin, and as such challenges the regard of mankind, should have evidence sufficient to support it. It can be only on this foot, that they are bound to receive it. If, in any case, we can suppose a stronger degree of evidence to be necessary than in another, the case of the Christian religion is that which requires it. It is intended to be of universal obligation; and therefore it is highly proper that the nature of its evidence should be so various and diversified, that none, to whom it is offered, might have just cause to pretend the least defect in it, as an excuse for rejecting it. To render the evidence such, it was, if not absolutely necessary, at least highly proper, that its publication to the world should be so long delayed. From thence there arises a very strong and accumulated evidence, which it would otherwise have wanted,—all the evidence that arises from the accomplishment of ancient prophecy.

No doubt there is evidence of another kind, which this religion has to plead in support of its claim to the faith of mankind: An evidence too, which, supposing that from prophecy to be wanting, would be sufficient to produce conviction in every unprejudiced mind. But still it must be owned, that the evidence which arises from this source, is no small accession to the degree of it, and—an evidence it is of that species (as shall be shown afterwards) that is particularly satisfying.

Sufficient as the above reasons may be, to account for the long interval betwixt the ceasing of prophecy and the publication of the Christian religion, there are not wanting others that might be mentioned.

The world laboured under disadvantages, some of a political,—others, of a moral, nature, that rendered the more early publication of it improper. It is well known, that, not only in the first, but through many succeeding, ages, the world was divided into many petty, independent, states, and that betwixt those there was little intercourse, but almost perpetual feuds and animosities. Those early ages were not more distinguished for the ferocity of their manners, than for their ignorance of true religion, and a blind, superstitious, and bigotted attachment to that which was false, under a variety of forms. In such a state of things, no words are necessary to show that the publication of a religion, which was intended to be of universal obligation, would have met with but a sorry reception.

T *The*

The world, it is evident, ought to be prepared for such an offer, before it should be made to it. It was only by degrees, that it could be thus prepared. And it is not unpleasant to consider, how, during this period, a variety of events obtained, which all contributed to this desirable end.

During this period it was, that first the Grecian and then the Roman empires started up; and who that knows the least of them, can be ignorant of that extension of knowledge, that was the happy consequence of the erection of both, and of some lucky events that fell out under them?

Alexander the Great, having, in the course of his conquests, subdued Egypt, built a city there, which he honoured with his own name *,—sent many of the Jews from their own country to it; and, to encourage their settling in it, he, besides many other advantages bestowed on them, continued the free use of their own laws and religion with them.

Soon after, *Ptolemy Soter* brought many more, and settled them in Egypt and the adjacent countries. The Kings of Egypt, finding Alexandria, from its situation and other circumstances, like to become a place of great importance, were willing to aggrandize it as much as they could. For this purpose, they thought it would be proper to make it a seat of learning, as well as a mart for trade and commerce.

---

* Alexandria was built about *A. ante Chrift.* 332.

commerce. And accordingly *Ptolemy Philadelphus* laid the foundation of a Museum or Library, which afterwards became famous, all the world over, for the number and value of its books. Such an institution as this could not be supposed long to want a copy of that book, which contained an account of the Jewish religion. A faithful copy of it was applied for, and obtained from the Jewish High-Priest. And that it might be the better understood, not only by the inhabitants of the country into which it was brought, but also by the Jews themselves, who now, like the other inhabitants, spoke the Greek, it was translated into that language: And, from the number supposed to be engaged in the translation of it, it obtained the name of the *Septuagint*, which it has ever since gone under. This circumstance, though seemingly of little importance, became of the greatest service, in making many acquainted with this religion, who would have otherwise remained strangers to it.

While the transactions of ancient times, or the discoveries of science, continued to be written upon tables of wood, or dressed skins called *Parchment*, it is evident that the communication of knowledge must have been both very difficult and very expensive*.

About

---

* We may judge of the expence of writing on parchment before this period, from what we are informed concerning it, at a much later one, when an improvement in the art of making it, had, no doubt, greatly reduced the price of it. From the

About the time that Alexandria was built, it deserves to be remarked, that the Egyptian *Papyrus* began to be used for writing. And by this means many copies of the sacred books could be procured at an easy rate.

What we have already taken notice of, are not all the remarkable occurrences of this period, which shewed God's gracious regard to the time of the discovery of the papyrus, till the Saracens conquered Egypt in the 7th century, it was generally used for writing on. But then, all communication between that country and the different parts of Europe being taken off, the papyrus was no longer in use among them, and they were obliged to betake themselves again to the parchment. And, as late as the 8th, 9th, and following centuries, we are informed that so dear was the parchment, for want of other materials for writing on, that, to make way for a performance that was judged valuable, they were wont to erase some other that was less esteemed From this circumstance, the reader will easily conclude that the number of books then written, could not be great. Nay, so small was it, that private persons seldom possessed any whatever. And the price of the few that were, was so high, that persons of a moderate fortune could not afford to purchase them. Let the price at which books then sold, be judged of by that which was paid by the Countess of Anjou, for a copy of the Homilies of Haimon, Bishop of Halbustadt, viz. 200 sheep, five quarters of wheat, and the same quantity of rye and millet. See more to this purpose in Dr Robertson's Hist. of the Emperor, Chap. V. note 10. Vol. I.

From the above account, we may form a judgment of the low state to which learning must have been reduced at this late period, for want of the papyrus, or some other cheap material for writing on; and, by consequence, what advantage must have been derived to learning, and the easy communication of knowledge in a more early period, from the discovery of the papyrus, whose leaves, according to some,—or the scaly coats or pellicles of the stem, according to others, supplied, at an easy rate, the place of parchment. From this plant, the substance on which we now write, is called *Paper*.

to it, and contributed to usher in the gospel-revelation with the greater advantage.

During this interval, when otherwise the world would have been without public teachers, did not God raise up a succession of eminent philosophers? And if these did not all the service that might have been wished for, on account of the many disadvantages they laboured under, did they not serve to check the rapid progress of vice, and, by the light they diffused, faint and glimmering as it was, to point out to mankind the dangers they ought to shun, and, in some measure, the path in which they ought to walk? Nay, was not that spirit of inquiry and investigation which they encouraged, of great use to qualify mankind for judging of the nature, evidence, and importance of Christianity, when it did appear*.

Towards the close of this period, the power of Rome was raised to a degree of greatness, unequalled by any that was ever heard of, either before or since that time. The Assyrian, Grecian, and Persian empires became absorbed in the Roman. And if the Romans had not then accomplished the conquest of the world, they had greatly enlarged the boundaries of their dominions. Over the East, where the Christian religion first made its appearance, their sway was universal. Their conquests greatly facilitated those of Christianity.

Many

* See the Comaprative View of the several methods of promoting religious instruction, &c. Vol. I. p. 123.

Many were the advantages it derived from them, which it muſt have wanted, had it appeared more early. By the ſucceſs of their victorious arms, an univerſal peace was diffuſed over the world,—an eaſy acceſs to the moſt diſtant parts of the empire was opened,—a connection of intereſts among neighbouring nations was eſtabliſhed,—a frequent intercourſe and commerce carried on,—the knowledge of different languages was acquired,—learning came to be encouraged and cultivated, and—leiſure was afforded for an attention to religion. Add to theſe, that, at this time, there prevailed an univerſal expectation over the Eaſt, that ſome illuſtrious Perſonage was to be born among the Jews;—that the Jews concluded the time was at hand, when their long-expected Meſſiah ſhould appear; and—that the reſt of the world waited, with anxious hope, for this great event: Let theſe things, I ſay, be conſidered, and I dare appeal to the candid reader, if this does not appear to have been the ſeaſon moſt fit for the publication of the Chriſtian religion, and therefore if it was not, with the greateſt propriety, reſerved to it *.

Had the religion of Jeſus been offered to the

---

* See a good deal on this ſubject in Dr Robertſon's Sermon, before the Society for Propagating Chriſtian Knowledge, and in Gibbon's Hiſtory of the Decline of the Roman Empire, Chap. xv. and xvi. Vol. I. In the firſt of theſe, many things, truly excellent, occur.—What a pity that in the laſt, there ſhould, under the appearance of a regard for Chriſtianity, be ſo much oblique and ſly inſinuation againſt it.

the world sooner, it must have failed of the success it had, little as it was, because, before this time, the world was comparatively but little prepared for it.

Besides, had it made its appearance more early, its enemies would not have failed to tell us, long ere this time, that it chose to make its appearance in some age of ignorance, to avoid the danger of a detection.

Aware of this, and conscious of the integrity of his own intentions,—the salutary nature of his doctrines, and—the strength of the evidence that supported them, the Founder of our religion delays the offer of it to the world, till, become highly improved by all the preceding dispensations, they were fully qualified to examine this. From such a manner of conduct, there arises not only the strongest proof of fairness upon his part, but also a strong presumption in favour of his religion:—a presumption, that, the more narrowly it were canvassed, the more thoroughly it would be believed, and—that, in the same proportion, the excellence of it would appear to the greatest possible advantage.

Thus we have carried down our observations, on both sacred and profane history, from the earliest times till that of our Saviour's appearance in the world; and I hope that, from the above deduction of facts, the tendency of them to spread the knowledge of the more early dispensations, and to prepare the way for the Christian, which should be the completion

completion of them all, is abundantly apparent *.

Nay, this not only appears to be their uniform tendency, but the very effect they have produced. For, from the moſt authentic vouchers, we well know, that the great empires of the Aſſyrians, Medes, and Perſians, were early acquainted with the Jews. And the Evangeliſt Luke informs (Acts ii. 5—12.) that, at Pentecoſt (that particular time when the Apoſtles were filled with the Holy Ghoſt), there were dwelling in Jeruſalem, devout men of every nation under heaven, Parthians, Medes, &c. Thus " the fall of the Jews be-
" came the riches of the world, and the di-
" miniſhing of them, the riches of the Gen-
" tiles †."

And as we find, that this was both the tendency and effect of the ſucceſſion of events we have taken notice of, are we not alſo naturally led to conclude that it was one great deſign of them? For, how can we behold ſuch a ſeries of events, and through ſuch a ſucceſſion of ages, all converging, like the radii of a circle, to one common centre, and yet imagine them unconnected with one another, or foreign to the great deſign they have conſpired to promote? This would require a degree

---

* See Dr Law's Conſiderations on the Theory of Religion, and Dr Taylor's Scheme of Scripture-Divinity; to which I own myſelf indebted for ſeveral of the hints in this ſection.

† Rom. xi. 12.

gree of credulity incomparably greater than even Christians are accused of.

It is true, any of these events taken separately, will not authorise the conclusion we have drawn. But this, surely, is no reason, why, accumulated, they should not. During the progression of this great design towards its accomplishment, it was not necessary that the tendency of every part should be discerned. It is enough, that it appears when (if I may use the expression) the drama is concluded. And I humbly imagine that, in the case under consideration, it is abundantly discernible.

An œconomy similar to what obtains in the natural and intellectual, we may observe in the moral, world. The ends of Providence are not to be precipitated in either. There are several stages of progression in them all. Any other course would have been unsuited to the nature of man and of his present state; and, in place of arguing superior perfection, would have been an evidence of the contrary.

The subject we have been contemplating in this section, is equally grand, pleasant, and interesting. Let us pause a little, and take a review of it. And may we not compare the several dispensations of God's grace to mankind to a piece of exquisite painting, sketched out by the most masterly hand, the several parts of which were not, all at once, but gradually, filled up,—the perfection of it requiring the greatest length of time to finish it, and to give it that colouring, lustre, and expression, which

was

was originally intended? The comparifon, fo far as it is carried, may be juft: But, it muft, at the fame time, be owned, that any idea it can convey of the gradual progrefs, and final perfection, of the Divine adminiftration in the glorious undertaking of man's redemption, is very defective. We fee enough to make us admire the greatnefs of the defign, and approve the propriety of the means ufed in the execution of it; but our faculties muft be greatly improved and enlarged, before we can comprehend the height and depth and breadth and length of that wifdom, goodnefs, and power, which run through the whole of this vaft, grand, and complicated fcheme.

PART

PART III.

That the GOSPEL *is the* LAST DISPENSATION *of* GOD's *grace to Mankind, in the way of Religious Discovery.*

WHAT I mean by this proposition is,— that the gospel is the most perfect dispensation we have reason to look for, and, therefore, the last. This is a doctrine that requires no laboured discussion. It admits of an easy and concise proof. All the dispensations of religion to mankind (except what may be called, if the phrase is allowed, the dispensation of natural religion) must be the subjects of pure revelation. From these alone it is, that we can derive our knowledge of their nature, succession, tendency, and respective completion. Taking therefore, for a moment, the sacred record as an authentic history of the Divine dispensations to mankind,

we

we can be in no doubt where to fix both their beginning and conclusion.

The firſt diſpenſation of God's grace to man, conſidered as a ſinner, was the benign interpoſition in his behalf, to ſuſpend the execution of the ſentence of death, to which he had ſubjected himſelf, and—to encourage his hopes of recovering that honour and happineſs from which he had fallen. For this purpoſe, God promiſes that the ſeed of the woman ſhould bruiſe the ſerpent's head. This firſt promiſe, it muſt be owned, was ſomewhat dark and obſcure. In the circumſtances in which it was given, it could not, with propriety, have been otherwiſe. It was, however, ſufficient, *even then*, to animate his ſervice in the hopes of the Divine mercy. And is ſufficient, now that it has met with its fulleſt diſplay, in the diſcovery of the riches of the Divine grace through Jeſus Chriſt, to juſtify the manner in which it was originally given.

For, if it is allowed that our Jeſus was the Meſſiah foretold and expected, there can remain no doubt, that by him the grand plan, which had been for ages gradually opening up, was to be cloſed. An attentive eye, in tracing the gradual progreſs of this amazing ſcheme, will be able to diſcern a plain reſpect to him in every part of it: And farther than him, it does not lead us.—Here the curtain is dropt, and the ſcene ſhut up.

Nay, leſt mankind might flatter themſelves with the hopes, that the grace of God, which,

in

in times paft, had made fuch abundant difcoveries, in almoft every age, would favour them with another, ftill more glorious than any of the former, we are exprefsly told, upon the authority of an Apoftle, that, could we fuppofe an Angel to come from heaven and preach another gofpel than this, we ought to reject it. And the reafon is plain, becaufe, this being intended to be the laft, we might be affured that any other would be an impofture. And indeed, if the nature of the Chriftian revelation is attentively confidered, it will evidently appear to be the laft difpenfation, becaufe it is impoffible to fay what is neceffary to the improvement of our nature in holinefs, or our preparation for happinefs, that is not herein clearly difcovered to us.

I know the facred records fpeak of a future period in the Chriftian church, truly glorious, that fhall continue, at leaft, a thoufand years. This is that period, which, from its duration, has been diftinguifhed by the name of, *the Millenium.*

Concerning the doctrine that refpects this ftate (and which, as it has been fince explained, was not known till the time of Papias, Bifhop of Hieropolis in Phrygia, who lived in the fecond century), there has been a great diverfity of opinions.

Some indulging their fancy, in the explication of certain figurative expreffions, in which this happy ftate of the church is defcribed, have maintained, that,—with thefe thoufand years, was to commence the temporal reign

reign of the Messiah upon earth;—that the highest pleasures of every kind, corporeal as well as spiritual, were to be enjoyed during its continuance; and—that, for this purpose, the saints and the martyrs, who had distinguished themselves, by their zeal and sufferings for religion, while on earth, were to return to it, and live again in it, while it lasted.

Others again, disgusted with the gross sense in which the passage * concerning this happy period has been interpreted, have expressed their hopes of it, with some degree of softening. While almost all who have written concerning it, have differed as to the time of its commencement. Some have maintained, that it was not to take place till after the general judgment: Others, not till after the conflagration: And some, like Dr Whiston, that it ought to have commenced some time ago.

My design does not lead me to inquire into, or attempt a confutation of, these extravagant opinions †. Let it suffice for the purpose, on account of which I have introduced the subject, to observe, that, from the passage referred to above, there is reason to expect a period of this duration, in which the church of God will enjoy great prosperity. In this period, our holy religion being allowed its full efficacy, and perhaps accompanied with the most powerful and benign influences of the Divine spirit, shall exalt it to as high a degree

of

---

* Rev. xx.   † See Dr Whitby's Treatise on the Millennium.

of perfection, and consequently of happiness, as the present state can admit. But, what though this should be allowed? This is no dispensation different from the present; but only the happy result and consequence of a sincere faith in the doctrines, and a submission to the precepts, of our holy religion:— A happy proof this, of what religion may, and will do, if not obstructed in its influence: And consequently a proof, that another dispensation is unnecessary, since this needs no more than to be allowed to operate, according to its spirit, to produce all the effects that could be wished for. And, if this is admitted, we surely have no reason to look for another dispensation of light and grace to succeed the present.

PART

PART IV.

Contains some general COROLLARIES, *from the subject of the preceding Treatise.*

HAVING finished the survey we proposed to take of the nature and constitution of the Jewish religion, he must have read it in a very cursory manner, who is not led by it into a train of useful reflections.

This subject, like an eminence in the midst of a wide and extensive plain, from which one may descry a beautiful landscape, diversified with grand and striking objects, opens a field of contemplation, at once the most pleasant, and the most instructive.

The reader will, I hope, indulge me a little longer, while I lay before him a few of the many hints, which this work, in the course of it, has suggested to me; and then I shall

shall leave him to pursue the subject in that tract, which shall to him appear the most proper: And I shall reckon myself happy, if I have advanced any thing, that may serve, either to direct his inquiries, or render them, in the progress, agreeable.

SECT. I.

That the preceding View of the Dispensations of the Divine Grace to Mankind, exhibits, to the devout and contemplative Mind, the richest Fund of moral Enterment and Improvement.

THAT the consideration of the Divine Providence, so far as it respects our important interests, both in this world and the next, may become at once the mean of our highest rational entertainment and moral improvement, it will be necessary that we study to form just conceptions of it; and, in order to this, that we view it in a true light. Without attending to the one, the other is not attainable:—The most beautiful object in nature, viewed through an improper medium, must be seen to great disadvantage, and, in some cases, may appear ugly and deformed.

In nothing, perhaps, has the justness of this observation appeared more striking to the attentive eye, than in the opinions which have been formed, and the decisions which have been given, upon the plan of the Divine administration

administration towards mankind, especially in their redemption.

Considering the several parts separately, some have too hastily concluded, and too unwarily represented, them to be so many different dispensations, unconnectd with, and independent on, one another. And others, taking the advantage of this account of the matter, have, with an impious pleasure, represented this scheme of the Divine grace, as an absurd and bungling one:—rude and undigested in its formation;—that needed to be mended in the course of its progress, acording to the occurrence of incidental circumstances; and—that required a series of ages to bring it to that degree of perfection which it has obtained. And what can have a stronger influence upon weak minds, than such a representation of the matter? Has it not a tendency to beget unfavourable sentiments of the Divine wisdom, and consequently to destroy all confidence in any of its schemes? And what else is this, but to lead to downright infidelity and irreligion? Such a mode either of conceiving or speaking of the Divine administration, is, it must be owned, very inaccurate. For, from the view we have given of the grand design of God in the redemption of mankind, I hope, it appears, that what are called so many dispensations, are, properly speaking, but so many branches of one. It is true, each had a separate end, which might be called the one immediately in view. But then, it must, at the same time, be owned, that all these were subordinate

ordinate to one noble purpose, and had this as their object.

This is the view which the preceding inquiry into the Divine administration, through the successive ages of the world, down to the Christian æra, naturally presents to us. And one it is, which, the more we consider, the more, I am persuaded, we will find it to be just.

No sooner had mankind sinned, than a hint of the Divine grace to be extended to them, was immediately given. And to unfold, illustrate, and diffuse the knowledge of this, and, by these means, promote their comfort and improvement, in the various stages of its progress, seems to have been the design of God, in the diversified manner of his conduct. Every opening into the design of God, while it had this tendency, was suited to that period of time at which it was made, and to the degrees of improvement in those whom it respected. For, it is easy to see from the above strictures, that a quicker method of procedure, would have defeated the very end proposed by it. The sublime discoveries made in later ages, had they been made much more early, would have met with the same reception, which the theological information given by one of Don Pizzaro's Priests to the Incas of Peru had,—that is, they would have been instantly rejected as absurd, because they would have been unintelligible. Let us then consider what is commonly called the different Dispensations of God to mankind, only as so many parts of one great whole,—all happily

pily harmonizing, and leading, by insensible, but sure, steps, to the accomplishment of a design worthy of himself and of such a vast apparatus. And what an exalted idea must it give us of the wisdom, power, and goodness of its great Author?

How deep, penetrating, and unsearchable, must have been that wisdom, that could, at the distance of thousands of years, have provided against all the obstructions that could be thrown in the way of the completion of his design?—Nay, that could so overrule these seeming obstacles, as to make them become the real means of advancing it*.—Thus, that very diversity, which some, from an imperfect view or conception of the subject, make the grand objection against the Divine wisdom, turns out, in the issue, to be a bright illustration of it.—Every part of it appears to be perfectly adapted, as was observed before, to the nature of man and the state of the world.

The power of God is no less conspicuous in the acomplishment, than his wisdom was in the contrivance, of this amazing plan.—Various (as appears from the history), and no less great than various, were the difficulties which occurred during the progress of it:—Difficulties arising from the passions, prejudices, ignorance, and vices of mankind,—from the pride of Philosophy, falsely so called,—the opposition of power, and—the intrigues of state: sometimes, from the one; sometimes, from

---

* See the note p. 196.—The instances there taken notice of, serve equally for the illustration of this remark, as of that for which they were adduced.

from the other; and often, from them all combined:—Difficulties which, to the greateſt human power, muſt have appeared inſurmountable, but were eaſily triumphed over by the Divine, and that in a manner which clearly evinces the power to be deſerving of this character. For when, in the ordinary courſe of things, his deſign might ſeem to be at a ſtand, who does not know that he often interpoſed, and, rather than permit this, ſuſpended, for a while, the very laws, by which he meant the world ſhould, at other times, be governed?

But are the wiſdom and power of God, the only perfections that are diſplayed in the contrivance, progreſs, and execution of this glorious plan?—No. It was goodneſs that ſet both to work, and was the firſt ſpring of this wonderful movement.—It could be no other than goodneſs and benignity of nature that prompted to ſuch a deſign; for, an increaſe of honour, intereſt, or happineſs to God, there could not be.

Neither is it in the firſt formation of the deſign only, that his goodneſs appears. It is diſtinguiſhed through all the ſucceeding periods of it.—For what but goodneſs, and that in a degree peculiar to himſelf, could have made God perſevere in carrying it on, notwithſtanding all the oppoſition given to him, even by thoſe who were the objects of it?—Such cauſeleſs diſobedience,—ſuch ſhameful ingratitude,—ſuch inſolent provocation, would have provoked any but a God, ſuch as he is, to to have given up the whole human race, and to have allowed them to remain in that misery, which they thus, as it were, pulled down upon themselves.—But his goodness triumphs over all these, and does not desist from its design, till it could be said, *It is finished.*— What an amiable character is here exhibited of the Deity?—A character, which, while it commands reverence, must inspire love, encourage hope, and sweetly incline to a dutiful homage and obedience:—a character of the Deity, which must determine the complexion of our religion, and make the services of it liberal, pleasant, and improving. Hence, therefore, we should be persuaded to study the most enlarged and extensive views of the plan of the Divine Grace, as we would either rightly understand the nature and design of it, or consult our own comfort and improvement by it.

A full discovery of it, in all its parts, and the manner in which each becomes subservient to the great design of it, modesty forbids us, at present, to aspire after. A dark cloud hangs upon a part of it. Many things in it lie beyond the reach of the most improved human sagacity to comprehend. Angels themselves, though their intellectual powers are far greater than ours, are incapable of this. They must be improved to a degree, far beyond what they are now possessed of, before they can reach it. But this, though a good reason for checking our pride of understanding, is no reason for checking the exercise

of

of it.—This, properly conducted, cannot fail to be the source of the richest pleasure, as well as the mean of our highest improvement.

SECT. II.

That the Jewish Religion is worthy of God for its Author, and was perfectly suited to the Purposes of its Institution,—the Genius of the People,—and the Circumstances of the Times, for which it was principally intended.

THE truth of the proposition contained in the title of this section, has, in some measure, been already evinced, in the preceding part of this treatise.—A farther illustration of it, however, may not be improper, as it will not only afford an additional confirmation of it, but lead us to elucidate some points of importance, connected with our primary design, which did not so naturally offer themselves to our consideration under any of the former divisions of our subject.

There can be nothing more apt to lead into error upon any subject, than either a partial or prejudiced view of it. This will ever prove a great obstruction to a successful investigation of the truth. And it seldom fails to make those who indulge in it, betray their ignorance, where they mean to display their knowledge. Some very striking instances of this we have had in the opinions that have been formed of the nature of the Mosaic institution of religion.

Taking but a cursory and superficial view of it, some, because they could not all at once discern the reasons of it, have attempted, rather than acknowledge their ignorance, to account for it in a way, which, could it be supposed to be just, would, instead of honouring, throw the greatest dishonour on that glorious Being whom they admit to be the author of it.

Thus, there have not been wanting who have roundly affirmed that it was an institution merely arbitrary; or, at least, intended with scarce any other view, than to display the power and authority of its Author, and keep in subjection a rough, stubborn, and uncultivated people, by the rigor with which he meant to treat them.

This is an hypothesis so evidently absurd, that I should affront the understanding of the reader, were I so much as to attempt a confutation of it. The ungainly appearance under which it presents the Deity, and the unfavourable sentiments of him which it is apt to beget in the mind, are enough to make it be rejected, as soon as it is mentioned.

That scheme is little better which would represent this mode of religion, not so much as the result of choice in the Deity, as of a force imposed upon him, for the reformation of his people, Israel. To this purpose does Lord Bolingbroke represent the matter. After observing that the first reformers of mankind,

having

having found them immersed in superstition and accustomed to licentiousness, were obliged to make their profit of the former, in order to cure them of the latter, he adds—" God, " therefore, was *forced* to indulge them in se- " veral superstitious prejudices."—And again, " To draw them off the more effectually from " some prejudices, he chose to indulge them " in others,—to indulge error, and suited his " institutions to the taste of the age*.

It is unnecessary to spend much time in a reply to these sentiments of the Noble Lord, if they could be his sentiments. They are far from being *noble;* and, before he published them to the world, he ought to have considered, that, while they were intended to throw a reproach upon the Deity, they really brought reproach upon himself for entertaining, or pretending to entertain, them. They contain an oblique compliment to the Deity for his philanthropy or regard to mankind, but it is paid at the expence of a very gross imputation upon his regard to truth and virtue:—and I may add, an imputation upon his wisdom and power also, as if he had been *forced* to yield to this necessity, for want of wisdom to devise a more proper scheme for this purpose, or power to carry it into execution.

Some, even of the zealous friends of revelation, and among the rest, the very learned Dr Spencer, have been of opinion, that the
Jewish

---

* See his Philosoph. Works, Vol. I. Essay ii. p. 312, 313. 8vo edit.

Jewish Religion was, in most points, formed upon the plan of the Egyptian:—That God's design in this new institution, was only to reform what was amiss in the other; and,—even in the parts that were altered, to preserve as great a similarity as possible, that so he might more easily draw Israel off from what was idolatrous in it, by making the difference betwixt them as small as possible. Whereas, say they, had he attempted such alterations, as might denominate it a religion formed upon quite a new plan, they would have been apt, all at once, to strike out against it.

I must confess that Dr Spencer, in particular, has said many things extremely plausible, in support of his favourite opinion; but I must be allowed to say, that they do not, after all, appear to me to be conclusive. He does, in a variety of instances, trace a very striking resemblance betwixt the rites of the Egyptian and those of the Jewish religion, and from thence he deduces this general conclusion,— That the first had given rise to many of the latter.

I will not take upon me to say, that there is no foundation, in any instance, for this conclusion. But I cannot help thinking, that he carries it too far. For the similarity which he observes betwixt them, will, by no means, authorise him to infer, that the rites of the Jewish, were taken from those of the Egyptian, religion. What if we should infer (would it not be as probable?) that the Egyptians have borrowed from the Mosaic institution, and not the Israelites from the Egyptian?

tian?—What makes this appear to be the truth, is—that it is highly probable that God would make a perfect discrimination betwixt them, as his great design in the selection of Israel and the erection of them into a peculiar church for himself, was, that, by their means, he might gradually restore the worship of the true God in the world, and banish idolatry from it. That God should gratify their taste for external pomp, so far as it could be done with propriety, is no more than, in their circumstances, might be reasonably expected, and seemed necessary to the success of their separation. But this is all that could be well expected:—A plan of symbolizing with it, would have been the way to strenghen their attachment to the old religion, by making them imagine that the difference betwixt them was very immaterial. Accordingly, it deserves to be remarked, that, in order to keep up their aversion to that idolatrous religion from which they were called, many rites and ceremonies were enjoined, the very reverse of what obtained in it. This remark might be illustrated from a view of the whole of their ritual, were it necessary. But it is not.

The resemblance betwixt the two religions, will, by no means (as has been hinted already) support the conclusion in favour of the greater antiquity of the Egyptian rites, or the derivation of the Jewish rites from these. Could it be made appear, that the rites and usages in the Egyptian religion, which are so like to the Jewish, did obtain long before them, I

confess

confefs it would fay a great deal for this hypothefis. But, as it is certain that all our accounts of them are long pofterior to the writings of Mofes, the probability rather is,—that the Egyptians having, from their vicinity to and intercourfe with the Jews, become acquainted with the leading features of their religion, had been pleafed with them, and, in fome inftances, copied them, though, from pride indifpofed to own this, they had blended them with fuperftitions of their own, that it might be more difficult to difcern wherein they were obliged to them.

Upon the whole, after all that has been advanced by Dr Spencer upon this head, I am ftill apt to imagine, that, however it might have been one part of the Divine purpofe to guard Ifrael againft a corruption from the Egyptian idolatry, by the inftitution of the Mofaic œconomy, this was not the principal defign of it. It feems to have been equally liberal, and far more extenfive: Not only to train up Ifrael by fuch a difcipline, in the knowledge, worfhip, and fervice of the true God, but alfo to make the ftatutes he gave them, the means of diffufing what deferved to be called *religion* among the heathen nations around. And of this Mofes gives a very ftrong hint, when he fays—" Behold, I
" have taught you ftatutes and judgments,
" even as the Lord my God commanded me,
" that ye fhould do fo in the land whither ye
" go to poffefs it. Keep therefore and do
" them; for this is your wifdom and your
" underftanding in the *fight of the nations*,
" which

"which shall hear all these statutes, and say,
"—Surely this great nation is a wise and un-
"derstanding people. For, what nation is
"there so great, who hath God so nigh unto
"them, as the Lord our God is in all things
"that we call upon him for? and what na-
"tion is there so great, that hath statutes and
"judgments so righteous, as all this law which
"I set before you this day*."

Those who have sat down to criticise this religion, have not only run into different sentiments concerning the primary design of its institution, but some of them have even gone so far as to arraign the tendency of it, and, in plain terms, to call it bad. This they have endeavoured to evince; some, by an attack upon the nature of its ritual; others, by animadversions upon the nature of its precepts.

With respect to the first, it has been represented as inconsistent, not only with the nature of true religion, but also of man who is the subject of it:—Inconsistent with the nature of the one, from the alleged tendency it has to turn off his attention from things important and interesting, to things of an acknowledged indifferent nature: Inconsistent with the other, from the tendency which it has, on account of its operose services, to employ mankind in such manner as to make them incapable of attending to the other offices of life.

This objection, which has often been urged
with

---

* Deut. iv. 5, 6, 7,

with great parade against all instituted religion in general, has been, in a particular manner, pointed against the Jewish. But it is only a superficial view, that can lead to the opinion contained in it; a thorough examination will immediately correct it.

It is readily granted that any religious service or worship, that is to be performed to, or accepted by, the Deity, must be spiritual. An opinion contrary to this, can only proceed from wrong notions of him. But this sentiment, if rightly understood, does, by no means, forbid the use of external rites, but a vain dependence upon them, in place of that sincere and inward devotion that ought to animate the use of them.

If we will allow God to be the only object of religious homage, must we not, at the same time, allow him a right to prescribe the manner of performing it, and, by consequence, a right to prescribe certain rites, if he shall so please? When I speak of any mode of service, as more acceptable to the Deity than another, I need scarce observe, that it cannot be on its own account.—No. These can be the sentiments only of the ignorant. The manner of worship is acceptable to God, in proportion to the devotion with which it is animated,—the tendency it has to promote the great ends of religion, and—its suitableness to the nature and situation of mankind. And who that considers these things, but must see the great use of certain rites?

In the nature of man, there is a strong bias
to

to something *sensible* in religion: and indeed, till the improvements made in the knowledge of it are become considerable, this seems, in some measure, necessary. The refinement of religion to a great degree of spirituality, would have been highly improper, at so early a period, and would have gone far to prevent the attainment of the end proposed by it.

That God might reach the great purposes of religion with his people, it was, in some measure, necessary, that he should condescend to their weakness, and, by the institution of certain rites, adapted to the sensitive part of their nature, not only recal the truths of religion to their remembrance, but give them a more powerful influence, by making a deeper impression, upon the heart.

Besides, if we will consider that the Mosaic ritual was instituted in a very early age,—if not before the knowledge of letters,—before the practice of writing was much in use, we must admit the propriety of it *then*, as almost the only permanent and safe manner of conveying knowledge, from one generation to another.

It ought to be remembered, that, at the same time religious rites were used for the preservation and communication of knowledge, they were also intended to express the devotion of those who joined in the use of them.

In the public services of religion (and of these only we speak at present), a social devotion is required. Is it not, therefore, proper, that

that it should be conducted with a becoming decorum and order? And yet, how could this be done without some instituted rites to be observed by the worshippers? Were there none such, how would they run into a thousand wild irregularities, each making his own fancy the rule of his conduct? Nay, so apparent is the propriety of some instituted rites, that no religion has ever been heard of that wanted them. Had not God made such an appointment, mankind would have done it themselves.

The Jewish ritual is not only justifiable upon the preceding considerations, but also from a regard to the temper and circumstances of the people for whom it was principally designed. They had, from their long residence in Egypt and the splendor of the Egyptian worship, contracted a taste for pomp and parade in religion;—a taste this, that was not, all at once, to be got the better of. And as, during their residence in the wilderness, it would, on many accounts, have been improper to thwart them in it, what could be more proper than the course that was taken? Did not the appointment of such a ritual, while it gratified their passion for external splendor, at the same time guard them against a growing passion for the Egyptian idolatry, with which they had been already a little infected, and were in danger of being still more corrupted? In this point of view, it has often been observed, that the nature of the Mosaic ritual was not merely arbitrary, but had a special regard to the temper and circumstances of the people of Israel, and was of such a particular structure, as to beget and keep up an aversion to the Egyptian idolatry, from which, among other valuable ends, it was intended to reform them.

And now, after what has been said in answer to this part of the objection, the reader may judge, what ground Lord Bolinbroke had for the impious sneer, with which he speaks of the Jewish ritual, in the following terms:—" In order to preserve the purity of
" his worship, he prescribes to them a multi-
" tude of rites and ceremonies, founded in
" the superstitions of Egypt, from which they
" were to be weaned, or in some analogy to
" them. They were never weaned entirely
" from all the superstitions: And the great
" merit of the law of Moses was teaching the
" people to adore one God, much as the ido-
" latrous nations adored several. This may
" be called *sanctifying* Pagan rites and ceremo-
" nies, in theological language: But is pro-
" faning the pure worship of God, in the lan-
" guage of common sense." *

The objections against this institution of religion have not been confined to its ritual. They have been more bold, and levelled, as I observed before, against its doctrines and morals. To judge of the regard due to such a charge, it will be necessary briefly to review the representation that has been given of this religion,

---

* See Bolingbr. Philosoph. Works, Vol. V. p. 377.

religion, and fee how its great and leading articles are affected by it.

The complexion of religion depends, in a great meafure, upon the character of that Being who is the Author of it. The one will always be of a piece with the other. If the fentiments entertained of him are unjuſt or erroneous, mean or grovelling, religion becomes tainted in its very fource; and, by confequence, all its parts, which, like fo many ſtreams, iffue from it, muſt be fo too.

It deferves to be taken notice of, that, in this œconomy of religion, the Deity hath taken care to make all whom it concerned, acquainted with his true character, by the titles which he affumed to himfelf, and which were admirably expreffive of it. Upon this article, one fhould imagine there was no great room for cavil or mifreprefentation. But it has not efcaped the envenomed cenfure of a Lord Bolingbroke. Hear how he would make Mofes fpeak of the fupreme Being. According to his reprefentation, if we would believe his Lordſhip,—" The fupreme Being condefcend-
" ed to be the tutelary God of Abraham,
" Ifaac, and Jacob; and, under this character,
" acted a part, which a fenfible heathen, not
" tranfported with prefumptuous notions of
" his own importance, nor by the impudence
" of enthufiafm, would have thought too
" mean and too low for any of his inferior
" gods or demons *." " He loves with a
                                              " ſtrange

---

* Philofoph. Works, Vol. V. p. 374.

"strange predilection and partiality for the
"Jews, who are not certainly the most love-
"ly of his human creatures. But, towards
"mankind in general, his anger is often fu-
"rious, his hatred inveterate, his vengeance
"unrelenting *."—" The other nations of
"the earth were plunged in idolatry: he left
"them in it: he neglected them, and thought
"it enough to preserve the knowledge of
"himself, and the purity of his worship, in
"Palestine †." "Can any man now presume
"to say, that the God of Moses is an amiable
"Being?—He is unjust, partial, and cruel,
"and delights in blood, commands assassina-
"tions, massacres, and even exterminations
"of people ‡."

Must not one who is but tolerably well acquainted with the genius of this religion and the character it gives of the Deity, stand astonished at the effrontery, as well as impiety, with which these bold assertions abound?

It is true, God is pleased to call himself the God of Abraham, Isaac, and Jacob; and the reason for doing so has already been taken notice of. But it is by no means true, that he is any where, through the sacred writings, represented as their tutelary God, in the restricted sense in which his Lordship would have it understood.

It is equally unfair to represent him, from his kindness to the descendants of these illu-

strious

---

* Ibid. Vol. V. p. 161.   † Ibid. Vol. V. 375.
‡ Ibid. Vol. V. p. 217.

strious Patriarchs, as influenced by a predilection for them, but cruel and unjust to the rest of mankind. Neither the one, nor the other, is the case, as I hope has been shown to the satisfaction of the candid reader. Nay, his conduct towards Israel, which is branded with the imputation of a narrow partiality, did really proceed from a true and most extensive philanthropy. And had his Lordship studied to understand his subject a little better, before he sat down to write upon it, he would not have exposed his ignorance or malevolence as he has done.

The charge of injustice and cruelty in the assassinations and massacres he is said to have commanded, is so vaguely laid, that we are left to conjecture what he means by it. If in this he alludes to the treatment of the seven nations in Canaan, there is not the least force in it, as has been shown already, whether the commission with respect to it be understood, in a restricted, or in an unlimited, sense. Or if, in this bloody charge, he alludes to any other part of the Divine conduct, he should have told us what it was, and I should not fear but it would be capable of a vindication, equally easy and satisfactory. Such a picture as this of *the God of Moses* (as his Lordship is pleased to call him by way of derision) could be drawn only by a hand guided by prejudice. Neither the features nor the colouring are just. No wonder, therefore, that it should not bear the least resemblance to the fair and divine Original.

Let

Let any one but confider the character of the Deity, as delineated by the pencils of the facred writers, or as defcribed by himfelf, and how different, nay how diametrically oppofite, muft it be to the account which his Lordfhip has fhamefuly given us of it? In place of confidering him in the light of an inferior or generated God, or of one whofe government was circumfcribed by the bounds of a fmall province or country, are we not taught to look upon him, as eternal, felf-exiftent, and independent,—unbounded in his dominion, and fupreme over all?

Before the Mofaic œconomy took place, idolatry had gained a great footing in the world: And moft nations had become fo intoxicated with the theology that was then current, which flattered their pride and foothed their paffions, that they were become worfhippers of the whole hoft of Heaven. One great defign, therefore, of this inftitution, though not the only one, was to give a check to this growing evil, and to call mankind back to the worfhip and fervice of the one true and living God. And this fo evidently appears to be the uniform tendency of it, that there are but few who would have the hardinefs to deny, or fo much as to difpute, it. This, however, has been done by the Author lately cited.

Thus fays he,—" If we confider his (God's) " laws, as means of preferving monotheifm " or the purity of worfhip, in oppofition to " polytheifm and fuperftition, we fhall find

" that no means could be worfe proportioned
" to this end *." Here he feems to admit
that one part of the primary defign of the
Mofaic inftitutes, was to abolifh polytheifm
and fuperftition; but he makes a poor compliment to the Author of this œconomy, when,
however laudable his defign in it might be, he
fo flatly charges him with impropriety, in the
choice of the meafures adopted for thefe purpofes. But we are, by this time, too well acquainted with his Lordfhip, to take his account of any thing relating to this religion,
upon his *ipfe dixit.* Let us examine the matter a little, and we fhall find that the reproach
intended to be thrown upon the Author of
this inftitution for the appointment of fuch
means, rebounds upon his Lordfhip, for not
perceiving, or rather wilfully mifreprefenting, the propriety of them. For furely, if,
in any thing, the intention of this ritual and
the revelation that attended it, is apparent, it
is in the difcouragement it gives to the belief
or worfhip of a plurality of gods. The unity
of God is not only afferted, in the ftrongeft
manner, at the delivery of the law, which
was accompanied with every circumftance of
awful folemnity, that was beft calculated to
ftrike Ifrael, and infpire them with fentiments
of reverence †: But, as God knew that the
impreffion made by this fcene would foon
wear off from that generation, and that the

account

---

* Bolingb. Philofoph. Works, Vol. V. p. 375.
† Exod. xx. 2, 3. Deut. vi. 3, 4.

account of it to succeeding ones would have but little effect upon them, the whole ritual of their religion was so framed, as was best calculated to keep them in mind of it. Thus, what else could be the tendency of but *one* Altar,—*one* Temple, and the constant residence of the Schechinah there? Was not this, in every respect, so different from the mode observed by the nations around them, as plainly intimates that the belief which influenced it, was equally different? The Pagan theology, while it admitted a plurality and subordination of gods, did, at the same time, admit and authorise an intercommunity of worship, and encourage those of one country to adopt the gods of another into their apotheosis. But the Jewish religion gave no such licenfe. Nay, as often as the people of Israel attempted any thing of this kind, they never escaped without feeling the severe displeasure of their own God, who not only told them he would admit of no rival, but took up a visible residence among them, that his presence might serve as a constant caveat against a defection from him, to the gods of the nations around them.

Let these things be considered, and I dare appeal to the candid and impartial, if they had not a most admirable tendency to undermine the foundations of idolatry, and guard Israel against a future infection from it, by conveying to them this important instruction,—that the Lord their God was *one* Lord, and that, besides him, there was none that deserved

ved to be called God: And therefore, that all the gods of the nations, of whatever rank or order, were but false gods,—the figments of a wild fancy and imagination.

Not only does the Noble Lord, whose character of the Deity we are now considering, represent him as descending below the dignity of a God, in the attention he paid to Abraham and his family, and as encouraging polytheism, by the very means appointed for abolishing it: He represents him also as one who delighted in scenes of blood and cruelty.

Such a representation as this is altogether unpardonable, not only because it is absolutely false, but because he must have known it to be so. How does it stand in direct opposition to the character which God assumed to himself,—*The Lord, The Lord God, merciful, &c.* Let us look back to the very occasion upon which the God of Israel was pleased to make himself known to them by this name, and does it not afford a striking proof of his title to it? It is true, he gave them an awful proof of his just displeasure against Israel, for their daring behaviour at the very foot of that Mount, where he had so lately manifested himself to them, in a manner equally expressive of his gracious condescension and tremendous majesty. And, in this, was there not the greatest propriety? Any thing less, would not have been sufficient to secure his authority over them. Such an early encroachment upon it, required a check of this nature. But, if he did then and afterwards chastise this people

people or his enemies, muſt it not be allowed that it was never done but in vindication of his honour and the authority of his government, and always in a manner that ſhowed that judgment is his *ſtrange work*, and ſuch as might beſt promote the greater happineſs of his creation? To charge his conduct with cruelty or injuſtice, is to deny to the Governor of the world, a privilege that muſt be allowed to the governor of the moſt petty ſtate. It is to condemn the exerciſe of it in a caſe, in which, had he neglected it, he would have been blamed for weakneſs and culpable indulgence. And the author of the preſent cenſure, would have been among the loudeſt in the cry againſt him.

Having thus offered ſome curſory animadverſions upon the vile inſinuations, or rather the impious reproaches, thrown out againſt the character of the God of Iſrael, it is unneceſſary to enter any farther into a vindication of it. Let the different traits of it, as they have been ſketched out, Part I. Chap. I. § 1. be attentively conſidered:—Let the whole of his conduct, either to the people of Iſrael in particular or to the world in general, be carefully viewed in the connection and dependence of its ſeveral parts, and he muſt renounce all pretenſions to diſcernment, who is not charmed with the beauty, greatneſs, dignity, and excellence of his character.

It might be expected that any ſyſtem of morals, of which ſuch a Being was ſaid to be the Author, would be every way worthy of him.
And

And such indeed was that which he offered to the world. But, pure and sublime as the morals recommended by this religion are, they have been struck at, by the impoisoned darts of this virulent adversary. "The law of the "Jews (says he) exacted from them all the "duties necessary to maintain peace and good "order among themselves: And if this be a "mark of Divinity, the laws which Rappa- "rees and Banditti establish in their societies, "have the same. But the first principles and "whole tenor of the Jewish laws, took them "out of all moral obligations to the rest of "mankind: And if Moses did not order them "to have no benevolence for any who were "not Jews, yet it is certain that their law, "their history, and their prophesies, determi- "ned them to think themselves a chosen race, "distinct from the rest of mankind, in the "order of God's providence, and that they "were far from owing to other men, what "other men owed to them and to one ano- "ther. This produced a *legal* injustice and "cruelty in their whole conduct: And there "is no part of their history wherein we shall "not find examples of both, authorised by "their law, and pressed upon them by their "Priests and their Prophets." *

It is not denied that the Jews, elated with pride, or an imagined superiority to other na- tions, did often behave with a supercilious haughtiness towards them. But can any
thing

* Bolingbr. Philosoph. Works, Vol. V. p. 357.

thing be more unfair than to charge this upon their law? It is not the neceſſary conſequence of any part of it. Nay, had they rightly underſtood the ſpirit of it, or the deſign in giving it, they could never have indulged in ſuch conduct.

It is true, their law did forbid a familiar intercourſe or correſpondence with Idolaters. But this it did, not from a principle of malevolence or hatred, but to prevent their forming any connections with them, that might occaſion their ſeduction from the worſhip of the true God. Nay, ſo far is it from being true, that examples of injuſtice and cruelty are to be found in every page of their hiſtory, authoriſed by their law and its miniſters, that not ſo much as a ſingle inſtance of either can be produced, that will bear examination. On the contrary, nothing can be more expreſs and in point againſt ſuch calumny, than that part of their law which required that they ſhould love their neighbour as themſelves. And of ſuch importance was this precept judged to be, that their Rabbins acknowledged a regard to it to be of much greater value in the Divine eſtimation, than all their ritual obſervances. And our Saviour confirms their judgment upon this point, by telling us,—that to love God with all the heart, and their neighbour as themſelves, was more than all whole burnt-offerings and ſacrifices*.

Not ſatisfied with ſuch an attack upon the morals

---

* Mark xii. 23.

morals of this religion, he audaciously represents the God of it, as glad to make the most mercenary bargain with his votaries. To secure their obedience and service, he scruples not to tell us, that he made use of motives the most mean and ignoble, and some of them even criminal. Thus he even dares to represent him, as becoming a party in their vices.

This is a charge so gross and impious, that, one might imagine, no man in his sober senses would have ventured to make it. But what would not a Bolingbroke dare to do against religion? Thus he writes.—" They (that is,
" the people of the Jews) are exhorted to
" keep the law, not for the sake of God, but
" for considerations of another kind, and
" wherein not only their wants were to be
" supplied, but all their appetites and passions
" to be gratified. If they hearkened dili-
" gently to the voice of God, they were to be
" set on high, above all nations of the earth:
" They were to be the *head* and not the *tail;*
" to be above only, and not beneath.—All
" the people of the earth were to fear them;
" all their enemies were to be smitten before
" their face; and they who came out against
" them one way, were to flie before them se-
" ven. These were objects of ambition.
" Their basket and their store were to be
" blessed: They were to grow rich: They
" were to lend to many nations, and to bor-
" row from none. These were objects of
" avarice. They were to be blessed every
" where, in the city and in the field, in the
" fruit

" fruit of their bodies, in the fruit of the
" ground, and in the fruit of their cattle, and
" of their flocks of sheep. These were ob-
" jects of all their other appetites and paf-
" sions. God purchased, as it were, the obe-
" dience of a people he had chosen long be-
" fore, by this mercenary bargain. It was
" ill kept upon their part, and the law with
" all these sanctions was continually violated,
" sometimes rejected, and had in no degree
" of force sufficient to maintain itself in ob-
" servation and reverence*."

It is readily granted that the principles which influence any piece of conduct, must be taken into the account in order to form a just estimate of it. And could it be made appear, that those proposed by this religon were unworthy of the Deity, we should not hesitate a moment in rejecting it.

In the account which his Lordship makes of the matter, the Deity is represented as willing to purchase the obedience of this people at any rate; and, rather than want it, to bribe them, not only by a connivance, but by an actual indulgence granted, to their meanest passions. But can this reasoning, in the cases alluded to, support the conclusion which he draws, and would have his readers admit? So far from it, that it serves in some things to expose his ignorance of human nature and of the ages under consideration, and, through the whole of it, to betray the malignity of his heart.

---

* Philosoph. Works, Vol. V. p. 358.

No doubt, the more liberal and ingenuous the principle of conduct is, the more excellent and praise-worthy it must be allowed to be. To serve God from a pure love to him and regard to virtue, would argue a very sublime degree of it. But who, that considers the state of the world at this early period, but must see that such a pitch of virtue was scarcely to be expected? At that time, the notions which mankind had of the Deity were but very imperfect:—and, therefore, to have urged religion merely from the liberal principles of its internal worth and excellence, would have had but little weight, considering the manner in which the service of the gods around them was promoted.

According to the system of the Pagan theology, they were made to expect clement seasons, plentiful crops, and worldly prosperity, from the superintendance of the gods they worshipped, over the elements and heavenly luminaries. And therefore, had not God rewarded the service of Israel by similar blessings, it would have been no easy matter to have drawn them off from the worship of those false gods, or to have convinced them of his superiority over them. Neither in this was there any thing unworthy of the Deity. It was no more than acting agreeably to the nature he had given man, and gratifying the passions of ambition and interest, (not avarice) no farther than was perfectly consistent with that subordination in which they ought ever to be kept to reason:—Or, in other words, it

was

was no more than showing them, in matter of fact and experience, that godliness was profitable unto all things, and was the trueeſt gain. And who that confiders the carnal and groſs temper of thoſe, to whom ſuch promiſes were addreſſed, but, in place of finding fault, muſt approve the wiſdom of them?

It is in vain to urge as a defect in this inſtitution of religion,—that it knew nothing of the doctrines of the immortality of the ſoul, or of a future ſtate of rewards and puniſhments, becauſe neither is urged as a ſanction of thoſe laws which required their obedience.

The ritual of this religion was peculiar to itſelf, and that which in a great meaſure diſtinguiſhed it from every other. There was no neceſſity, therefore, for uſing a doctrine, as a ſanction to its laws, which was common to every other mode of religion. It was enough that it was the popular belief in all nations and ages of the world:—and ſuch indeed it was, however ſome philoſophers may have reaſoned themſelves into a doubt of it. It is no objection againſt this,—that the doctrine is no where mentioned expreſsly in the Moſaic writings. Many things there are in them that indicate the belief of it. Has not the hiſtory of angels and their intercourſe with the world,—the tranſlation of Enoch,—the prohibition of necromancy, ſuch an aſpect? But, above all, was not the commiſſion given to Moſes, for delivering Iſrael from Egyptian bondage,

bondage, a proof of this*, if there had never any been given before? Does not God, in this, reprefent himfelf, as the God of Abraham, Ifaac and Jacob? and, as they had long before this removed out of this world, what lefs could this infer, than that they continued to exift in another, at prefent, invifible to fenfe? For certain it is, that God is not the God of the dead, but of the living. This inference is fo very obvious, that it could not efcape any; much lefs, we may believe, did it efcape Mofes. And yet Lord Bolingbroke has, without the leaft hefitation, taken upon him to affure us—" That Mofes did not be-
" lieve the immortality of the foul, nor the
" rewards and punifhments of another life;
" though (as he adds) it is poffible he might
" have learned thefe doctrines from the
" Egyptians, who taught them very early †".

What a ftrange account is this which he makes of Mofes! He allows him, when it anfwers his purpofe, to have been abundantly fagacious; but, at other times, he, without the leaft blufh, makes him equally ftupid. But we may know his character as well as he. Let us judge of it from his own conduct, in the circumftances in which he was placed. From all the accounts we have of him in hiftory, he appears to have been a man of very diftinguifhed parts and abilities. And if this is but admitted, Lord Bolingbroke, diftinguifhed as his were, would have found it difficult

* Exod. iii. 6.
† Philofoph. Works, Vol. V. p. 355.

ficult to account for his conduct upon any other suppofition than that which his Lordfhip denies,—Mofes's belief of the immortality of the foul and a future ftate. For, had Mofes entertained the leaft doubt or fufpicion as to thefe, it is not to be imagined that he would have acted the part he did. None could have had higher or more flattering profpects before him, than he had. The pleafures of the moft brilliant court in the world,—the favour of a mighty prince, and— the hope of all that could be derived from thence, were ftrong arguments to diffuade him from taking any concern in Ifrael, efpecially as he muft have feen that he could take none without forfeiting all thefe profpects. And yet no fooner did God intimate his intention of making him the deliverer of his people, from that bondage under which they groaned in Egypt, than, regardlefs of every danger to which it could expofe him, he undertakes it. Now whence, pray, could he be prompted to venture upon fo many fcenes of danger, as the execution of this fcheme muft have prefented to him? It is in vain to fuppofe him to have been animated in this arduous enterprife, by the flattering profpect, which the expected conqueft of a rich, plentiful, and delicious country prefented to him. This will, by no means, account for fuch extraordinary conduct. He muft have been quickfighted enough to fee the many and great dangers that were infeparable from fuch an undertaking,

undertaking, and the uncertainty of succefs in it at laft.

But, putting thefe entirely out of the queftion, let us fuppofe him certain of the poffeffion of this pleafant country, the alleged object of his ambition; muft it not be admitted, that, even in this cafe, he could hope for nothing fuperior, nor indeed equal, to what he renounced in Egypt? And therefore, after figuring out every apology for his conduct, that imagination itfelf can fuggeft, we muft, I apprehend, be obliged to refolve it into the refpect he had to the recompence of reward, in another world. Any other principle muft be inadequate to fuch a greatnefs of behaviour. This is entirely equal to it. This accounts for it in a moft rational manner, and in perfect confiftence with that character for wifdom, knowledge, prudence, and good fenfe, which he feems to have fupported through the reft of life.

But, to draw to a conclufion of this fection, I hope I may now appeal to the candid reader, if there be any juft ground for the objections that have, with no fmall degree of virulence, been thrown out againft the fubject of it. Nay, I hope, I may, by this time, take upon me to fay, that this religion, run down as it has been by many, does carry the cleareft evidence of wifdom and propriety in the inftitution of it; and—that it has the beft tendency to infpire its votaries with reverence for the great Author and Object of it, and powerfully to incline them to all the duties of the most respectful homage and liberal service to him.

SECT. III.

That, if we would rightly understand the New Testament, we must accurately study the Old.

IT is the observation of a learned writer,—
" That nothing can be more natural, no-
" thing thought more divine, than that, in a
" system composed of two dependent dispen-
" sations, the study of the former should be
" made necessary to the comprehension of the
" latter: And that the very uniformity of
" style and colouring should admonish us of
" the intimate connection, which each has
" with the other, to the end that we might
" the better conceive the meaning and fathom
" the design of the Divine counsels in both*."
And the reasons that support this observation, are both many and strong.

In the Christian dispensation, that grand scheme has had its accomplishment, which had been gradually unfolding under the Mosaic: And therefore ought not these dispensations to be considered as having the relation of parts to one another? If we attempt to explain them separately, without any regard

---

* See Dr Hurd's 10th Sermon, at the Bishop of Gloucester's Lecture.

to one another, we muſt inevitably run into many errors. And from this ſource, have many of thoſe errors proceeded, with which moſt of our commentaries abound. By a proper attention to this obſervation, they might have been eaſily prevented.

But the connection betwixt theſe parts of the Divine revelation, though a ſufficient reaſon to ſtudy them as thus related, is not the only one. There is another of very great weight. A great part of the Old Teſtament was written in a very early period; the cuſtoms, uſages, and language of which, were pretty well underſtood in the Apoſtolic age, and therefore often brought into view in the writings of the New, without any explanation offered of them. But now it is otherwiſe. They need it very much. This is, in a particular manner, the caſe with every thing that regarded the ſacrifice-ſervice of the Jews. The practice of ſacrifice, and the rites that attended it, had their origin in ages and countries, both of them remote from that in which we live; and therefore it is no wonder; if, in many things, we ſhould be at a loſs with reſpect to the meaning of either. He who would underſtand it aright, ought to be well acquainted with the import of that emblematical and ſymbolical language, in which every thing connected with this practice, was firſt expreſſed. No doubt, when this ſimple, and, according to the genius of thoſe times, energetic mode of expreſſion was adopted, a preciſe and determinate meaning was affixed to every part of it. And, in proportion as

the

the progress of improvement in language was slow, it would continue the longer in use.

There was another thing that contributed to prolong the use of it; and that is,—that the rites and usages of this religion, which, at first, were adopted from a kind of necessity,—an accommodation to the low state of improvement in literary discoveries, or of refinement in the feelings and manners of mankind, became, at last, so wrought into it, that they made a part of its very constitution.

This circumstance, besides many others that might be taken notice of, secured that attention to them, that was necessary to make them understood. But when, by the introduction of a new system of religion, the old was abrogated, the meaning of a thousand things in it, which before were well understood, became in a short time involved in obscurity, from which we shall find great difficulty in extricating it.

In those parts of the Apostolic writings which were immediately addressed to the Jews, the Jewish phraseology does greatly abound; and therefore we must conclude that, at that time, it was sufficiently understood. But who that applies to the study of these writings now, will not find it difficult to satisfy himself, not to say others, as to the true meaning of them, in many places? While a mere novice in such exercises,—a mere smatterer in the learning of those remote ages, dogmatises in proportion to his ignorance,—boldy pronounces upon the meaning of every part

part of the sacred text, and—sometimes even proceeds so far, as to anathimatise him as a heretic, who shall dare to differ from him, or even so much as to hesitate. What Christian church, or what particular period since the commencement of the Christian æra, has not produced many sad instances of this intolerant spirit? Early did the expounders of the sacred text, take up with such an interpretation of it, as, in the mean time, suited their own taste and preconceived opinions, and saved them from the trouble of a laborious search into the writings of antiquity, for the true meaning of it. And having, by some lucky concurrence of circumstances, once obtained a character for sanctity and learning, their sentiments were greedily swallowed by their admirers, and soon formed into systems. The names of their Authors,—the pride of agreeing with them, and—the fear of losing reputation should they venture to differ, made those systems very quickly become venerable, nay be considered as sacred—as truth itself. And then it is easy to see what must have been the consequence of so much as an attempt to deviate from them.

This proved an early bar to improvement in theological knowledge. But now,—happy times in which we live! a more liberal spirit begins to prevail, and a freedom of inquiry is encouraged. This, it must be acknowledged, may, in some cases, lead into wild conceits and extravagant flights of fancy. But even these, however strange it may seem at first

first hearing, have not been without their advantage. They have often served to strike out a new light, which has led others of a more solid judgment into the most useful discoveries; while, at the same time, the flights complained of, have generally carried such evidence of their whim along with them, as was sufficient to prevent any danger that might have otherwise flowed from them.

But still, notwithstanding all the advances we have made in the cultivation of this spirit of inquiry and improvement, much, very much, remains to be done. And, if I might venture to offer what occurs to me on this subject, I should say, that, till ancient literature is more studied, our modern discoveries in theology will be but few and trifling. And in particular, it appears to me indispensably necessary to bestow more attention, than is commonly done, upon every thing related to the Jews.

Besides the acquisitions that are to be made from an acquaintance with such of the Jewish writings as have come down to us, there is another source of instruction, very valuable, to which we have now more frequent and easy access than before. What I mean is,— The accounts we have of the Eastern countries that border upon, and have always had a communication with, Judea. These have hitherto remained pretty much secluded from the rest of the world, and, by the little intercourse they have had with neighbouring nations, have retained, in a great measure, the

ancient

ancientcuftoms and ufages of their own. Of the advantages arifing from an inquiry into the manners of fuch a people, and the veftiges of ancient learning to be found among them, what ftriking inftances have we in *Maundrel*'s and *Shaw*'s travels, through only a fmall part of the Eaft? Were the fcene of the travels of learned men more diverfified,—could any plan be concerted, by which the illuftration of the fcripture hiftory would be one of the great objects kept in view through the whole of them, what advantages might we not look for? Might we not, once more, expect a light from the Eaft, like the ftar that guided the Magi, to conduct us into the knowlege of the religion of that infant Saviour to whom it led them? Nay, in the anticipated profpect of this fpreading light, I greatly rejoice, and cannot but felicitate my country.

This pleafing light, like the harbinger of the approaching fplendor for which we hope, already begins to dawn. Providence feems to be difpelling thofe thick fhades, through which it would be difficult to penetrate, by the laudable attempt of Dr Kennicot, in collating all the manufcript copies of the Old Teftament, that can be found in the original language; and by the equally laudable zeal, with which Chriftians of all denominations, forgetting the little diftinctions of party, have contributed to promote it. An exact copy, with the various readings, is now publifhed. And when it comes to be read with a critical, but unprejudiced, eye, valuable difcoveries discoveries will, I am persuaded, be made, and a more perfect knowledge of the Scriptures will be acquired. Such an acquisition will greatly tend to illustrate the nature of true religion,—to conquer the prejudices of its enemies, and—confirm the attachment of its friends.

SECT. IV.

That a serious review of the subject of this inquiry, will furnish a proof of the Divine origin, both of the Jewish religion and of the Christian.

THAT the Mosaic institution of religion derives its origin from God, we are naturally led to conclude, whether we consider the several parts of it separately, or in their union with one another.

The view we have taken of the nature and genius of this religion, and its happy accommodation to the temper of the Jews, and the circumstances of that early period at which it first took place, cannot but lead us into favourable sentiments of it. It might also, by an easy train of reasoning, lead us into a firm belief of its Divine origin: because, should this be refused, it would be difficult to say upon what principles any one could have devised such a system, and have got so large a body of people to submit to the heavy yoke imposed by it, contrary to all the prejudices they

they entertained against it. But the proof I mean, at present, to produce, is of another nature. It is from the facts which constitute some of the most shining parts of the history of this people.

If the authenticity of the record which conveys their history to us is admitted, we must, by consequence, admit the Divine origin of the religion it contains; because it will be found to rest upon a series of facts, which can be accounted for in no other way.

To pass over many things which might be taken notice of, let our attention be restricted,—to the manner in which the people of Israel were delivered out of Egypt,—conducted through the wilderness,—preserved amidst the dangers of it, and—at last put in possession of the land promised to their ancestors; and it will be evident to every one, that the acknowledgment of a Divine conduct and direction through all these scenes, must be the consequence of an admission of these facts.

The adversaries of revelation are so sensible of this, that they, all at once, deny the authenticity of the history that conveys the account of these things to us, and labour with all their might to bring it into discredit. Of them all, none have spoke with less reserve on this subject, than the author we have had occasion so often to cite already. " The au-
" thority of the Pentateuch, to say nothing
" of the other books of the Old Testament,
" has been established (says he) *entirely and
" solely on affirmation; the affirmation of the
Jews:*

"*Jews:* or, at best, upon seeming and equi-
" vocal proofs, such as Josephus brings, against
" such evident marks of falsehood, as can be
" objected to no other writings, except to
" professed romances, nor even always to
" them *." " Incredible anecdotes are not
" mentioned seldom and occasionally in them.
" The whole history is founded on such. It
" consists of little else; and if it were not a
" history of them, it would be a history of
" nothing. When I sit down to read this hi-
" story, with the same indifference that I
" should do any other, I am ready to think
" myself transported into a sort of fairy-land,
" where every thing is done by magic and
" enchantment:—Where a system of nature
" very different from ours prevails; and all I
" meet with is repugnant to my experience
" and to the clearest and most distinct ideas
" I have. The history of the Old Testament
" is founded in incredibility. Almost every
" event contained in it is incredible in its
" causes or consequences, and I must accept
" or reject the whole †."

My design does not lead me to offer a particular answer to what has been thrown out by his Lordship, with equal injustice and scurrility. We are no farther concerned with it, than as it seems intended to affect the credibility of the history.

The Pentateuch, which was written by Moses, must be admitted to contain the platform

* Bolingbr. Philosoph. Works, Vol. V. p. 333.
† Philosoph. Works, Vol. V. p. 343. 344.

form of the religion and government of the Jews; and therefore we shall confine our inquiry, at present, to the credibility of it.

Our author, with a boldness and assurance that could be justified only by demonstration itself, asserts, that the authority of the Pentateuch rests *entirely and solely upon the affirmation of the Jews.* Such an assertion, one should think, would need to be supported with a strong proof, before he could expect it should be admitted. But it is pretty remarkable, there is not so much as any offered. Had the credibility of the Mosaic history rested solely, as he alleged, upon the affirmation of the Jews, I will not say that this would have been sufficient of itself to have established it beyond all degree of suspicion. Though even in that case, it would have deserved considerable regard, if nothing could be brought to discredit it. And the reason is,—because it is not easy to conceive why they should have received it, unless they had evidence of a proper nature and degree laid before them, for the truth of it.

It would be to no purpose to allege, that nations have fondly admitted a history, evidently blended with fable, when the tendency of it was to flatter their pride, by ascribing to them a high antiquity, and a distinguished rank among neighbouring states. It is true, there have been some instances of this. But I cannot recollect an instance, in which their pride has had so much the ascendent over them, as to make them court the gratification of it in some cases, at the expence of exposing them in others, in which their national character was still more concerned. And yet this was the case with the history under consideration.

But we are under no necessity of resting the authority of the Pentateuch upon this foundation.

Let us consider it atttentively, and it will be found to carry internal evidences of truth, sufficient to procure it credit. If it be admitted, that this history was delivered to Israel, in the lifetime of its author, is it to be imagined that, by such a publication, he would have appealed to those of that generation, who must have been intimately acquainted with many of the facts contained in it, if he had not been conscious that the account given of them, was such as could stand the most critical examination? Few, if any, there are, or have been, who would be so hardy as this. This would have been such a risk of character, as no man could be suspected of running, who had the least value for it, or any thing depending upon it. Neither gratitude for the favours he had done them, nor fear of his resentment if they ventured to offend him, will account for the reception of this history, upon any other supposition, than a conviction of the truth of it. The character and conduct of this people, show that they had no such blind attachment to, or such timid respect for, him:—Nay that, upon many occasions, they were not indisposed to dispute,

and

and even attempt to throw off, his authority over them. And might it not have been expected, that, in some of those surly moods, the imposture, if there had been any, would have been laid open? Or, if we shall suppose this history not to have appeared till after his death, what should have hindered some of the many thousands who survived him, and were capable of bringing a proof of the falsehood of it, from doing it?

It will be to equally little purpose to alledge, that the vitiation is of a much later date. The later it is placed, the more incredible it becomes. For certain it is, that, at no time, could this have been attempted, but it must have been discovered, and consequently easily prevented. Many are the things which afford a security against an attempt of this kind. The religious reverence, which, it is well known, the Jews had for their law,—the appointment for depositing a copy of it in the tabernacle, to be appealed to in all cases, where any corruption was so much as suspected,—the frequent perusal of it which was enjoined,—the commentaries offered upon it by the Levites, and—the little feuds that sometimes subsisted among themselves, made the least attempt of a vitiation dangerous, and must have discovered it before it was capable of being carried into execution.

The writings of Moses may, in a certain sense, be considered as an introduction to all the other writings of the Old Testament. And

And do not the latter afford a strong corroboration of the history contained in the former? In every page of them, do we not find their authenticity acknowledged, in the respect shown by all ranks of people, to the rites and ceremonies of this religion, as laid down by Moses? And whence could this come, but from an entire conviction of their Divine origin?—A personal regard or attachment to Moses, it is allowed, might be supposed to work upon those of that generation among whom he lived. But surely there could be no room for such supposition, in the distant periods of their commonwealth, upon any other ground than this,—that the account transmitted to them of him was just, and admitted to be such. All this may be considered as a species of internal evidence, such as arises from the writings themselves.

It is true, it may be alleged, from the discovery of a copy of the law in the temple, in the reign of Josiah; the attention which it drew, and the astonishment it excited; that it was a perfect novelty to king, priests, and people. And therefore, that, before this period, a vitiation might have been attempted and acomplished, without danger of discovery.

What has been just now supposed, may, at first, appear specious and plausible; but, upon examination, will be found to have less weight in it, than is imagined.

Whether the copy of the law found by Hilkiah was the autograph or original manuscript deposited by Moses in the tabernacle and afterwards

terwards in the temple, or only an authentic copy of it: Whether the whole of the Pentateuch, or only the book of Deuteronomy, the learned are not agreed. But whichever be supposed, it does not matter much. It is readily acknowledged, that, at this period, the knowledge of religion had fallen very low; but it will, by no means, follow, from the surprise with which the High-Priest and the king received the book of the law, that the Knowledge of it was entirely lost. Nay, from the character that is given of Josiah, that he did that which was *right in the sight of God*, and the rites of religion still observed by the Priests and people, I humby think, there must have remained a more than tolerable knowledge of it. Without supposing this, it will be difficult to say how Josiah could have regulated his conduct, or the Priests, the worship of God. We need but suppose, that the book of the law found by Hilkiah, was either *the original*, or *an authentic copy of that deposited in the tabernacle by Moses;* and this will account both for the surprise and joy expressed upon this occasion. From the above mentioned circumstances, it is, I think, highly probable, that no material vitiation was made in the sacred text. And what gives additional weight to this conjecture is,—that we have no mention made of such vitiation. Had there been any, it would have been branded with just infamy. But should a vitiation be admitted, may we not observe, by the way, that

the

the discovery of this book of the law, would have enabled Josiah to set all to rights again.

To what has been offered in support of the authority and authenticity of the Pentateuch, let me add what must be allowed to have considerable weight in it,—that the great and leading facts in the Mosaic history seem to have been known to Pagan writers of the greatest antiquity, and are handed down in their works, with such evident resemblance in their features, as must discover the orignal from which they were copied, notwithstanding all the artful disguise which their pride has made them use to conceal it. This analogy betwixt scripture-history and heathen mythology, learned men have traced in a great variety of instances; some respecting the Creation; and others, the Flood, Noah, Abraham, Isaac, Joseph, Moses, &c.*—Or, if it should be alleged, that the Pagan writers of Greece and Rome knew little of the Jews so early as, in their writings, they exhibit the striking resemblances alluded to, and therefore could not have borrowed them from the Mosaic history, this will, by no means, weaken the argument from thence in favour of the Divine origin of the Jewish religion. It will lead to the same conclusion, though by an intermediate step. If these likenesses were not immediately derived from the writings

---

* See a pretty large collection of these resemblances in, Stillingfleet's Origines Sacræ, Book iii. chap. 5.—Grotius de Veritate Relig. Christ. lib. i. cap. 16. and lib. iii. cap. 16.— Allix's Reflections, Vol. I. chap. 5. and Vol. II. chap. 2.

writings of Moses, they must have been derived from the common source of *tradition*. And does not the exact correspondence betwixt this and the Jewish history, speak very strongly in its favour, because it cannot be suspected, nor was it indeed possible, to have proceeded from collusion. Thus, without having intended it, their works serve as excellent evidences for the truth of the Mosaic history, and consequently for the Divine origin of the Jewish religion; for, as I hinted already, it is in vain to own the one and deny the other. They must stand or fall together.

Let any one who admits the facts contained in this history try, and he will find it difficult to account for them, in any other way than Moses does. Is it to be imagined that Moses, without any commission or assistance from God, had, if not art to persuade, power enough to oblige, Pharoah, to let Israel go, notwithstanding all the loss he must have sustained, for the want of their labour? That, by a wonderful skill he had acquired in magic, he was able, when pursued by the Egyptian host, to save himself and the people under his care, by making the Red Sea, that opposed their progress, afford a dry passage to the one, and a wet grave to the other?—That he could provide for such a numerous body, in a barren wilderness, for no less than 40 years; and, at length, introduce them into, and secure them in the possession of, a country, full of people, strong and warlike?—That he should be able, by his sole skill, to contrive and digest

gest a plan of religion and a code of laws, so
different in their nature from every other in
the world, and yet so rational in themselves,
and so well adapted to the great designs in
view for this people?—That, by his address
and authority, he should be able to make this
numerous and refractory people, renounce a
religion of which they were so passionately
fond, and embrace another, to which, in many
respects at least, they were almost equally
averse?—That not only his immediate successor, but those who followed him, should
adopt the same plan, and concur in carrying
on the same fraud upon Israel? That, all this
time, there should not one start up among
them, who had either the ability, or the
honesty, to discover it? Nay, that all Israel
should, through the several periods of their
commonwealth, continue to act in a manner
that showed the strongest conviction of the
Divine origin of this religion, though, according to the supposition made, there was not
the least rational foundation for such a belief?
There are none so credulous as to be capable
of believing these things.

It is true, it may be alleged that Moses, by
his education in Egypt, had acquired such an
acquaintance with science, as might procure
him great fame among his countrymen the
Israelites, and make them, in hopes of recovering their liberty, and, at last, obtaining a
settlement in some better country, follow his
fortune through a wilderness. But, what if
this should be allowed? Still new difficulties.

equally unsurmountable as the former, present themselves to us.

In the first place, will it not be difficult, if at all possible, upon this supposition, to account for the conduct of Moses, either in the first steps, or future progress, of his scheme? By the step he took, what could he propose to himself? He must, all at once, not only renounce the flattering prospects which presented themselves to him in Egypt, but expose himself to the resentment of its highly provoked sovereign? and all he could hope for, was no more than the small honour of being at the head of a body of slaves,—the greatest difficulty in governing them, and—the danger of perishing, at last, with them, in an howling wilderness. Were not these, and many such, the difficulties that seemed to embarrass a scheme of this kind? And were they not too obvious to escape the discernment of Moses? A scheme, even as wild and romantic as this, might have been adopted by one who had nothing to lose, and might have some hopes, however faint, distant, and uncertain, of gaining by it. But the situation of Moses was, in every respect, so different from this, that it could not admit his so much as thinking of such an adventure, upon any other ground than that which he himself assigns for it. Thus, his conduct, viewed in every possible light, justifies the integrity of his intentions and the wisdom of his plan, and leads us to infer, that the authority by which he, all along, acted, was directly from God; and that,

that, by confequence, fo was the religion which he taught the Ifraelites.

Another conclufion to which we are led from the preceding inquiry into the conftitution of the church of Ifrael, is—that the religion of Jefus is derived from the fame fource. The divinity of the latter, becomes the juft confequence of a proof of the divinity of the former. The manner of evincing this, is not at all difficult. They have a clofe connection. It can fcarce efcape the notice of any. And perhaps it is becaufe the argument from the divinity of the one, to that of the other, is fo obvious, that fome, with more malevolence than art, have denied it to the firft. A variety of reafons, that may be eafily figured out, might make them unwilling to attack Chriftianity directly. They take the other equally fuccefsful, but lefs honeft, method of fubverting it. They know that, if they can bring the evidence for the one into fufpicion, they, of courfe, leffen the regard that is due to the other.

The train of reafoning that leads us to infer the Divine origin of the Chriftian religion, is neither obfcure nor operofe. We find the Author of it and his firft minifters, when pleading its caufe among the Jews, frequently referring to the prophecies of the Old Teftament, in proof of the religion contained in the New. And indeed this argument, properly purfued, muft be admitted to carry evidence with it, next to irrefiftible; becaufe the completion of the one, in the principal characters

characters and events of the other, must, for ever, remain unaccountable upon any other suppofition, than that he who forefaw and predicted the one, did alfo direct the other, and fo may be confidered as the author of both.

I know that the argument derived from the completion of prophecy has (ftrong as it is in itfelf) been objected to by many.

Difpofed to cavil at all hazards, there have not been wanting fome who laugh at prophecy, and reprefent it as a thing altogether abfurd:—Some, who, admitting what is called by this name, deny the confequence drawn from it, and hold it to be no more than a fhrewd conjecture, founded upon an extenfive knowledge, long experience, and a feries of probabilities: And others, feeing that neither of thefe opinions are tenible, cut the knot which they cannot loofe, and boldly deny that there ever were any fuch prophecies as thofe referred to, till of late, and that they were fabricated to correfpond with the events of which they fpeak.

From this account of the manner, in which the oppofition to the argument in favour of Chriftianity, from prophecy, has been carried on, one muft fee a formed defign to refift it as long as poffible. Driven from one entrenchment, thofe who carry on the oppofition retire into another, and from that into a third, and all along behave like an adverfary who fights, not with the hopes of fuccefs,

but

but for the vain honour of not yielding till he can hold out no longer.

The objections againſt prophecy juſt now mentioned, could any one of them be properly ſupported, would indeed be deciſive upon the point. They are urged with uncommon aſſurance. It may not be improper to examine them a little. And I hope that, in the iſſue, we ſhall find, that notwithſtanding all the boaſted force aſcribed by ſome to them, they are poſſeſſed of very little.

Some, as I have obſerved already, make ſhort work of the controverſy concerning prophecy, by alleging that the very belief of it is abſurd, becauſe, ſay they, it is a thing in itſelf impoſſible. In their attempt to evince this, they diſcover ſome art; but it is ſuch art as betrays a conſciouſneſs of weakneſs. They employ all their invention and rhetoric in expoſing the ridiculous nature of Pagan inſpiration; and then, by transferring the idea of it to what is pleaded for among the Jews, they hope to make it be conſidered in the ſame diſadvantageous light. This is the unfair manner in which Lord Bolingbroke has gone to work. " The cauſes of inſpiration (ſays he) " were principally theſe,—an intoxicating " wind or vapour that blew into the inſpired " perſons, or the action of demons or genii, " on their bodies, or in them." And in the very next page, he adds, " Now nothing " could reſemble more a heathen, than a " Jewiſh vaticination. Egypt and the Eaſt " were the great ſchools of ſuch philoſophy

" and

"and theology. They abounded with feers
"of vifions, and dreamers of dreams, with
"prophets and diviners, with wizzards and
"cunning men, with theurgic as well as na-
"tural magic, and all the occult fciences *."
And again he fays,—" That an hiftory of in-
"fpiration, like one of divination, would be
"a collection of fuch extravagancies and ab-
"furdities, as might be fufficient to make our
"fpecies forfeit the character of reafonable
"creatures, if it did not fhow, at the fame
"time, that by a free ufe of their reafon,
"men have detected, one after another, moft
"of the fallacies, the groffeft at leaft, that
"had been impofed on them by Heathens,
"Jews, or Chriftians, for even of thefe it
"cannot be denied †."

To this it might be fufficient to reply, that fuch a mode of infpiration was never fo much as alleged to have obtained among the Jews. It is well known, that there were three ways, in which, the Jews fay, the knowledge of future events was communicated to them. The firft was the refponfe from the oracle of Urim and Thummim; and this, they allege, was the common mode, during the fubfiftence of the tabernacle and firft temple. When this was withdrawn, it was communicated either by vifion, that is, a fenfible reprefentation before their eyes while awake:—Or, by dreams, that is, an impreffion made upon their

---

* Philofoph. Works, Vol. I. p. 145, 146.
† Philofoph. Works, Vol. I. p. 152.

their imagination when asleep. The third method was by what they called the *Bath-kol*, that is, by a voice speaking to them in some audible and articulate manner. They called it by this name, which signifies, *the daughter of a voice*, either to signify its inferiority to the oracle of Urim and Thummim, which they considered as immediately from God: or because, according to some of their Rabbins, it was commonly attended with thunder, which they considered as the voice of God, and was never heard till the peal was over.

After the mention of these several modes of prophecy among the Jews, the reader cannot omit remarking the injustice done to the Jewish manner of inspiration, by representing it as similar to that which obtained among the Heathens, when no two things could be well more different.

Concerning the first of the Jewish methods of information, or rather, of prophecy, I have spoken already. And as to the last, it seems to have been the invention of some of their Rabbins in a late period, perhaps to save the honour of their nation, which they considered as suffering by the want of the prophetic spirit, to which they had been accustomed in former periods. And what makes this the more probable is,—that we not only have no mention of such method of prophecy in the history of this people, but also that we seldom hear of its being applied, except to the purposes of superstition, as the

sortes

fortes virgilianæ were among the heathens*. The other method is that which we are principally concerned with.

It will be needlefs to obferve to the reader, than an explanation of the manner of the Divine afflatus, impulfe, or call it what you will, upon the mind, cannot fo much as be looked for. It can only be fully underftood, by being felt. It will be enough to our prefent purpofe, if it can be fhown that fuch a communication betwixt the Divine Spirit and ours, as is fuppofed, is not impoffible; and that there were many wife reafons, for which it might have been expected.

Thofe who object to prophecy, will not take upon them to deny the Divine prefcience of future events. The only difficulty is to account for the communication of this knowledge to mankind, by the inftrumentality of fome employed for this purpofe.

It is readily acknowledged, that we are not fo well acquainted with the nature and power of created fpirits, as to be able to fay what is within, or what beyond, their reach. Much lefs can we take upon us to determine with refpect to the Divine. And therefore, though we dare not attempt an explanation of the manner of the operation of the Divine Spirit upon the human mind, it would be too forward to deny the poffibility of it. For, are there not a thoufand things, which every day occur to us in the natural world, the truth of which

---

* Dr Prideaux's Connection, &c. Vol. II. p. 328.

which we are satisfied of though the manner of exiſtence remains a ſecret to us? Nay, upon the principles of reaſon itſelf, may not the poſſibility of it be eaſily vindicated? To deny this, would be to ſuppoſe that God, having once made man, had reſerved to himſelf no other poſſible method of communicating knowledge to him, but by the help of his external ſenſes, and the exerciſe of his rational faculties. But what is there in the conſtitution of our nature, that can, upon the principles of reaſon, ſupport ſuch a concluſion? Nay, is not the reverſe what we would be rather led to infer? Conſidering the human frame as the work of God, is it to be imagined that he ſhould have ſo made it, as to place it beyond the reach of his own agency? We evidently ſee the material part of it, not only ſubjected to thoſe temporary laws by which his Providence is conducted, but, in ſome caſes, to the leſs common and extraordinary interpoſitions of it. And what reaſon can be aſſigned, why the ſpiritual part of our compoſition may not be under a mode of government, ſomething ſimilar and analogous to this, and equally ſuited to its nature? From the notions we are taught to form of pure ſpirits, we muſt admit, that, by their natures, they are made capable of intercourſe with each other. And why ſhould it be thought impoſſible that they might, either by the intervention of our bodily ſenſes, or without them, make impreſſions upon the human

man mind, and communicate to it the knowledge of things and events, of which it was otherwife incapable? As it is by the means of our fenfes that our firft ideas are received, we too haftily conclude that the intervention of thefe is neceffary for the communication of knowledge to the human mind. And becaufe any other method is not fo familiar to us as this, we are apt to deny the poffibility of it; not confidering, that the manner in which one fpirit may act upon another, is not more unintelligible to us, than the manner in which body acts upon fpirit. Nay, if we may reafon from analogy, fhould we not imagine that the operation of fubftances of an homogeneous nature upon one another, would be much more eafy, than that of thofe which are heterogeneous?

It will be to no purpofe to object againft the admiffion of this doctrine, that it would give encouragement to the wildeft enthufiafm. No doubt fome have miftaken emotions, which were no more than the effects of mere mechanifm and a bodily frame, for the motions and influences of the Divine Spirit. But it will by no means thence follow, that there can be no characteriftic by which the one may be diftinguifhed from the other,—the motions of the Divine Spirit, from the delufions of enthufiafm, or the extravagancies of an overheated imagination. On the contrary, if the thing is admitted as poffible, we furely cannot doubt but God might, nay we have reafon to believe

believe that he certainly would, give such evidence of the genuineness of the communication made, as would leave no room to suspect whence it came. Nay, may we not advance a step farther and say, that such communications are not only possible, but also that it is highly probable that such have been made, as there are many wise and good ends, that, in the administration of his moral government, might be answered by them? And therefore may we not, in conclusion of what has been advanced on this part of the subject, take upon us to affirm, that nothing can be more unfair, than to allege, as Lord Bolingbroke does,—" That an history of inspiration, " like one of divination, would be a collec- " tion of such extravagancies and absurdities," &c.?

When driven from one post, the adversaries of revelation are glad to fly to another, rather than give up the cause; and are not ashamed to say, that, if such a thing as prophecy must be admitted, it is no more than a shrewd conjecture with respect to future events, founded on a serious of probabilities.

In support of this opinion, is adduced the noted story of Romulus and the twelve vultures, and the commentary put upon it, in the time of Varro, by Vetius Valens the augur, by which he would ascertain the continuance of the city and the state (the foundations of which Romulus had laid) to 1200 years. This, say they, is an instance of a

prophetic

prophetic spirit, without the necessity of admitting a divine inspiration*.

Another instance, thrown out with an air of ridicule against the argument in favour of Christianity from the completion of prophecy, is the famous prophecy (as it is called) of Seneca†, concerning the discovery of the New, or American, World, upwards of 1400 years before it took place.

If these are admitted, it might be inquired, by what distinctive characters we can know

---

* The story, as quoted by Cicero, is as follows.
Certabant urbem Romam, Remamne vocarent.
Omnis cura viris, uter esset induperator—
Cedunt ter quatuor de cœlo corpora sancta
Avium, præpetibus sese, pulchrisque locis dant.
Conspicit inde sibi data Romulus esse priora
Auspicio regni stabilita scamma, solumque.
Cic. de Divin. lib. i. cap. 48.

One would think that nothing could be more obscure or general than such a prediction, if it deserves the name. But let us see how it is explained by Vetius Valens.—Quot sæcula urbi Romæ debeantur, dicere mecum non est. Sed quod apud Varronem legerim, non tacebo, qui libro Antiquitatum duodevicesimo ait,—fuisse Vetium Romæ, in augurio non ignobilem, ingenio magno, cuivis docto in desceptando parem: Eum se audisse dicentem,—si ita esset ut traderent historici, de Romuli urbis condendæ auguriis, & duodecim vulturibus, quoniam CXX. Annos incolumis præteriisset populus Romanus, ad mille & ducentos perventurum.
Censorinus de Die Natal. c. xvii. p. 47.

† ——————————Venient annis
  Secula feris, quibus Oceanus
  Vincula rerum laxet, & ingens
  Pateat tellus, Tiphysque novos
  Detegat orbes: Nec sit terris
  Ultima Thule.   Sen.

that the Prophets in the Jewish state spake by the Spirit of God.

It is readily granted, that, in a long succession or revolution of ages, there may happen such a coincidence of circumstances, as may show a wonderful likeness, betwixt the wildest random conjecture and certain events. But, could any thing be more unphilosophical, than, upon such similarity, to found a relation betwixt these things, or to suppose that the one had a view to the other*. Take a piece of marble from the block, and, either in a lateral or horizontal section of it, you will perceive, when it has received a polish, such a beautiful assemblage of figures, that it would seem to be the representation of some grand scene in miniature:—Such exact resemblances of trees, flowers, &c. that, with some, it has passed for a mere petrifaction of them. Nay, what can be more beautiful and picturesque than the scenery upon our chamber-windows in the morning, after a frosty night? Will any one, from thence, take upon him to say, that a delineation, such as his inventive fancy has made out, was intended in either of these cases? Would he not rather consider these as altogether fortuitous, or, if you will, as the effects of those bold strokes of nature, which are altogether inexplicable to us?

Upon a foundation, similar to these in some respects, are raised those shrewd conjectures, which

---

* It may be worth the reader's pains to consult Dr Hurd's Sermons, Vol. I. at the Bishop of Gloucester's lecture, on this subject.

which some form to themselves, and with which they amuse the credulous part of mankind, with respect to future events. After-ages, still as credulous as the former, are fond enough to dignify them with the name of prophecies, from an imagined resemblance betwixt them and certain persons, events, or things, to which they make them look forward. But who may not see that such application would be entirely fanciful? And the reason is plain. Because there is no standard to which to appeal in the interpretation, each is left to give that which to him appears best, without being able to prove, either to himself or another, that he is right. But this is not at all the case, with respect to the prophecies of the Old Testament.

In some respects, a certain degree of obscurity may, for wise reasons (as has been observed already) have hung upon them. But, with respect to most, if not all, of them, the general design is abundantly evident.— One thing is remarkable of them, and that is,—That they are not to be considered as unconnected, but all of them as so many links which form a great chain, and unite in forwarding one grand scheme or design; and— that the correspondence betwixt the prophecy and the events to which it has a relation, is such as can scarce apply to any other. Let these things be but duly considered, and must they not be credulous to the highest degree, who can believe all these coincidences to be

no

no more than the effect of chance, or the creatures of fancy and imagination?

There remains only one resource more for infidelity upon this point. Being forced to own the possibility of prophecy, and that these prophecies we have transmitted to us are more than shrewd conjectures concerning the events referred to in them, infidels have nothing left them but to deny their authenticity. And this some of them have done, by insinuating, that they have been fabricated since the events took place: Others, at a more early period: And some have satisfied themselves with an inuendo of a vitiation or corruption of the text, in general. Hints to all these purposes have been thrown out by that *candid* inquirer after truth, Lord Bolingbroke.—" The Jewish history (says he) never
" obtained any credit in the world, till Chri-
" stianity was established. The foundations
" of this system, being laid partly in these
" histories, and in the prophecies *joined to*
" *them or inserted in them*, Christianity has re-
" flected back upon them an authority which
" they had not before, and this authority
" has prevailed wherever Christianity has
spread*." In another place, he says—" The
" ancient manner of recording events made
" it easy to practise all these frauds. The
" priests in Egypt, Judea, and elsewhere,
" were intrusted to make and keep these re-
" cords; and they were under a double obligation

---

* Miscellan. Works, on the Study of Hist. Vol. I. p. 54.

"gation, if I may say so, for such they
"thought it, no doubt, to keep them with
"greater regard to the system of religion,
"whose ministers they were, than to the truth
"of things. They were to keep up the cre-
"dit of ancient lies, and to invent as many
"new ones as were necessary to propagate
"the same fraud. By these means, and on
"these motives, the whole of history was cor-
"rupted in those nations, as we may easily
"believe that it could not fail to be, when
"we consider the connexity between civil
"and ecclesiastic affairs, and their mutual
"influence upon one another*."

To render the objection against prophecy, from the alleged vitiation of the sacred record, of greater force, those who make it should have told us, if they could, when, and by whom, these vitiations were made. Such hints might have served as a clue to guide us through an intricate inquiry: but, as they have not favoured us with any such, we must make our way through it the best we can.

Could it be made appear that the predictions now contained in the writings of the Old Testament, did not exist till after the appearance of Christianity in the world, this circumstance alone would justly bring their credit into question, or rather would entirely destroy it. But this, which indeed is almost the only thing that could invalidate the argument drawn from them in favour of it, has been

---

* Philosoph. Works, Vol. V. p. 275.

been urged, so far as I can recollect, positively by none. Not that the adversaries of Christianity would have hesitated to urge it, could they have hoped to serve their cause by it; for, on other occasions, they have not shown themselves overscrupulous: But because they saw, that an assertion of this kind could have gained no credit,—or rather, could have been easily refuted. Had any attempt to vitiate the prophetic writings been made since the introduction of Christianity, the Jews would not have failed to charge its friends with a fraud of this kind. But this they have never done.—Nay, they admit the same prophecies, and only differ from Christians in the interpretation and application of them.

Besides, as a farther vindication of the Christians from the suspicion of such a design, it deserves to be taken notice of, that, before the appearance of Christianity in the world, a considerable progress had been made in learning; and there are many books still extant, both of Jewish and Pagan authors, which unite in ascertaining the existence of prophecies long prior to this event. Here, then, I might rest the cause, and from the acknowledged existence of prophecy before the events of which they speak, proceed to make the use we intend of it, in favour of Christianity. But as the insinuations thrown out against the authenticity of the writings of the Old Testament, may be apt to make an impression upon some weak minds, it may not be improper to observe, that, when they come

A a 2

to

to be examined, there appears to be no ground for them.

That, in tranfcribing them, fome miftakes may have happened, is not at all difputed. But thefe are all fo trivial, as no way to affect the authority of the record. And could we figure out to ourfelves any, whofe defign it could have been to have vitiated them, it might be eafy to fhow that it was next to impoffible to have fucceeded in it.

I obferved to you already with refpect to the Pentateuch (and the obfervation is of nearly equal force, as to the other writings of the Old and New Teftament) that the command for frequently reading it, was one great fecurity againft a vitiation of it. The erection of fynagogues, and the frequent performance of their fervice, had the fame tendency. Moft of the Prophets lived within a fhort time of one another. Betwixt Ifaiah, who began to to prophefy in the reign of Uzziah, and Malachi, who died about 500 years before Chrift, was no more than a period of about 300 years. And is it to be imagined that their prophecies could, during this interval, be fo little attended to, as to give room for a defign to vitiate them, if we could fuppofe any perfon to find his intereft in doing it? The Prophets were required, not only to deliver the meffages with which they were charged, but alfo to commit them to writing, that fo future ages might not only have the benefit of them, but alfo that, by thus fecuring againft all corruption,

their

their confidence in them might be strengthened.

It deserves farther to be remarked, that the commissions given to the Jewish Prophets, were not always confined to the people of the Jews. They often extended to neighbouring kingdoms, and led them to foretel the fate of some of these, so far as it seemed connected with, or might have any influence upon, that of Israel. And was not the knowledge of the prophecies, by these means, more extensively diffused, and the corruption of them rendered much more difficult? The connexity (to use Lord Bolingbroke's own words) betwixt the civil and ecclesiastic affairs of the Jews, and their mutual influence upon one another, he takes notice of, to give a credibility to the alleged vitiation of their sacred writings. But I humbly think this argument makes against him, and goes a good way to establish the authority of the writings, which it was intended to destroy. For, as the history of their nation and state was warped with the history of their religion, it became the object of every one's care, to guard against any persons taking the least freedom with either. For reasons mentioned above, it must be allowed highly probable, that no attempt to vitiate the prophecies could have been made at an early period. And luckily there happened an event, that must have effectually secured against such an attempt, at any late period of their state. About 300 years before the Christian æra, the the Septuagint translation of the Old Testament

ment Scriptures was made out. From this a double advantage was derived. It served not only to diffuse the knowledge of the religion which it contained, but also to put it out of the power of any to interpolate or mutilate those writings. For, by means of it, the Jews and Heathens became a mutual check upon one another, and both of them are become a joint security to us, for the faithful transmission of them to our times.

Every body knows the veneration, even to a degree of superstition, which the Jews had for their sacred writings, and the care they were at to preserve them pure and uncorrupted. There was a whole society, whose profession was to attend to the purity of the Hebrew text. For this purpose (they tell us) they were at the greatest pains, not only to fix the true meaning by the use of vowels, but also to number the books, chapters, sections, verses, words, and even letters of the text. This was the business of those whom the Jews called *Massorites* *. But, whatever veneration this institution might have been in among the

---

* They received this name from the Hebrew word, *Masar*, which signifies, *Tradidit*, in consequence of a tradition held among the Jews. Their Rabbins maintain, that, when God delivered the law to Moses at Sinai, he not only delivered the true interpretation, but also the true reading, of it: And that this last, as well as the former, was handed down, from one generation to another, by tradition, till, at last, it was fixed by the use of vowels and accents. And hence, say they, this work was called *Masora*,—the hedge or fence of their law, as they esteemed it,—and those who were engaged in it, *Masorites*.

the Jews, I own I have no great veneration for it, nor any great opinion of its ufefulnefs, and therefore I choofe not to lay any ftrefs upon it.

In this induction of arguments in favour of an incorrupted tranfmiffion of the Old Teftament record to us, I have, to avoid being tedious, barely mentioned fome things, which might have been greatly enlarged on. But I hope enough has been faid, to convince the reader of the force and importance of the arguments that have been made ufe of, and to enable him to judge of the regard that is due to what Lord Bolingbroke has advanced on this fubject. And I perfuade myfelf, the candid reader will, by this time, think himfelf fufficiently authorifed, to pronounce his Lordfhips audacious charge againft the writings of the Old Teftament, equally incompatible with the good manners, which might have been expected from one of his rank,—and with that inviolable regard to truth that fhould be paid by all, and efpecially by thofe who profefs to inquire after it. But when one, hurried on by the impetuofity of paffion and prejudice, allows himfelf to forget the dignity of character, and to mingle with fome of the meaneft fcribblers of the unbelieving tribe, in their attacks upon Chriftianity, what that is handfome or liberal can be expected?

To draw near to a conclufion of this part of our fubject. If what has been offered upon it, is admitted as fufficient to fupport the authenticity and credit of the Old Teftament re-

record againſt all ſuſpicion of vitiation, the concluſion we would draw from it,—that the Chriſtian religion is of Divine, and not of human, origin, will be found to be perfectly juſt and logical. Neither are we led to this concluſion, by an intricate and tedious, but, on the contrary, by an eaſy and ſhort, proceſs of argument.

Thus, we can eaſily conceive how one well verſed in aſtronomy, and acquainted with the laws of nature, may foretel all eclipſes of the ſun or moon, that may happen for a ſeries of years, nay, and of ages. In this, there is nothing ſurpriſing, becauſe it depends upon fixed and invariable laws, and the accuracy of calculation. We can alſo ſuppoſe that one, who, by years and experience, has acquired a more than ordinary acquaintance with human nature,—the temper, genius, circumſtances, and interfering intereſts of different nations, may make ſome very ſhrewd and probable conjectures, concerning future events relating to them. This contains as little ſurpriſing as the other. For, though the principles upon which mankind act, are leſs to be depended on than thoſe general laws, according to which the movement of the heavenly luminaries is conducted, yet are they, in certain ſituations, ſo uniform and ſo much the ſame, that one who has been attentive to them, may form more than a probable gueſs, how, in certain circumſtances, they would act who are under the influence of them. But that different perſons,—in different

rent countries and ages of the world, and—under circumstances the most different, should all unite in speaking of one Person, and make what related to him the subject of their writings:—that some of them should fix the time and place of his appearance; and—that others should give a particular description of his person, character, and undertaking,—the manner of his life and death,—the triumphs of his religion, and—incompatible as it might appear with the account of his death,—the glory to which he should be exalted after it:—that, I say, any should fortel such a series of important events with the utmost precision, without a spirit of prophecy; would be a supposition much more unaccountable than the gift of prophecy itself: And the reason is plain, because there can be no principles assigned, upon which it was practicable. For, to finish the argument in the words of an excellent writer upon the subject of prophecy, may we not draw the same conclusion he does, from premises similar to these we have been considering? "That, though some co-
"incidences may fall out, by accident, and
"*more* might be imagined; yet when so *many*
"and *such* prophecies are brought together,
"and compared with their corresponding
"events, it becomes ridiculous (because the
"effect is, in no degree, proportioned to the
"cause) to say of such coincidences, that
"they are the creatures of fancy, or could
"have been the work of chance *."—" Pro-
"phecies

* See Dr Hurd's Sermons at the Bishop of Gloucester's Lecture. Serm. IV. ad fin.

"phecies fulfilled, I mean, such prophecies as these in question, prove invincibly the Divine inspiration of the Prophets. But, if the Prophets were inspired, the Divine mission of him, in whom the predicted marks of the Messiah met, must needs be acknowledged. And what more is required to prove the truth of Christianity? Not even the evidence of *miracles* performed by Christ, if the prophecies had not made them one mark of his character*." Thus, the testimony of Jesus is the spirit of prophecy †.

---

* Hurd's Sermons. Serm. V.   † Rev. xix. 10.

INDEX

A

ABEL, the principle upon which he offered his facrifice to God, p. 50.

Abraham, why God was called his God, p. 45. Reafons of his call, p. 45 et feq. 273. His call no evidence of a partiality to his pofterity, inconfiftent with the regard due to the reft of mankind, p. 221 et feq. 271. Converfed with the Egyptians upon the fubject of religion (Note) 68. His fame through India and Perfia, (N.) p. 104. The intended facrifice of Ifaac, not what gave rife to the practice of human facrifices, p. 102—106. Particular reafons why he might be pitched upon to be the Founder of a New Church, in the world, p. 273.

Alexander the Great fent many Jews to Egypt; this the means of fpreading the knowledge of their religion, p. 290.

Alexandria, when built, p. 290 (N.) A mufeum or library founded there, by Ptolemy Philadelphus, p. 291.

Allegorifing humour, the danger of indulging it, p. 200.

Apollo, the infcription on his temple at Delphi, and the meaning of it, p. 50.

Appearances, vifible, of the Deity, early vouchfafed to mankind, p. 34. Why there was no vifible appearance of the Deity at Sinai, p. 36. Sometimes, in the fimilitude of a man, and fometimes, without any particular fhape, (N.) p. 150. In the firft of thefe ways, the Deity was wont to appear in the more early ages of the world, and to this there are frequent allufions in the feveral modes of facred phrafeology, (N.) p. 150. Why the manner of appearance afterwards changed, p. 150. The excellent tendency of fuch appearances, p. 209. Admirably calculated to perfuade Ifrael, that the religion taught by Mofes was from the Supreme God, p. 209. To fupport *their* fpirits under the difadvantages of their fituation, and Mofes in the adminiftration of government, p. 110 et feq. Neceffary, not only to give mankind, in the early ages of the world, proper inftruction in religion, but alfo to gain credit to it, p. 257. Calculated, not only for communicating the knowledge of religion, with greater eafe and advantage, but alfo for making a proper impreffion upon the mind, p. 260. Why thefe appearances were not more frequent, p. 261. Abraham

ham, not the first, as Dr Shuckford alleges, to whom they were vouchsafed, p. 262, et seq. Appearance, Divine, the propriety of the first to man, p. 268.

Ark, why a more settled residence of it became necessary after the Israelites had obtained possession of Canaan, p. 146.

Asiatics, their language, why so figurative, accounted for, p. 195.

B.

Babel, the dispersion at it, a temporary check to idolatry, p. 271.

Barrington quoted, p. 19.

Bath-Kol, what, p. 361.

Beards, cutting off and strowing the hair of them upon the bodies of the deceased, a funeral rite frequent among the Heathens, to render the infernal deities propitious, p. 217.

Blood, used by way of lustration, among the Heathens, p. 181

Bolingbroke, Lord, quoted, p. 172, 313, 321, 322, 323, 326, 330, 333, 336, 347, 360, 369.

Books, the expence of writing and publishing them, before the discovery of the papyrus, p. 291, (N.)

C.

Calf, golden, the reason of the Israelites worshipping it, p. 55, (N.)

Canaanites, the order with respect to the destruction of them, represented as cruel and unjust, p. 226. Vindicated from such imputation, p. 227 et seq. The commission with respect to them, no encouragement to the licentious ravages of others, p. 229. Nothing in the Divine command, that made an excision necessary, p. 230.

Christianity, the opposition given to it, accounted for, p. 18.

Circumcision, the opinion of Herodotus concerning the origin of it, p. 67. The opinion of Diodorus Siculus, p. 68. Remarks on these opinions, p. 68 et seq. What seems to have been the opinion of Josephus concerning it, p. 68. (N.) When enjoined to Abraham, p. 71, (N.) Arguments against the derivation of it from the Egyptians, p. 71 and seq. Probable that the Egyptians borrowed it from the Israelites, p. 72 and seq. Different opinions concerning the original design of it, p. 75 and seq. The propriety of such an institution, p. 83 and seq.

Cloud, that covered the mercy-seat, a symbol of the Divine presence, p. (N.) 140. The opinion of Mr Toland concerning it, considered, p. 140, (N.) te seq. Pillar of cloud and fire, the opinion of Mr Toland concerning it, p. 143, (N.)

D.

Deities, local, believed by the Heathens, p. 61. Infernal, a fanciful method of apeafing them, p. 217.

Demons, fuppofed to prefide over the feafons, p. 119.

Difpenfation, how to be underftood through this treatife, (N.) p. 83. Difpenfation of God's providence and grace, the feveral branches of it confidered by fome, as fo many diftinct difpenfations, p. 249. This a very imperfect view of the fubject, p. 249. What are called different difpenfations, more properly fo many branches of one grand fcheme or difpenfation, p. 250. Difadvantages arifing from the confideration of it, in any other point of view, p. 306. The wifdom, power, and goodnefs of God, confpicuous in the difpenfation of his grace to mankind, p. 307.

E.

E I, The infcription on the temple of Apollo at Delphi, the meaning of it, p. 50.

Elohim, the name by which the Deity was firft fpoken of, p. 39. The propriety of the ufe of it, p. 41. A plurality of perfons in the Godhead, inferred from thence by fome, p. 41. Why this word in the plural number, applied to God, p. 42. Elohim-Jehovah, why God fpoken of by this title, p. 42.

Empires, Grecian and Roman, the erection of them becomes the mean of extending knowledge, p. 290.

Expiation, the day of, the defign of it, p. 123. The folemnities that attended it, p. 124. The propriety and ufefulnefs of it, p. 124.

F.

Feafts, folemn, of the Jews, advantages refulting from the religious obfervance of them, p. 115.

Flax and Wool, the increafe of, fuppofed by fome heathens, to be owing to Siderial influences, p. 217. The reafon why garments of thefe were worn by the heathens, ibid. Why the ufe of fuch forbidden to the Jews, p. 218.

Forbes, Prefident of the College of Juftice in Scotland, his opinion concerning circumcifion, p. 75.

G.

Gentiles, court of the, inftruction fuggefted by its appointment, p. 152.

Glory, that bright or refplendent cloud, in which the Deity fometimes appeared, why fo called, p. 150.

God, the meaning of the word, p. 39. God, the Lord God, merciful, &c. when God affumed this title, p. 55. The inftruction and comfort fuggefted by it to Ifrael, p. 56 et feq.

seq. God of the hills and of the plains, whence this distinction took its rise, p. 61. God of gods, the reason of this title, p. 61.

Gospel, the last dispensation of the Divine grace to mankind, p. 299 et seq.

Groves, why the Jews were prohibited to worship in them, p. 147, (N.) The purposes to which they were devoted by the heathens, ibid.

H.

Heliopolis, a temple built near it by Onias, upon the spot where the temple of Bubastis or Isis stood, p. 158.

Herodotus quoted, p. 67.

Hieroglyphics, what kind of writing was so called, and why so called, p. 187. By some thought to have given rise to idolatry, p. 189.

Holy of holies, why God took up his residence in it, p. 164.

Hosannah, the meaning of the word, and the application of it, at the feast of feast of tabernacles, p, 120, (N.)

I.

Hosts, Lord of, the meaning of this title, and whence it took its rise, p 56 et seq.

Hume, Mr David, quoted, p. 25 and 27, (N.)

Hurd, Dr, quoted, p. 339, 377, 378.

I Am, the meaning of this title, when applied to God, p. 50. Explained by the inscription on the temple of Apollo at Delphi, p. 50. By the inscription on the temple of Minerva at Sais, p. 51. By the translation of the Septuagint, ibid. The reason of this mode of translation, ibid. This name intended to strengthen the expectations of Israel, from his superiority over the gods of the Egyptians, p. 54.

I Am, the First and the Last, some observations on the beauty and propriety of this character, p. 62.

Jehovah, the meaning of this title, p. 50. The propriety of the time, when it was first used, p. 52. Conceits of cabbalistical writers concerning it, p. 52, (N.)

Jews, their captivity, and the destruction of their temple and polity, nowise inconsistent with the regard which God had shown for them, p. 235. Good ends answered by these, p. 236. Arguments used by them for the continuance of the Mosaic œconomy, p. 241. It was never intended to be of more than a temporary duration, p. 242 et seq.

Immortality of the soul, that it is not expresly mentioned in the writings of Moses, this no proof that it was not a doctrine of the Mosaic institution of religion, p. 335. This institution of religion proceeds upon the acknowledged belief of it, p. 335. Believed by Moses, p. 336.

Inspiration, Lord Bolingbroke's account of it, p. 359. Such as was acknowledged by the Jews carries no absurdity in it, p. 362. Gives no encouragement to enthusiasm, p. 364.

Instructions, the first given to mankind, not of the abstruse kind, p. 267. Given in a gradual manner, and as they could bear, p. 269.

Josephus quoted, p. 68, 201. His character of the Jews, p. 238, (N.)

Isis worshipped under the emblem of a bull, p. 55, (N.)

Israel, the selection of them, and the privileges bestowed upon them, represented by some as incompatible with the character of God, considered as the parent of all, p. 220. The Divine conduct in this vindicated, p. 220 et seq. The selection of Israel, the means of accelerating the spread of the true religion, p. 221 et seq. The different accounts of the time of their residence in a strange land, reconciled, p. 275. Their descent into Egypt, the advantages derived from it, p. 276 et seq. The manner of their deliverance from Egypt, had a tendency to spread the knowledge of the God of Israel and his religion, p. 280 et seq. Their long stay in the wilderness, had a tendency to make the nations around them acquainted with the character of the God of Israel, p. 282. The manner in which they were ushered into the land of Canaan, and almost all the remarkable events relating to them during their settlement in it, means of spreading the knowledge of religion, p. 283.

Judaism, the character given of it by D. Hume, Esq; p. 25.

Judges, who they were, p. 214.

Julian, the Roman Emperor, the attempt made by him to rebuild the temple at Jerusalem, and the manner in which it was prevented, a strong intimation that the worship wont to be performed in it, was not to be restored, p. 248.

K.

Kennicot, Dr, great advantages may be expected from his collation of the Hebrew manuscripts of the Bible, p. 344.

L.

Law, the sense in which it is generally understood in this treatise, p. 23. The manner in which the Apostle Paul speaks of it, a proof of its divinity, p. 24.

Laws, political, of the Jews, subservient to the interests of religion, p. 215 et seq.

Letters, the uncertainty of the time of their invention, p. 186. The honour of it claimed by many, p. 187. Why ascribed to the gods, ibid. Their progress from the hieroglyphic to the alphabetic kind accounted for, p. 188. Moses supposed to have altered the form of those used in his time, and why, p. 190.

Levites, the design of their institution, p. 168. Cities of the Levites, p. 169. Levites employed in matters of a forensic or civil nature, p. 214, (N.)

Literature, ancient, the study of it necessary to the right understanding the scriptures, p. 343.

Longevity of mankind, in the early ages of the world, a reason assigned for it, p. 267.

M.

Malachi, the length of the interval betwixt his death and the appearance of the Messiah accounted for, p. 284 et seq. Disadvantages the world laboured under, before this period, for the extensive publication of religion, p. 289. Events which occurred, in this period, to facilitate it, p. 290.

Mankind, the situation of, with respect to religion, in the rude state of society, p. 254. The instructions vouchsafed to them in the first ages, proportioned to their circumstances, p. 257.

Massora, what, and whence so called, p. 374, (N.)

Massorites, who, p. 374.

Millenium, what so called, p. 301. Different notions concerning it, p. 301.

Minerva, the inscription on her temple at Sais, p. 51.

Miracles, could be no proof of a divine revelation, in the first ages of the world, and why, p. 258.

Moloch, who, and why, so called, p. 180. Why children made to pass through the fire to him, ibid.

Monotheism, the Mosaic religion admirably calculated to promote it, p. 326.

Moses, a probable reason why he inquired of God, by what name he would choose to be spoken of to Israel, p. 48. The difficult part he had to act in the wilderness, p. 210. Believed the immortality of the soul, and the existence of a future state, p. 336. The authenticity of the account he makes of the extraordinary things done for Israel, p. 348. This account supported by heathen writers, p 353. The manner of his delivering Israel from Egypt, and conducting them through the wilderness, an evidence of the agency under which he acted, p. 354.

Mountains, lettered, near Senai, what they were, p. 190.

N.

Names originally expressive of the nature or qualities of the things

things to which they were applied, p. 48. Inftances of this, p. 38, (N.) Names of God, no lefs than ten reckoned up by Rabbinical writers, p. 39. Many of them thought by Heathens, to be of fuch wonderful compofition, that oracles might be obtained, difeafes cured, and miracles performed by them, p. 48.

Noah, a mean of preferving the knowledge of the learning and religion of the old world, p. 270.

Noahic precepts, what, p. 243.

O.

Onias's temple in Egypt, p. 157.

Oracles, heathen, whence their origin, p. 165, (N.)

Ofiris worfhipped under the emblem of a bull, p. 55, (N.)

P.

Papyrus, the difcovery of it contributed, and how, to the extenfive communication of knowledge, p. 292. Gave name to the fubftance on which we now write, p. 292, (N.)

Paffover, whence fo called, p. 112, (N.) The wifdom of fuch an inftitution, p. 113 et feq. The moral inftruction conveyed by it, p. 115. Among other reafons, it might have been inftituted to guard Ifrael againft being corrupted by fome of the religious feftivals of the heathens, which were celebrated annually about the fame time, p. 116.

Pentateuch, evidences of its authenticity, p. 348.

Pentecoft, whence one of the Jewifh feafts fo called, p. 118.

Philofophers, ancient, what great fervice they were of to the interefts of religion, p. 293.

Pillar of Fire and Cloud, the opinion of Mr Tolland concerning it, p. 143, (N.)

Plato quoted, p. 38, 64.

Preparation required for the fervices of religion, extended to the priefts and people, p. 177. The moral defign of the previous preparation required, p. 178. Might he alfo intended to guard Ifrael againft the fuperftition of their heathen neighbours, p. 179.

Priefthood, Jewifh, hereditary in one family, p. 161. In the Patriarchal ages, priefthood the privelege of primogeniture, p. 161. What might have given rife to the inftitution of the Levitical or Aaronic priefthood, p. 161.

Priefthood, high, hereditary in the family of Aaron, p. 162. Great privileges belonging to it, p. 162.

Priefts, their bufinefs, p. 168. The chief of the priefts, why fo called, p. 168. The external fplendor that attended every thing relating to them, vindicated, p. 169. Employed in matters of a forenfic nature, p. 214, (N.)

Promifes of worldly bleffings, the propriety of them, under the Mofaic economy, p. 334.

Prophecy could be no proof of a Divine revelation, in the firft ages of the world, and why, p. 259. The ceafing of prophecy had a tendency to recover their regard for it, p. 285. The belief of it includes nothing abfurd, p 362. Different kinds of it among the Jews, p. 360. Is more than a fhrewd conjecture with refpect to future events, p. 365. Prophecies of the Old Teftament, not fabricated fince the events took place, p. 369. The conclufion in favour of Chriftianity, drawn from the completion of prophecy, p. 376.

Prophets, fchools of the, when firft erected, p. 159. The original defign of them, p. 159. Why fo called, p. 159. The injuftice done by Lord Bolingbroke and others, in the reprefentation given of them, p. 172. Their ftyle alleged to be dark and enegmatical, p. 194. Whence the obfcurity of it arofe, p. 196. In many cafes highly proper, p. 196, (N.)

Profelytes of the gate and of righteoufnefs, who fo called, p. 242, (N.)

Profeuchæ, what, p. 156.

Purification, water of, what, and why fo called, p. 181.

Purgations by wind, fire, and water, ufed by the Heathens, p. 179.

R.

Rabbins, who, p. 175.

Religion, Chriftian, the difadvantages it would have laboured under, from a more early publication of it, p. 294.

———Mofaic or Jewifh, the time required to be fpent in the fervices of it, no objection againft it, p. 134. Nay, highly proper and neceffary in their circumftances, p. 134. The alleged rigour and feverity of it, no obftruction to the extenfive communication of the knowledge of it, p. 272. Different opinions concerning the nature and defign of it, p. 312.

Revelation, the propriety of, in the firft ages, p. 257.

Robertfon, Dr, quoted, p. 255, 257.

Romulus, the ftory of him and the twelve vultures, p. 365.

S.

Sabbath, the defign of it, p. 108. The wifdom and propriety of fuch an inftitution, p. 108 et feq. By fome thought

not

not to have been inflituted till the giving of the law, p. 126. Reafons againſt this opinion, p. 127. Whether the command concerning the Sabbath required only one day in feven, or the feventh in rotation from the creation of man, p. 129. A reafon for the change of the day, from that obferved by the Jews, to that obferved by Chriſtians, p. 133.

Sacrifice, the opinion of Tindal concerning the origin of it, p. 84. The opinion of the author of Philemon and Hydafpes, p. 86. The opinion of Dr Spencer and Grotius, p. 87. Probable that it derived its origin from the pofitive command of God, p. 88. The different kinds of facrifice, p. 91. Different opinions concerning the defign of this practice, p. 91. The ufefulnefs of fuch a fervice, confidered as an act of devotion, p. 96. The defign of the ceremonies that preceded and accompanied this fervice, p. 100. The inftitution of animal, thought by fome to have given rife to human facrifice, p. 101. This fhown to be improbable, p. 102.

Sanhedrim, the alleged caufe and time of its inftitution, p. 213, (N.)

Schechinah, what meant by it, and the different manner of its appearance, p. 150, (N.)

Scribes, who, p. 174.

Sects, Jewiſh, unknown, till prophecy ceafed, p. 285. What may have given rife to them, p. 286.

Seneca, his alleged prophecy, p. 366.

Septuagint tranſlation of the Old Teſtament, when made, p. 51. Contributed to fpread the knowledge of the Jewiſh religion, p. 291. and to prevent the vitiation of it, p. 373.

Signatures, or marks, the votaries of different deities diſtinguiſhed by them, p. 81.

Suetonius quoted, p. 27, (N.)

Symbolic ritual of religion, the meaning of it well underſtood, p. 183. Proper at the time of its inſtitution, p. 184.

Synagogues, when firft built, p. 155. Why fo called, p. 156.

Syſtems, the danger of an undue attachment to them, p. 205.

T.

Tabernacle, what the defign of it, p. 138.

Tabernacles, feaſt of, why fo called, p. 120. The miſtaken opinion of Plutarch concerning it, p. 121.

Tacitus quoted, p. 27, 80.

Temple, Jewiſh, built upon the plan of the tabernacle, p. 151. The place of the celebration of the more folemn part of the Jewiſh worſhip, p. 152. The propriety of this inſtitution

tion, p. 152. Thought by Dr Spencer to be an imitation of the Egyptian temples, p. 153. What might have given rife to erection of temples, p. 153. A probable reafon for building the firft Jewifh temple, p. 154.

Temple of Gerizzim, when, and upon what occafion, built, p. 157.

———In Egypt, for the Jews, when built, p. 157. What the occafion alleged for it, p. 158. Where built, p. 158.

Teraphim, what, p. 264.

Teftament, New, the beft commentary on the Old, p. 204.

———Old, the ftudy of it neceffary to underftand the New, p. 340.

Tindal quoted, p. 84, 175.

Travelling into the eaft, if properly conducted, might prove a mean of greater acquaintance with the facred oracles, p. 344.

Treatife, this, what gave rife to it, p. 19. The defign of the feveral parts of it, p. 20.

Type, the meaning of it, p. 198, (N.) How far types are to admitted, p. 199. The danger of pufhing the application of them too far, p. 200.

U.

Urim and Thummim, different opinions concerning it, p. 163, (N.)

V.

Voltaire quoted, p. 227.

W.

Water, the ufe of it, by way of purgation, p. 179. Thought to be an allufion to the flood, p. 180.

Weeks, feaft of, the defign of it, and the propriety of fuch an appointment, p. 117.

Wildernefs, the long ftay of Ifrael in it, no objection to the wifdom of the Divine adminiftration, p. 223. Attended with many advantages, p. 223.

Wool and Flax, the growth of thefe thought to be owing to fiderial influences, p. 217. This the reafon why they were wrought into garments by the Heathens, p. 217. Why the ufe of fuch garments forbidden to the Jews, p. 218.

Writing, what the firft kind of it, p. 187. The progrefs from this to the ufe of letters, or alphabetical characters, p. 188.

F I N I S.

www.ingramcontent.com/pod-product-compliance
Lightning Source LLC
Chambersburg PA
CBHW030555240426
43664CB00048B/294